THEOLOGY IN A SOCIAL CONTEXT

Over the last 30 years a number of theologians have been using aspects of sociology alongside the more traditional resources of philosophy. In turn, sociologists with an interest in theology have also contributed to an interaction between theology and sociology. The time is right to revisit the dialogue between theologians and sociologists. In his new trilogy on Sociological Theology, Robin Gill makes a renewed contribution to the mapping of three abiding ways of relating theology and sociology, with the three volumes covering: *Theology in a Social Context; Theology Shaped by Society*; *Society Shaped by Theology*.

Theology in a Social Context argues that a sociological perspective, properly understood, can make an important contribution to theology. Part I looks carefully at various objections raised by both theologians and sociologists, maintaining instead that a proper understanding of social context is a prerequisite for effective theology. Part II suggests that a sociological perspective offers crucial insights into resurgent forms of fundamentalism. Part III offers a fresh account of social context in the modern world, once thought by sociologists and theologians alike to consist simply of increasing secularization.

Ashgate Contemporary Ecclesiology

Series Editors
Martyn Percy, Ripon College Cuddesdon, Oxford, UK
D. Thomas Hughson, Marquette University, USA
Bruce Kaye, Charles Sturt University, Australia

Series Advisory Board
James Nieman; Sathi Clarke; Gemma Simmonds CJ; Gerald West;
Philip Vickeri; Helen Cameron; Tina Beattie; Nigel Wright; Simon Coleman

The field of ecclesiology has grown remarkably in the last decade, and most especially in relation to the study of the contemporary church. Recently, theological attention has turned once more to the nature of the church, its practices and proclivities, and to interpretative readings and understandings on its role, function and ethos in contemporary society.

This new series draws from a range of disciplines and established scholars to further the study of contemporary ecclesiology and publish an important cluster of landmark titles in this field. The Series Editors represent a range of Christian traditions and disciplines, and this reflects the breadth and depth of books developing in the Series. This Ashgate series presents a clear focus on the contemporary situation of churches worldwide, offering an invaluable resource for students, researchers, ministers and other interested readers around the world working or interested in the diverse areas of contemporary ecclesiology and the important changing shape of the church worldwide.

Theology in a Social Context
Sociological Theology Volume 1

ROBIN GILL
University of Kent, Canterbury, UK

ASHGATE

Published by
Ashgate Publishing Limited
Wey Court East
Union Road
Farnham
Surrey, GU9 7PT
England

Ashgate Publishing Company
Suite 420
101 Cherry Street
Burlington
VT 05401-4405
USA

www.ashgate.com

British Library Cataloguing in Publication Data
Gill, Robin.
 Theology in a social context : sociological theology.
 Volume 1. -- (Ashgate contemporary ecclesiology)
 1. Religion and sociology. 2. Christian sociology.
 I. Title II. Series
 261-dc23

Library of Congress Cataloging-in-Publication Data
Gill, Robin.
 Theology in a social context / Robin Gill.
   p. cm. -- (Ashgate contemporary ecclesiology)
 Includes index.
 ISBN 978-1-4094-2595-3 (v. 1 : hardcover) -- ISBN 978-1-4094-2594-6 (v. 1 : pbk) -- ISBN 978-1-4094-2596-0 (ebook) 1. Christian sociology. 2. Theology--Methodology. I. Title.
 BT738.G465 2012
 261.5--dc23

2011041806

ISBN 9781409425953 (hbk)
ISBN 9781409425946 (pbk)
ISBN 9781409425946 (ebk)

Printed and bound in Great Britain by the MPG Books Group, UK.

Contents

Introduction

Theology in a Social Context returns to the theme of my very first book *The Social Context of Theology*.[1] Although it is part of a wider project in what, for convenience, will be termed *Sociological Theology*, it is self-contained and stands alone. At a distance of almost four decades it was unthinkable simply to reissue my youthful book unchanged. Too much has happened to make this credible and, besides, it was much more enjoyable to revisit and revise earlier themes afresh. Instead, this present book and the two related but stand-alone books to be published later– *Theology Shaped by Society* and then *Society Shaped by Theology* – are intended as a summary of my academic work in sociological theology, as an update and even correction of that work and, in many places, as an entirely new contribution.

This academic venture started almost by accident. My PhD 'The Model of Purpose Explored as a Christological Model' now seems to me absurdly jejune and ambitious (I was only 25 when it was completed). It started from the broad consensus of New Testament scholarship in the 1960s that the Synoptic Gospels' metaphor or model of The Kingdom of God really did represent an unambiguously historical and key element in the teaching of Jesus. The PhD argued that, shorn of the monarchical metaphor in which it was framed, this model could be re-interpreted as 'God's Purposeful Action in the World' (with both present and future aspects) and seen as having parallels with the Fourth Gospel's concept of Logos. It could then be explored as a modern-day Christological model that offered an alternative voice in a social context of increasing secularization and loss of any sense of objective purposefulness.

My two examiners, the late C.F.D. Moule and Maurice Wiles, were as ever kind and understanding. They clearly disagreed with each other on theological issues (Moule was a traditional evangelical whereas Wiles started as an evangelical but by then championed more liberal theology). They also mentioned several times that my PhD submission was 'unusual' and 'independent'. However, it never occurred to me at the time to write otherwise, since I saw this naively (a term

---

[1]   Oxford: Mowbrays, 1975.

that they were too considerate to use) as an extended intellectual opportunity to work out my faith. After making numerous small changes, often pulling in different theological directions to satisfy each of the examiners, the degree was awarded. Ever ambitious I was keen to publish it, but Wiles simply said 'Don't!' Despite a bruised ego, I soon realized how wise he was. Two obvious deficiencies in my thesis, not mentioned by the examiners, soon emerged. The first perhaps should have been noticed. While there were (and still remain) strong grounds for concluding that the concept of the Kingdom of God really does go back to the historical Jesus, there were also strong grounds for concluding that the more troublesome concept of the Son of Man does too. But the problem was that while New Testament scholars generally agreed on the broad meaning and significance of the Kingdom of God sayings, they were thoroughly divided on the meaning and significance of the Son of Man sayings. By focusing upon the former and paying much less attention to the latter, I had oversimplified (in the interests of scholarly consensus) the evidence from the Synoptic Gospels.

The second problem would have been much less obvious to theologians at the time. Soon after completing my PhD and while working as a curate in a busy, multicultural Midland's parish, I started to read sociology. Media research had obvious relevance to my work with local newspapers (this will be reflected in Chapter 11), as did ethnicity research to my engagement with local minority groups. The late 1960s was a time of considerable religious debate and ethnic tension both within the media and in the parish. As everyone knows, it was also a time of changing sexual behaviour. This caused serious tensions and divisions within local congregations. My PhD clearly assumed a social context of increasing secularization. The late Eric Mascall, my pellucid supervisor, too assumed like many other theologians (as will be seen in Chapter 6) that secularization unambiguously characterizes the modern world. I had never previously questioned this assumption and neither, apparently, had my two examiners. However, once I started to read the books of sociologists such as David Martin, Bryan Wilson and Peter Berger, it was evident that the status of the secularization paradigm *was* being vigorously discussed. Most theologians, including myself, had not yet caught up properly with this discussion. I decided to use my day off from the parish for a serious engagement with sociology by enrolling for an MSocSc at Birmingham.

The modules that I took – urban industrial society, ethnicity, and sociology of religion – all related closely to parish work. That, after all, was my primary motivation at the time. It was only when planning a dissertation that the organizational sociologist Bob Hinings, my supervisor at Birmingham (now at Edmonton), suggested applying sociology to theology rather than just to parochial work. Now that I understood better what a sociological perspective involved in a number of different areas (not just religion), his suggestion made good sense. I could also see what was missing from my PhD and from the work of other theologians at the time. The present book and the two that will follow are the result of this shrewd piece of advice.

It later transpired that the Canadian theologian Gregory Baum was making a very similar transition at almost exactly the same time. Baum, unlike me, was already in mid-career as a theologian when he discovered and then trained in sociology, taking a two year leave of absence to be at the New School for Social Research in New York. His primary motivation for doing so was theological at the outset, as he recorded in his influential book *Religion and Alienation*, written in the aftermath of this training:

> I was interested in sociology largely because I could not understand why the Catholic Church, despite the goodwill of clergy and laity and the extraordinary institutional event of Vatican II, had been unable to move and adopt the new style of Catholicism outlined in the conciliar reports. I thought that sociology, as the systematic inquiry into society, should be able to answer this question. But what I did not expect was the profound influence that the study of sociology would have on my entire theological thinking. I became convinced that the great sociological literature of the 19th and early 20th centuries records human insight and human wisdom as much as philosophical writings, and that it ought to have a special place in the education of philosophers and theologians.[2]

Published in the same year as *The Social Context of Theology*, we found ourselves quite independently expressing the hope that 'more theologians will turn to

---

[2]   Gregory Baum, *Religion and Alienation: A Theological Reading of Sociology*, New York: Paulist Press, 1975 [reprinted Ottawa: Novalis, 2006], p. 1.

sociological literature and enter into conversation with it'.[3] Baum's theological interest turned especially to the sociology of knowledge both in this and subsequent books.[4] The relevance of this interest will be seen later in *Theology Shaped by Society*.

Our joint hope did have some immediate fruits. In the introduction to *Sociology and Theology: Alliance and Conflict* (to which we both contributed) in 1980, the Dominican John Orme Mills wrote cryptically:

> In 1975 one of the contributors to the present volume (a theologian) asked another (a sociologist) to review for a journal the book *The Social Context of Theology*, the first of the studies in this area to be written by yet another contributor here, Dr Robin Gill. The sociologist asked the theologian to comment on the review he wrote; a lively correspondence on the relationship between sociology and theology ensued, and its outcome was the meeting in January 1978 of twelve sociologists and theologians, of different denominations, and a philosopher, at Blackfriars, the Dominican house of studies at Oxford, in order to debate the matter further.[5]

The identity of the sociologist and theologian and the contents of their lively correspondence were never revealed. However, the Blackfriars Symposium in Theology and Sociology continued to meet annually for 10 years. Instructively a bright, young academic, John Milbank, joined the Symposium just before it ceased. While it lasted it was an invaluable forum for sharing and debating concepts that united and divided theology and sociology. The Dominicans, as hosts and active participants, played a crucial role in enabling this to happen.

The sociologist John Brewer has helpfully set the Blackfriars Symposium into a wider context of sociologists engaging with a variety of other disciplines: history,

---

[3]   Ibid.

[4]   See Gregory Baum, *The Social Imperative: Essays on the Critical Issues that Confront the Christian Churches*, New York: Paulist Press, 1979; *Theology and Society*, New York: Paulist Press, 1986; and *Essays in Critical Theology*, Kansas City, MO: Sheed and Ward, 1994.

[5]   John Orme Mills, 'Introduction: Of Two Minds', in David Martin, John Orme Mills and W.S.F. Pickering (eds), *Sociology and Theology: Alliance and Conflict*, Brighton, Sussex: Harvester, 1980 [reprinted Leiden, NL: Brill, 2003], p. 10.

social anthropology, demography and, more exotically, art history, law, evolution theory and human geography.[6] He argues that interdisciplinarity has characterized the work of many famous sociologists, including C. Wright Mills in his seminal 1959 book *The Sociological Imagination*.[7] Of course such work is likely to attract those who already have an interest in sociology and the 'other' discipline (whatever it is). The Blackfriars Symposium was no exception. Sociologists who disdained theology (perhaps a majority of sociologists) were never likely to join it, nor for the most part were the many theologians who disdained sociology:

> Any discussion of the relationship between theology and sociology has first to confront sociology's fixation with secularization. The secularization debate is a meeting place of sociology and theology that to sociologists renders theology redundant. The emptying pews, boarded-up windows, deconsecrated buildings and elderly and dying congregations in some churches suggest that sociology's prediction of imminent religious decline is partly right. One of the paradoxes of the sociology of religion, however, is that the secularization debate with which it seems obsessed only proves that religion remains relevant to sociology. At first sight it appears ironic that religion is important enough for many sociologists of religion to want to continue to deny its importance.[8]

Chapter 10 will return to this issue, noting that one of the leading proponents of the secularization paradigm, the sociologist Steve Bruce (a colleague of John Brewer at Aberdeen), has devoted three separate books mainly or entirely to the paradigm over the last 15 years.

Equally paradoxical was the denunciation of sociology by the theologian John Milbank. Later chapters will respond, as they must, to the detailed challenges he laid down in his remarkable book *Theology and Social Theory: Beyond Secular Reason*.[9] However, at a more general level, it is paradoxical that he should have

---

[6] John D. Brewer, 'Sociology and its strange "others": introduction,' *History of the Human Sciences*, 20:2, 2007, pp. 1–5.

[7] Oxford: Oxford University Press, 1959.

[8] John D. Brewer, 'Sociology and theology reconsidered: religious sociology and the sociology of religion in Britain,' *History of the Human Sciences*, 20:2, 7–28, 2007, p. 8.

[9] John Milbank, *Theology and Social Theory: Beyond Secular Reason*, Oxford: Blackwell, 1990 [revised 2006].

spent so much energy reading and criticizing at length a discipline that he so clearly despises. It will be seen in Chapter 2 that *Theology and Social Theory* made the startling claim that it had deconstructed *the entire subject* of twentieth-century sociology of religion as a 'secular policing of the sublime'.[10] This claim was made just three years after Milbank attended the Blackfriars Symposium and without mentioning the work of any of the sociologists of religion who were also present. Perhaps he had forgotten their work. Or perhaps he had chosen to forget because sociologists such as David Martin, W.S.F. Pickering, John Orme Mills and Robert Towler (all key members of the Symposium) had so obviously never engaged in a 'secular policing of the sublime'. Sadly this latter verdict seems the more likely.

The most stinging of Milbank's critics have been those who have objected to *Theology and Social Theory* on moral grounds. Gregory Baum, for example, acknowledged early that 'it is an original, brilliant and enormously learned treatise'.[11] Yet, being old enough to remember Jewish German members of his own family murdered in the Holocaust and being convinced that anti-Semitism carried by various forms of Christianity had contributed to this, he was appalled by Milbank's Christian exclusivity:

> John Milbank, a young man, belongs to a generation born after the Holocaust and, hence, not as profoundly challenged by it as the older generation of theologians. Milbank's exclusivist Christology re-introduces the traditional negation of Jewish existence into Christian theological discourse and interrupts the recent conversion of the Church to universal solidarity.[12]

He was particularly offended by Milbank's claim elsewhere[13] that the Church's stance toward other religions should not be dialogue but 'suspicion'. With obvious vehemence Baum stated bluntly: 'In my opinion, to defend such a position in contemporary England troubled by racial, cultural and religious diversity creates a

---

[10] Ibid. p. 106.

[11] Gregory Baum, *Essays in Critical Theology*, p. 52.

[12] Ibid. p. 71.

[13] John Milbank, 'The End of Dialogue', in Gavin D'Costa (ed.), *Christian Uniqueness Reconsidered*, Maryknoll, NY: Orbis, 1990, pp. 174–191, 190.

discourse that encourages violence.'[14] Perhaps it was some of Milbank's polemical rhetoric that invited such a sharp moral response.

Over the course of this book and the two that will follow I hope to take a more eirenic path. British sociology of religion has been greatly indebted to the courteous debate about secularization between David Martin and the late Bryan Wilson in the 1960s (discussed in Chapter 10). These two pioneers were very different in style, method and religious commitment. However, both were immensely generous to younger colleagues and, by their example, encouraged us to be generous to each other (whatever our secular/religious differences). So if Steve Bruce was naturally inclined to treat Wilson as a mentor, I was more inclined towards Martin. Yet both of us received help and encouragement from our opposite mentors and have long cooperated with each other in our research. Would that theologians could always be courteous to each other.

In the present book the first six chapters contain material (with many additions and changes) drawn from the first six chapters of *The Social Context of Theology* (itself long out of print). However, I have tempered the youthful rhetoric that some of those original chapters contained. Chapters 7 to 9 contain material (again with many additions and changes) from *Competing Convictions*,[15] written 14 years later (also long out of print) and more temperately. It was, however, necessary to bring Chapter 8 up to date in order to reflect more recent academic accounts of the rise in fundamentalist violence. Chapters 10 and 11 have been largely researched and written afresh. The final chapter is an extended version (published with permission) of the opening chapter of *Churchgoing and Christian Ethics*,[16] written a decade later (and still in print).

---

[14] Gregory Baum, *Essays in Critical Theology*, p. 70.
[15] London: SCM Press, 1989.
[16] Cambridge: Cambridge University Press, 1999.

PART I
Theology and Sociology

Chapter 1

Three Sociological Approaches to Theology

In 1975, when *The Social Context of Theology* was first published, the literature on ways of relating sociology and theology was thin. With the notable exceptions of Peter Berger[1] in the States and David Martin[2] in Britain very few sociologists of religion had written on theological themes. Conversely, very few theologians – with the important exception of Gregory Baum noted in the Introduction – had attempted any sophisticated form of cooperation with sociologists. In complete contrast to the immense body of literature devoted to the inter-relation of theology and philosophy, that concerned with theology and sociology was extraordinarily limited.

Doubtless there were and remain many reasons for this comparative neglect. The language barrier between the two disciplines may in part be responsible. Both sociology and theology have constructed autonomous specialist terms which only those trained in sociology or theology may fully appreciate. However, the situation is no different if one compares the languages of philosophy and theology. It should not in principle be too difficult for the competent theologian to acquire a certain measure of expertise in sociological terms, or for the sociologist to acquire a similar expertise in theological terms. More crucially, though, the possibility of conflict may have daunted some who might otherwise have explored relations and interactions between sociology and theology. The chapters that follow will examine some of these conflicts, at both the methodological and empirical levels. However, it is as well to realize at this stage that such conflicts do exist and that they may have dissuaded some from studying this area of scholarship.

Again, the attitude of some of the pioneer sociologists of religion was often construed by theologians as effectively 'anti-religious' – a quality not designed to

---

[1] Peter Berger, *The Social Reality of Religion*, London: Faber & Faber, 1969, Appendix II [US title, *The Sacred Canopy of Religion*, Garden City, NY: Doubleday, 1967] and *A Rumour of Angels*, Garden City, NY: Doubleday, 1969 and Harmondsworth: Penguin, 1970.

[2] David Martin, *The Religious and the Secular*, London: Routledge & Kegan Paul, 1969 and *Tracts Against the Times*, Cambridge: Lutterworth, 1973.

endear sociologists to theologians. Certainly it was known that few of the pioneer sociologists of religion themselves had theological commitments. Even Max Weber, as sympathetic towards religion as he was, depicted himself (probably inaccurately) as being 'religiously unmusical'. Chapter 3 will return to this issue, examining the role of explanation within both the sociology of religion and theology.

Whatever the exact reasons for this comparative neglect, a recurrent theme throughout this and the following two volumes will be that this is a fruitful area of scholarship if it is done with sufficient rigour and sophistication. Chapter 4, in particular, will be critical of some of the 'amateur' social assumptions that theologians in the 1970s offered. I will argue that a far more sophisticated form of scholarship is necessary if justice is to be done to both sociology and theology. However, it would have been equally possible to criticize some of the correlations that sociologists have sometimes offered. To redress the balance two examples of inadequate correlation on the part of social theorists might be noted – the first by Ernst Troeltsch and the second by J. Milton Yinger.

Troeltsch's analysis of religious institutions[3] was particularly influential within sociology of religion in the 1970s for accounts of Church/Sect typology (the study of differing types and dynamics within religious institutions). Under the influence of Bryan Wilson and David Martin, at the time, religious institutions were often classified in terms of Church, Denomination and Sect, rather than Troeltsch's Church, Sect and Mysticism. Nevertheless, the broad outline of his analysis proved invaluable to the sociologist.

Troeltsch believed that the social structures of religious institutions are theologically rooted. He argued that the Church/Sect/Mysticism structure of the Christian Church was neither fortuitous nor simply the product of organizational pressure. Instead this structure is inherent in the Gospel itself, and, so long as Christianity survives, this triadic structure will also survive. Troeltsch believed that each type of structure complemented the other; the inclusive Church was strengthened by the exclusive Sect, and both were further strengthened by the individualistic Mysticism. The Church could offer objective grace, the Sect a community of love, and Mysticism individual experience free from formalized

---

3   Ernst Troeltsch, *The Social Teaching of the Christian Churches*, vols I and II, New York: Harper, 1960 [1912].

worship and belief. Together these three types of structure could present to society differing, but complementary, facets of the Christian Gospel.

In view of the influence of Troeltsch's typology within the sociology of religion, it is interesting that he offered this theological interpretation of his analysis. I will argue in the next volume that, from a *theological* perspective, his interpretation is still insightful (even if it has been largely neglected by theologians themselves). However, from a *sociological* perspective, it faced at least two important difficulties.

Firstly, sociologists, with their focus on religion in general rather than Christianity in particular, have tended to argue that an adequate Church/Sect typology should be applicable to world religions. So, for example, both Roland Robertson[4] and Bryan Wilson[5] were careful to frame typologies which did not simply apply to Christianity. Wilson's sevenfold system of classifying Sects, in particular, introduced types which are at times only very marginally concerned with Christianity. It was argued that a typology which is too close to the Christian Gospel would prove inadequate in this wider context.

Secondly, sociologists tended to point to the confusion of criteria that is apparent in Troeltsch's typology. He employed several sets of criteria to determine whether or not a particular religious movement should be identified as Church, Sect or Mysticism. Sometimes these criteria are theological; for example, the predominance within a particular religious movement of certain theological models such as 'grace' or 'love'. At other times the criteria correspond more closely to organizational theory; for example, the presence or absence of professional functionaries within a particular movement.

In reaction to this sociologists such as Nicholas Demerath[6] argued that almost any criteria were preferable to those which are theologically or religiously rooted. Typologies which are so rooted fit uneasily into general sociological theory and make comparative study difficult if not impossible: on the other hand, typologies

---

[4]   Roland Robertson, *The Sociological Interpretation of Religion*, Oxford: Blackwell, 1970.

[5]   Bryan Wilson, 'A Typology of Sects', in Roland Robertson (ed.), *Sociology of Religion*, Harmondsworth, Middlesex: Penguin, 1969, and *Magic and the Millennium*, Oxford: Heinemann, 1973.

[6]   Nicholas J. Demerath III, 'In a Sow's Ear: a Reply to Goode', *Journal for the Scientific Study of Religion*, 6:1, 87–88, 1967.

based solely on organizational theory might provide a more adequate sociological foundation for further analysis.

Yinger also provided an interesting, although again inadequate, socio-theological correlation in the way he derived his functional definition of religion. He took his initial cue from the theologian Paul Tillich:

> Paul Tillich has said that religion is that which concerns us ultimately. This can be a good starting point for a functional definition. While there are important disagreements concerning the 'ultimate' problems of man, a great many would accept the following as among the fundamental concerns of human societies and individuals: How shall we respond to the fact of death? Does life have some central meaning despite the suffering, the succession of frustrations and tragedies?[7]

From this theological definition Yinger attempted a formal sociological definition of religion:

> Religion, then, can be defined as a system of beliefs and practices by means of which a group of people struggles with these ultimate problems of human life. It is the refusal to capitulate to death, to give up in the face of frustration, to allow hostility to tear apart one's human association.[8]

One of the important consequences of this dependence was that the sociologist Yinger exposed himself to the same weaknesses as the theologian Tillich. The philosopher H.D. Lewis at the time depicted Tillich's concept of 'ultimate concern as a confusing attenuation of faith ... the standing temptation of liberal minded thinkers to gain recognition of Christian truth and adherents'.[9] For Lewis it was an attempt to claim that everyone was ultimately a Christian believer – 'the only way in which we could make Tillich's statement plausible would be by identifying

---

[7]   J. Milton Yinger, *Religion, Society and the Individual*, New York: Macmillan, 1957, p. 9.

[8]   Yinger, p. 9.

[9]   H.D. Lewis, *Philosophy of Religion*, London: English Universities Press, 1965, p. 127.

belief in God with seriousness'.[10] Similarly, the sociologist Betty Scharf argued that Yinger's definition 'is cast in wide terms which allow almost any kind of enthusiastic purpose or strong loyalty, provided it is shared by a group, to count as religion'.[11] Thus both Tillich and Yinger were criticized for the same reason; they allowed almost any form of strongly held ideology to count as religion.

In contrast to these two attempts by sociologists to use theological concepts in the service of sociology, I argued in *The Social Context of Theology* that there are three basic sociological approaches to theology which might prove to be more adequate: a study of the social determinants of theological positions, a study of the social significance of theological positions, and a study of the social context of theology.

A Study of the Social Determinants of Theological Positions

By the late 1960s and early 1970s there was emerging a small, but growing, amount of interest among sociologists in the social determinants of moral ideas[12] – an interest previously more typical of anthropologists than sociologists. The social determinants of specifically religious beliefs and practices had long been a preoccupation of sociologists of religion. But there had been comparatively little attention paid to the social determinants of theological positions as such. Yet it was clear that sociology, like psychology,[13] could play an important role in examining particular theological positions – although not, of course, the validity of these positions.

Theologians inevitably interact with society at large, and, however, much they may seek to influence that society, they themselves are influenced by it. Peter Berger argued that this is necessarily the case:

---

[10]   Lewis, p. 127.

[11]   Betty Scharf, *The Sociological Study of Religion*, London: Hutchinson, 1970, p. 33.

[12]   For example, Alasdair MacIntyre, *A Short History of Ethics*, London: Routledge & Kegan Paul, 1967; Maria Ossowska, *Social Determinants of Moral Ideas*, London: Routledge & Kegan Paul, 1971; and John H. Barnsley, *The Social Reality of Ethics*, London: Routledge & Kegan Paul, 1972.

[13]   For example, Michael Argyle, *Religious Behaviour*, London: Routledge & Kegan Paul, 1958.

> Sociology ... raises questions for the theologian to the extent that the latter's
> positions hinge on certain socio-historical presuppositions. For better or for
> worse, such presuppositions are particularly characteristic of theological thought in
> the Judaeo-Christian orbit, for reasons that are well known and have to do with the
> radically historical orientation of the Biblical tradition. The Christian theologian
> is, therefore, ill-advised if he simply views sociology as an ancillary discipline that
> will help him (or, more likely, help the practical churchman) to understand certain
> 'external' problems of the social environment in which his church is related. On
> strictly methodological grounds it will be possible for the theologian to dismiss
> this new perspective as irrelevant to his *opus proprium*. This will become much
> more difficult, however, as soon as he reflects that, after all, he was not born as
> a theologian, that he existed as a person in a particular socio-historical situation
> before he ever began to do theology – in sum, that he himself, if not his theology,
> is illuminated by the lighting apparatus of the sociologist.[14]

Berger's argument was significant. Theology is written by theologians, and the latter are human beings living in a human society. This platitude carries the obvious implication that theologians, like all other thinkers and writers, can properly be examined by the sociologist.

Sociologists concerned to study the social determinants of theological positions might achieve this by examining either the work of a single theologian or a theological position in general. Adopting the first approach they might, for example, attempt to trace the influence of two world wars on the theology of Karl Barth.[15] Very little sociological research at the time had employed such analysis.

Adopting the second approach, sociologists might, for example, be concerned to explore the influence of social structures on theological positions in general. Some of the research in the field of Church/Sect typology had indeed been concerned with just such an influence. At many points the socio-historical surveys of both Troeltsch[16] and Werner Stark[17] illustrate the social determinants of general theological positions.

---

[14]   Peter Berger, *The Social Reality of Religion*, pp. 182–183.

[15]   Cf. John Bowden, *Karl Barth*, London: SCM Press, 1971.

[16]   Ernst Troeltsch, *The Social Teaching of the Christian Churches*.

[17]   Werner Stark, *The Sociology of Religion*, vols I–III, London: Routledge & Kegan Paul, 1966–67.

The latter's interpretation of the origin of Sects, in particular, provided an example of an attempt to use this approach:

> The last root of all sectarianism lies in the alienation of some group from the inclusive society within which it has to carry on its life. It is a kind of protest movement, distinguished from other similar movements by the basic fact that it experiences and expresses its dissatisfactions and strivings in religious (rather than political or economic or generally secular) terms. The causes of alienation can be many, but hunger and humiliation easily come first. All through history, the lowest ranks of society have been the prime recruiting ground of heresies and schisms.[18]

Bryan Wilson was less concerned with such sweeping historical generalizations than with a detailed study of contemporary Sects. Nevertheless, he too attempted to trace the varied social determinants of sectarian theology. His sevenfold typology of Sects was based on the single criterion of a Sect's 'response to the world' – a variable manifestly influenced by a Sect's theology. Wilson argued that this criterion 'recognizes the ideological character of sects, without nevertheless neglecting the way of life of the sect's members, which also necessarily affect the manner in which they accept, reject, neglect or attempt to transcend, to improve or to transvaluate the opportunities which worldly society may offer'.[19]

Wilson's attempt to trace the social determinants of theological positions can also be seen in his account of the process of secularization.[20] He argued that ecumenical theology in the 1960s acted as a 'new faith' within an overall situation of secularization. Far from being a sign of strength within churches, or a 'return to the Gospel', ecumenical theology was in fact a sign of organizational weakness and a product of the process of secularization within the West:

> In general, organizations amalgamate when they are weak rather than when they are strong, since alliance means compromise and amendment of commitment. Of all social organizations, religious movements have most difficulty in altering their

---

[18]   Stark, p. 5.

[19]   Bryan Wilson, 'A Typology of Sects', in Roland Robertson (ed), *Sociology of Religion*, Harmondsworth: Penguin, 1969, pp. 363–364.

[20]   Bryan Wilson, *Religion in Secular Society*, Harmondsworth: Penguin, 1969 (although it was first published by the secularist press C.A. Watts three years earlier).

commitment, since their purpose is supposed to be 'given' from a higher source. The truths of religion are generally supposed to be apprehensions of the divine, and particular movements have come into being to give expression to truths which they found unrepresented in existing religious practice. The ecumenical tendency illustrates the extreme weakness of religious commitment and belief, since, much more markedly than for organizations which have purely instrumental ends, amalgamation implies surrender of principles, or their attenuation.[21]

Finally, Weber's interactionist approach to religion provided numerous examples of an attempt to establish the social determinants of theological concepts. His account of the rise of monotheism well illustrates this point:

> Among the Greeks, philosophers interpreted whatever gods were found elsewhere as equivalent to and so identical with the deities of the moderately organized Greek pantheon. This tendency towards universalization grew with the increasing predominance of the primary god of the pantheon, that is, as he assumed more of a 'monotheistic' character. The growth of a world empire in China, the extension of the power of the Brahmin caste throughout all the varied political formations in India, and the development of the Persian and Roman empires favoured the rise of both universalism and monotheism, though not always in the same measure and with quite different degrees of success.[22]

The rise of monotheism and universalism, then, was correlated by Weber with the rise of political imperialism.

A Study of the Social Significance of Theological Positions

Whereas the first approach took seriously the possibility that society has influenced theological positions, this approach suggested that the latter may at times influence society. An interactionist approach demands that both sociological approaches be

---

21   Wilson, *Religion in Secular Society*, pp. 152–153.
22   Max Weber, *The Sociology of Religion*, London: Methuen, 1965 [1920], p. 23.

treated as viable possibilities. I argued at the time[23] that theology had all too often been ignored as a possible independent variable in the sociology of religion. I attempted to show in the British context that both the debate centring around John Robinson's *Honest to God* in 1963 and the breakdown of the proposed Anglican/ Methodist Union in 1969 showed the possibility (countering Bryan Wilson) that theology itself could act as an independent religious variable. The *Honest to God* debate contained certain non-theological factors which may have influenced the general public in Britain at the time, whereas the breakdown of the proposed Union apparently defied most sociological theories of ecumenism and suggested the possibility that specifically theological differences of opinion were a causal factor in it. Both of these examples indicated only a possibility – albeit a possibility which required a more serious attempt on the part of sociologists of religion to examine the role of theology as an independent religious variable.

The comparative neglect of this approach in contemporary sociology of religion was, perhaps, somewhat surprising in view of the importance that Weber placed on it. The latter's radical thesis in his *The Protestant Ethic and the 'Spirit' of Capitalism*, which first appeared in 1905, suggested that one of the variables responsible in some way for the rise of capitalism in the West may have been Calvinist theology. In particular, Weber singled out the theological concepts of vocation, predestination, inner-worldly asceticism and sanctification as being of peculiar relevance to the rise of capitalism. Important criticisms of this thesis were certainly made in the 1970s,[24] yet the thesis itself was more modest than it was sometimes portrayed. In an important footnote Weber cautioned:

> We have no intention whatever of maintaining such a foolish and doctrinaire thesis as that the spirit of capitalism … could only have arisen as the result of certain effects of the Reformation, or even that capitalism as an economic system is a creation of the Reformation. In itself, the fact that certain important forms of capitalistic business organisation are known to be considerably older than the Reformation is a sufficient refutation of such a claim. On the contrary,

---

[23] Robin Gill, 'British Theology as a Sociological Variable', in Michael Hill (ed.), *A Sociological Yearbook of Religion in Britain*, London: SCM Press, 1–12, 1974.

[24] Betty Scharf, *The Sociological Study of Religion*, London: Hutchinson, 1970, pp. 132f.

we only wish to ascertain whether and to what extent religious forces have taken part in the qualitative formation and the quantitative expansion of that spirit over the world.[25]

Weber's thesis became the object of a considerable amount of sociological research,[26] particularly since 1961, when Gerhard Lenski[27] claimed that it could be used as a model to explore modern-day differences between Catholics and Protestants. Gary Bouma, however, argued that much of the research which used the Weberian thesis as a modern-day, rather than historical, model was inadequately based. His main criticism of this research – a criticism that is highly relevant in the present context – was that it ignored important theological differences between Protestants. Bouma maintained that researchers 'did not check whether any of the people who are classified Protestant believed in predestination, viewed their jobs as a calling, felt as though they ought to do all for the glory of God, actually held ascetic norms, or felt it necessary to order their lives rationally … in the attempt to determine the effect of inner-worldly asceticism as contrasted with that of otherworldly mysticism, most researchers simply fell back on the assumption that Protestants are inner-worldly ascetics and Roman Catholics are other-worldly Mystics.'[28]

One area, however, which was comparatively well researched was that concerning a possible correlation between theology and racial prejudice. On the specific issue of anti-Semitism, Glock and Stark claimed that there was a strong correlation between it and a high level of Christian 'orthodoxy'. In their major empirical study of 3,000 church members, however, they found no similar correlation between 'orthodoxy' and attitudes towards Black Americans. They eventually concluded that specifically theological notions, especially those based in religious particularism, acted as independent variables within the area of anti-Semitism. They pictured the causal sequence as follows:

---

[25]   Max Weber, *The Protestant Ethic and the 'Spirit' of Capitalism*, New York, NY: Scribner, 1958 [1905], p. 91.

[26]   See Gary D. Bouma, 'Recent "Protestant Ethic" Research', *Journal for the Scientific Study of Religion*, 21:2, 141–155, 1973.

[27]   Gerhard E. Lenski, *The Religious Factor*, Garden City, NY: Doubleday, 1961.

[28]   Bouma, p. 152.

Orthodox faith that claims universal truth and specifies in detail what that truth is leads persons to take a particularistic conception of their religious status. They think of themselves as having a patent on religious virtue and hence discredit all persons who do not share in their faith. Particularism leads Christians to be especially negative in their historic image of ancient Jewry, to see the Jews as implicated in the Crucifixion of Jesus. The combination of these factors markedly predisposes Christians to hold a negative religious image of the modern Jew as unforgiven for the 'sins' of his ancient forebears, and suffering God's punishment.[29]

They did not claim that these theological factors were either the sole or the indispensible cause of anti-Semitism, but they did claim that they were important. Even this limited claim, however, was unlikely to appeal to theologians.

It is significant, perhaps, that both 'orthodoxy' and anti-Semitism appeared to be higher among sectarian groups than among mainstream churches in the Glock and Stark survey. This was perhaps hardly surprising since their scale of 'orthodoxy' involved an arguably sectarian understanding of religious 'certainty'. Nevertheless, even this observation did not destroy their claim that certain types (albeit sectarian) of theological concept predispose people towards anti-Semitism. There was, though, the claim of other researchers at the time[30] that the predisposing factor was not so much Christian 'orthodoxy' as generalized dogmatism or authoritarianism. On this understanding, both sectarian 'orthodoxy' and anti-Semitism would have common roots in authoritarian attitudes.

A rather different way of approaching the possibility that theology may act at times as an independent sociological variable was suggested by Roderick Martin. After a brief analysis of Durkheim, Weber and Marx, he suggested that their work demonstrated the inseparability of social diagnosis and social research. Their concepts 'were initially presented as part of a critique of contemporary society

---

[29]　Charles Y. Glock and Rodney Stark, *Christian Beliefs and Anti-Semitism*, New York: Harper, 1966, pp. 94–95.

[30]　Dean R. Hoge and Jackson W. Carroll, 'Religiosity and Prejudice North and South', *Journal for the Scientific Study of Religion*, 12:2, 181–197, 1973: though see Richard L. Gorsuch and Daniel Aleshire, 'Christian Faith and Prejudice: Review of Research', *Journal for the Scientific Study of Religion*, 13:3, 281–301, 1974.

that was often moral and ideological in origin'.[31] He believed this was particularly true of the concept of alienation in Marx, of that of disenchantment in Weber and of social disintegration in Durkheim. An adequate appreciation of pioneer sociology must see that 'it drew its theoretical concepts from sources as diverse as Christian theology, enlightenment rationalism, German idealism, the conservative reaction to the French and industrial revolutions, and many others'.[32] A sociology of sociologists, then, suggested that theology may act as an independent variable in this context too.

This second approach as a whole goes hand in hand with the first. It would doubtless be possible to study the social determinants of theological positions in isolation. Yet it would be hard to justify such study from a sociological perspective if in fact theology can never act as an independent sociological variable. That is, if theology is without social significance, an analysis of its social determinants may command little attention.

A Study of the Social Context of Theology

This last approach is the one that will be explored in this volume. I will argue at length that theologians inevitably make certain societal assumptions and that in doing so it is important that they turn to sociologists. Accordingly, the latter can perform an important function in discerning the social context which theologians need take into consideration if they are to communicate effectively.

This approach is different from the first in that it is not concerned with discerning the social determinants of particular theological positions. Rather it is concerned with the general social context within which the theological perspective operates. Nor is it specifically concerned with the possibility that this perspective may act as an independent variable within modern-day society.

It is clear that this approach is primarily oriented towards the needs of the theologian rather than those of the sociologist though, hopefully, it will not be entirely irrelevant to the latter. It employs sociological evidence and explanations

---

[31]   Roderick Martin, 'Sociology and Theology', in D.E.H. Whiteley and R. Martin (eds), *Sociology, Theology and Conflict*, Oxford: Blackwell, 1969, p. 34.

[32]   Martin, p. 34.

only in so far as these are relevant to theology and to the theological enterprise. By following this approach I hope to show that sociology is indeed of central importance to theologians and that the latter ignore it at their peril.

Precisely because this study handles both theological and sociological material it raises fundamental methodological problems in both disciplines. The sociologist might suggest that this work is simply an exercise in what used to be termed 'religious sociology', whereas the theologian might argue that sociology is ill equipped to handle theological material. Accordingly, in the next chapter I will examine critically the traditional, and somewhat disparaging, distinction that was made in sociology in the 1970s between 'religious sociology' and the 'sociology of religion'. This examination will lead naturally to the subsequent chapter on the role and status of 'explanation' in both theology and the sociology of religion.

Since the social context of theology is still a relatively unexplored area these preliminary methodological considerations are vital. There is no universally accepted 'sociological method', just as there is none in theology. Consequently, it is important to make explicit the distinctions that I intend to use in subsequent chapters. However, the full force of these preliminary considerations will only become clear in the final chapters.

It will soon become apparent that this study is very different from that of the French 'religious sociologists' half a century ago. Whereas they were concerned to apply sociological findings to the mission of the church, I intend in addition to apply sociology to theology. Nevertheless, 'religious sociologists' such as Ferdinand Boulard were faced in part with similar problems. The latter described his work as follows:

> Religious sociology has a modest role in mission. It is an auxiliary science of pastoral policy, in the same way as psychology, pedagogy or medicine. It is at the service of pastoral theology, which directs the work of the Church towards 'the edification of the Body of Christ,' by making available a better understanding of human milieus and their influence upon the behaviour of the individuals who live in them. By so doing it indicates to responsible authority those sectors which are most menaced and the influences which cause the danger. It brings

into the open, over and above the Christian history of individuals, the course of salvation in geographical regions and social milieus.[33]

Despite repeated criticism from both sociologists and theologians, Boulard maintained that this is a legitimate exercise. To the latter he suggested that 'religious sociology' has not 'undertaken the task of calculating the chances of Christianity in our world, as if we thought they depended only on immediate results'.[34] To the former he suggested that sociology can indeed be a pragmatic discipline. It is to this debate that I must turn next.

---

[33]   Ferdinand Boulard, *An Introduction to Religious Sociology*, London: Darton, Longman & Todd, 1960, p. 74.

[34]   Boulard, p. 74.

Chapter 2

The Critique of Religious Sociology

'Religious sociology' tended to be treated with disdain by both sociologists and theologians in the 1970s (today it has been largely forgotten altogether). Whereas sociologists tended to regard it as a distortion of 'authentic' sociology, theologians were inclined to treat it as an intrusion of the 'secular' social scientist into matters that properly belong to a transcendental perspective. Despite its early and enthusiastic adoption by groups in France, the United States and indeed Britain,[1] 'religious sociology' had come to be regarded with a good deal of suspicion.

Sociologists in the 1970s often distinguished between the 'sociology of religion' and 'religious sociology'. Sometimes a further distinction was made, 'Christian sociology', although it had little in common with what was typically understood to be sociology: it referred instead to a theological critique of the social order,[2] a task that might or might not require the assistance of the academic sociologist. In the distinction between the 'sociology of religion' and 'religious sociology', it was only the first which was generally thought by sociologists to belong to their particular perspective.

Sociological Objections to Religious Sociology

There were several reasons for sociologists thinking it important to distinguish between 'religious sociology' and the sociology of religion', and for claiming that the former does not come within the province of academic sociology. Three reasons were deemed particularly important.

---

[1]   See John D. Brewer, 'Sociology and theology reconsidered: religious sociology and the sociology of religion in Britain', *History of the Human Sciences*, 20:2, pp. 7–29, 2007.

[2]   See M.J. Jackson, 'Introduction to the English Edition', in F. Boulard, *An Introduction to Religious Sociology*, London: Darton, Longman & Todd, 1960, p. x.

In the first place, it was sometimes argued that sociologists of religion attempt to adopt a neutral stance in relation to the beliefs, practices and experiences that they are examining.[3] Essentially, they are not concerned with validity.[4] Whether or not there really is a God, or whether or not Christ was the Son of God, are not issues that sociologists as sociologists could decide or even matters with which they should be concerned. Nor can the Holy Spirit be given a place within a sociological perspective to act as an independent religious variable. Sociology must be strictly neutral on the issue of transcendence, since only in this way could both religious-minded and non-religious-minded sociologists work within the sociology of religion.

In contrast, it was held that religious sociology is not strictly neutral in this sense. It demands a prior act of religious commitment from its adherents, or at least a prior act of commitment to furthering religious ideals or structures – whether in the form of the technical area of theology or in the shape of institutional churches. It was pointed out that some of the main pioneers of religious sociology in both France and the United States were Roman Catholic priests, whose basic aim was to further the work of the Catholic Church.[5] So it was argued that, however commendable this study might be in itself, it is not a part of sociology and should be contained within the seminary rather than the university.

Secondly it was argued that the sociology of religion and religious sociology are dependent upon different traditions. Whereas the former is dependent upon the sociological tradition, the latter relies upon a theological one'.[6] Those engaged in sociology of religion in the 1970s usually, though not always,[7] maintained that it belongs to the sociological tradition as a whole and can be used to test and illuminate sociological theories lying outside the sociology of religion.

---

[3]　See Thomas Luckmann, *The Invisible Religion*, London: Macmillan, 1967, p. 115.

[4]　See Michael Argyle, *Religious Behaviour*, London: Routledge & Kegan Paul, 1958, p. 1.

[5]　Even John Brewer, who offers a much more nuanced and comprehensive account of religious sociology than sociologists writing in the 1970s, defines the discipline as 'sociology in support of the ethical tenets of faith', in 'Sociology and theology reconsidered', p. 8.

[6]　Michael Hill, *A Sociology of Religion*, London: Heinemann, 1973, p. 3.

[7]　Benjamin Nelson, 'Is the Sociology of Religion Possible? A Reply to Robert Bellah', *Journal for the Scientific Study of Religion*, 9:2, 89–96, 1970.

So, for example, the sociology of knowledge,[8] the sociology of deviance[9] and organizational sociology[10] had all been related at the time to the sociology of religion. Arguably, the comparative neglect of the sociology of religion within both Britain and the United States between the 1930s and the 1950s was only overcome by sociologists of religion acting in this way and justifying their study in relation to sociology as a whole.

Religious sociology, on the other hand, was usually thought by sociologists to have a theological, rather than sociological, dependency. As a discipline it was primarily answerable to a church or to a theological perspective and not to sociology as a whole. It simply used sociological techniques: it did not seriously test sociological theory. On this basis it could be maintained that, whereas the sociology of religion is a subdivision of sociology in general, religious sociology is essentially a parasitic discipline. The latter might at times produce data which are of interest to the sociologist – after all, sociologists of religion did refer at times to the work of Boulard[11] or Fichter[12] – but its primary reference lies outside sociology.

Finally, it was argued that the sociology of religion, like any other legitimate academic discipline, pursues knowledge for its own sake, whereas religious sociology has a far more pragmatic orientation. Sociologists are not concerned about the 'usefulness' of their discipline. In studying religion they are not ideologically motivated: they are not interested in how far their analysis of religion will be useful either to the religious or the non-religious. Instead, they typically find religion an interesting phenomenon in its own right, which can be studied in the same spirit in which one might study Homeric mythology. The academic study of anything is self-justifying – as long as there are people who wish to study it, it can be studied.

---

[8]   See Peter L. Berger, *The Social Reality of Religion*, London: Faber & Faber, 1969 [US title, *The Sacred Canopy of Religion*, Garden City, NY: Doubleday, 1967].

[9]   See Peter L. Berger, *A Rumour of Angels*, Garden City, NY: Doubleday, 1969 and Harmondsworth: Penguin, 1970.

[10]   See Kenneth A. Thompson, *Bureaucracy and Church Reform*, Oxford: Oxford University Press, 1970.

[11]   F. Boulard, *An Introduction to Religious Sociology*, London: Darton, Longman & Todd, 1960.

[12]   J.H. Fichter, *Social Relations in the Urban Parish*, Chicago, IL: Chicago University Press, 1954.

The position of the sociologist in relation to religious sociology, then, seemed clear. The sociology of religion and religious sociology were entirely separate disciplines, despite their common use of the word 'sociology'. Further, the academic sociologist regarded religious sociology with caution because it was not neutral, it did not relate to sociological theory as a whole and it was not a self-contained and detached discipline. Instead it was religiously committed, theologically dependent and pragmatically oriented in a way that the sociology of religion was not.

Theological Objections to Religious Sociology

If religious sociology tended to be dismissed by sociologists, it fared little better in the hands of theologians. Despite an apparently growing use of sociological techniques by churches in the West at the time, there was also evidence of considerable resistance to these techniques.

The reaction to Leslie Paul's report *The Deployment and Payment of the Clergy* in 1964 well illustrates this resistance. Paul, although a theologian himself, deliberately adopted the techniques of the social scientist in the hope that 'the rejection of emotive terms will enable us to keep a certain coolness and objectivity in assessing the evidence'.[13] Whatever the specific sociological deficiencies of the report,[14] it undoubtedly revealed discrepancies both in deployment and payment within the Church of England at the time. Writing six years later, however, Paul pointed out that, due to a sharp decline in ordinands, the situation had actually deteriorated in the Church of England. Somewhat bitterly, he wrote:

> Briefly the present ministry of the Church of England is an aging group, a
> declining group, a misused group and (in urban areas) an overworked group.
> The Church has rejected the rationalising proposals of my report and the severer
> Fenton Morley Report. These would at least have led over a period to the most

---

[13]   Leslie Paul, *The Deployment and Payment of the Clergy*, London: Church of England Information Office, 1964, p. 11.

[14]   See, for example, Margaret Hewitt, 'A Sociological Critique', in F.G. Duffield (ed.), *The Paul Report Considered*, Chester: Marcham Manor Press, 1964.

effective use of the existing ministry. The Pastoral Measure (1968) provides some way round problems of shortage and of mission needs if dioceses have the courage to use it – it does make provision for the complete re-organisation of areas in the light of missionary needs – but it is a slow and piecemeal means of reform. It looks, by the temper of Church Assembly, July 1970 (which rejected Fenton Morley and proposed yet another commission), as though the Church will wait in inertia for the shocks of erosion to shove it into action. But a Church aging in more senses than the historical may be impeded by hardening of the arteries when the time comes and may deeply regret the wasted decade of the sixties.[15]

Paul's obvious disillusionment was caused, not simply by the 'inertia' of the Church of England, but also by the fact that his report was rejected in part on theological grounds. So, for example, the then Bishop of Pontefract, Eric Treacy, claimed that 'whilst not denying the need for clear heads and a recognition of facts in ordering the life of the Church, we must ever have in mind that the Spirit bloweth where it listeth, and that the Spirit can make nonsense of statistics and sociological surveys.'[16] Treacy suggested that the 'character' of the Church of England – 'a mixture of cunning, laziness, and peasant simplicity' – renders it 'absorbent and impregnable' and impervious to sociological techniques.[17]

One of the central objections of theologians to sociology was that it tended to ignore the transcendent. This objection could be expressed at both an institutional and an individual level. At the institutional level, the sociologist systematically excludes the possibility that the Holy Spirit may in any way guide or influence the church. That is, the Holy Spirit is never treated as an independent religious variable. Precisely because the sociological method adopts a thoroughly finite system of causality, it excludes any system of transcendent causality. Such a method might be deemed adequate for sociologists of religion, but it was likely

---

[15] Leslie Paul, 'The Role of the Clergy Today – An Organizational Approach: Problems of Deployment', in C.L. Mitton (ed.), *The Social Sciences and the Churches*, Edinburgh: T&T Clark, 1972, p. 170.

[16] Eric Treacy, 'Approaching the Report', in F.G. Duffield (ed.), *The Paul Report Considered*, Chester: Marcham Manor Press, 1964, p. 9.

[17] Treacy, p. 10.

to be most inadequate for theologians, since it ignored the one element that they typically considered to be significant about the church.[18]

At an individual level, theologians may well have felt uneasy about attempts by sociologists to quantify religiosity. For the theologian the concept of 'faith', which is essentially unquantifiable, may be more apposite than that of 'religiosity' – since the concept of 'faith' takes into account the transcendent role of grace within the individual believer. No sociological account of individual religiosity – whether it is based on the data from questionnaire-surveys or on generalized statistics of religious practice – would ever be able to provide an adequate theological account of individual faith. Indeed the 'religious maps' provided by Boulard or John Gay[19] – based as they were on churchgoing statistics – would hardly give the theologian an adequate impression of the locality of individual faith in France or Britain at the time.

The second major criticism that theologians typically made concerned the apparent tendency of the social sciences to 'explain away' religious phenomena. It was evident to them that some of the most distinguished pioneers of the social sciences – notably, Marx, Durkheim and Freud – were inclined to 'explain away' religion and religious phenomena – whether as 'a sop for the masses' in a situation of elitist stratification, as the product of human 'sociability', or as a neurotic perpetuation of childhood fantasies. Further, it was known that all three men were inclined to be somewhat hostile towards conventional religiosity in the West.

The apparent 'neutrality' of contemporary sociologists of religion did not totally immunise them from this criticism, despite claims that they were no longer concerned with the validity of religion. It was always possible to argue that the tendency of the pioneer sociologists to 'explain away' religious phenomena remained implicit within the sociological perspective. The very fact that sociologists seek social determinants of all human behaviour seemingly commits them to the view that religion must be 'explained away'.

In 1990 John Milbank, in his highly influential *Theology and Social Theory*, argued that contemporary sociology of religion in its entirety is a 'secular policing of the sublime':

---

[18]   Paul, 'The Role of the Clergy Today', p. 171.

[19]   John D. Gay, *The Geography of Religion in England*, London: Duckworth, 1971.

I am going to show how all twentieth-century sociology of religion can be exposed as a secular policing of the sublime. Deconstructed in this fashion, the entire subject evaporates into the pure ether of the secular will-to-power.[20]

Amazingly it is not just the declared atheists Marx, Durkheim and Freud that he has in mind, but practising Christians such as Peter Berger, Robert Bellah and Mary Douglas as well (within the text he ignores altogether more explicitly theological sociologists of religion such as David Martin and Kieran Flanagan). He concludes provocatively:

If the analysis in this chapter is correct, then sociology of religion ought to come to an end. Secular reason claims that there is a 'social' vantage point from which it can locate and survey various 'religious' phenomena. But it has turned out that assumptions about the nature of religion themselves help to define the perspective of this social vantage. From a deconstructive angle, therefore, the priority of society over religion can always be inverted, and every secular positivism is revealed to be also a positivist theology. Given this insight, sociology could still continue, but it would have to redefine itself as a 'faith'.

Milbank's claims here depend upon a number of elisions. As the paragraph stands it is not at all clear why the sociology of religion ought to come to an end, what the connection is between secular reason and the sociology of religion, what the assumptions about the nature of religion are, or what the relation of the sociology of religion is to secular positivism. However, in the Preface to the Second Edition he explains more helpfully (in response to sociological critics such as Kieran Flanagan):

At first, there was a certain amount of outraged protest from sociologists, many of whom took it that I was objecting to a supposed 'reduction' of religion to the social, when I was explicitly arguing that 'the social' of sociology was itself an unreal, unhistorical and quasi-theological category. Today, this sort of reaction survives only amongst theologians themselves – who are still so often belated. Within secular social theory by contrast, there is a widespread recognition (only

---

[20]   John Milbank, *Theology and Social Theory: Beyond Secular Reason*, Oxford: Blackwell, 2nd edition 2006, p. 106.

a very little indebted to my book) that 'sociology' is an unexploded paradigm and in part because of its inbuilt secular bias.[21]

Now it can be seen that Milbank believes that sociology in its entirety has an *inbuilt social bias*. Clearly this inbuilt bias does commit sociologists to a reduction of religion to the social (even among those sociologists who have conventional theological commitments), although this reduction is not itself the main focus of his thesis. Instead his main thesis is that the *inbuilt social bias* constitutes a form of (secular) faith or positivist theology (presumably even for theologically committed sociologists). Armed with this explanation, his central claim against the sociology of religion might be reformulated as follows (the words in italics are my additions):

> If the analysis in this chapter is correct, then sociology of religion *in its entirety* ought to come to an end. *The inbuilt* bias of secular reason *within the sociology of religion* claims that there is a 'social' vantage point from which it can locate and survey various 'religious' phenomena *without remainder*. But it has turned out that *the inbuilt* assumptions *of the sociology of religion* about the nature of religion themselves help to define the perspective of this social vantage. From a deconstructive angle, therefore, the priority of society over religion *within the sociology of religion* can always be inverted, and every secular positivism *inbuilt within the whole of twentieth-century sociology of religion* is revealed to be also a positivist theology. Given this insight, sociology *of religion* could still continue, but it would have to redefine itself as a 'faith'.

Milbank's position, then, assumes that the sociology of religion is inescapably reductive,[22] even though his focus is upon the theological implications rather than the existence of this (faith based) reductionism. So he too appears to believe that the very fact that sociologists of religion seek social determinants of all human behaviour commits them to the view that religion must be 'explained away'.

---

[21]   Milbank, *Theology and Social Theory*, 2nd edition, p. xii.

[22]   See Richard H. Roberts, 'Theology and the Social Sciences', in David F. Ford and Rachel Muers (eds), *The Modern Theologians*, 3rd edn, Oxford: Blackwell, 2005, pp. 378–381.

A part of this theological criticism remained even when it was admitted that it rests upon two obvious errors. The first is that few of the pioneers of the social sciences really did attempt to 'explain away' all religious phenomena. Certainly they were concerned to provide explanations of the origins and function of religion, but both Durkheim and Freud claimed at various points that this was not tantamount to 'explaining away' religion, whatever their own personal religious beliefs.

The second error followed from the first. The confusion of origins with validity is a fundamental philosophical mistake (the genetic fallacy). To say that x is caused by y is to say nothing logically about the validity of x on logical grounds, no matter how disreputable y might be. Nevertheless, a point remained. Suppose, for example, that John Allegro's thesis in his controversial 1970 book *The Sacred Mushroom and the Cross*[23] about the origins of Christianity being linked with a psychedelic mushroom cult really had been substantiated (although it is extremely difficult to imagine just how it ever could have been substantiated). How would this affect Christian belief? Logically, it need not, since Christians could always have claimed that the origins of their beliefs do not affect their validity. So, it would be logically possible for the Christian to remain a Christian, claiming that God could have wrought salvation through a mushroom cult if God had so desired. However, there is something rather odd psychologically about this claim. It would seem more likely that many Christians would lose their confidence in the validity of Christianity, since they would find it psychologically difficult to remain adherents of such an extraordinary faith. While admitting on logical grounds that God could have acted in this way, in practice they would be inclined to think otherwise. Evidently, then, the origins of beliefs are not altogether irrelevant to their validity – at least, for most people they are not.

The theologians' suspicion of at least some social scientists may well be justified precisely at this point. It is not necessary for the latter to be attempting to 'explain away' religion: it is enough that they seek causal explanations while studying religious phenomena. The social scientist can give no guarantee to the theologian that these causal explanations will always prove harmonious with religious belief. Indeed, the accounts of the function of religion provided especially by Marx

---

[23] See Judith Anne Brown, *John Marco Allegro: The Maverick of the Dead Sea Scrolls*, Grand Rapids, MI: Eerdmans, 2005.

and Freud may well prove psychologically distressing for Jews, Christians and Muslims alike.

A more recent example of the genetic fallacy is provided unwittingly by the philosopher Daniel Dennett in his polemical book, *Breaking the Spell: Religion as a Natural Phenomenon*.[24] Dennett argues that belief must have given humans some evolutionary advantage. He suggests that early forms of folk religion (animism and then shamanism) provided their adherents with a crucial sense of agency in an otherwise complicated world and perhaps health benefits as well. In time more organized forms of religion provided evolutionary benefits in terms of group cooperation and social altruism. Religion is thus a purely natural phenomenon helping its adherents to survive in the competition for life. As an atheist he then challenges religious people to make a rigorous and scientific analysis of the claimed benefits and evident dangers of religious faith today. Dennett is prepared, for example, to concede that religious beliefs may continue to deliver health benefits to adherents (alongside wars of terror), but he challenges others to investigate whether specifically religious beliefs are the only or even the best way of delivering these benefits in the modern world. Only a rigorous and impartial use of the social sciences, he believes, can establish whether or not this is so.

But the problem here is that neither evolutionary theory nor the social sciences are capable of delivering the kind of convincing verdicts that are likely to persuade the religious to renounce their beliefs or the non-religious to espouse them. And only a moment of careful thought is necessary to realize this. At most evolutionary theory can speculate about how religion might have arisen. There have been many attempts at such speculation in the past and doubtless there will be many more in the future. Yet they remain speculations and there is no possibility whatsoever of finding evidence to support or refute them. And even if a religious person is convinced by Dennett's speculation, she could still argue (as the Catholic natural law theologian Stephen Pope does)[25] that such evolutionary paths are simply God's way of embedding belief. It seems that Dennett, too, has confused origins with validity and then he has confused benefits with truth.

---

[24]   New York: Viking and London: Allen Lane, 2006.

[25]   Stephen Pope, *Human Evolution and Christian Ethics*, Cambridge: Cambridge University Press, 2008.

Both of these criticisms – based on a tendency to ignore the transcendent and to provide distressing causal explanations – are really overall criticisms of the social sciences in so far as they consider religious phenomena. A third criticism, however, was peculiar to religious sociology. It was based on the tendency of religious sociologists to move too quickly from sociological descriptions to theological prescriptions. Chapter 4 will return to this criticism in relation to Harvey Cox's *The Secular City*. This tendency is, however, a major weakness in socio-theological correlations. From both the theological and the sociological perspectives it might be unwise to assume too readily that there is a logical link between sociological analysis, explanations and even predictions, and the sort of prescriptive language the theologian employs.

Objections Reviewed

I have suggested, then, that six fundamental criticisms were made of religious sociology in the 1970s – three from the sociologist and three from the theologian. The former criticizes the discipline because it is religiously committed, theologically dependent and pragmatically oriented in a way that the sociology of religion is not. The latter criticizes it because it tends to ignore the transcendent, to provide distressing causal explanations and to move too easily from sociological descriptions to theological prescriptions. An examination of these criticisms should help to clarify some of the methodological distinctions that are important here.

Even by 1975 the sociological argument based on 'neutrality' was becoming increasingly difficult to maintain with conviction. An examination of the spread of interests among sociologists was sufficient to confirm that sociology was seldom value-free. Some notable theorists, both in sociology in general,[26] and in the sociology of religion in particular,[27] argued that the values and ideologies of sociologists do exert an influence upon their work. If this were not the case, the lack of interest among sociologists in religious phenomena between the 1920s

---

[26]   For example John Rex, *Key Problems of Sociological Theory*, London: Routledge & Kegan Paul, 1961, pp. vii f.

[27]   For example David Martin, *The Religious and the Secular*, London: Routledge & Kegan Paul, 1969.

and 1950s would have been hard to explain. Inevitably, the particular interests of sociologists are, at least partially, determined by the contemporary interests of the academic community as a whole. So at a time following the logical positivists, when academic interest in religion was at a fairly low level both in Britain and in the States, the comparative neglect of religious phenomena by sociologists was understandable – understandable, certainly, but incredible if sociology is to be regarded as value-free.

It increasingly seemed possible that the notion that sociology was in some sense 'neutral' sprang from an outdated system of induction. Once it was commonly thought that scientists employed an inductive method of approaching reality. That is, they dispassionately observed phenomena until the latter suggested laws, which they could then frame into theories and which, in turn, they could test empirically. On the assumption that sociology is a science some sociologists apparently did view their work in this way.[28] However, by the late 1960s there was already a greater readiness to admit that the scientist's own imagination – creative imagination – plays an important role in the formation of scientific theories. Scientists do not approach their work in a dispassionate and value-free way: instead they approach it creatively.[29]

Among some contemporary social theorists, too, there was a greater readiness to admit that sociological theory is based not on a system of induction but on the creative use of models.[30] Consequently, it became increasingly difficult to maintain that the sociology of religion is indeed a 'neutral' or value-free enterprise and to criticize religious sociology for not being so. Instead a genuinely scientific methodology would seem to demand the admission that we all have value-biases and that we should make these explicit in so far as this is possible, rather than retain them implicitly in a seemingly value-free theory.

However, it was unnecessary to claim that personal values and religious orientations dominate *all* social scientific examinations of religious phenomena. Ninian Smart suggested two reasons for supposing that this may not be the case:

---

[28]   See Rex, ch.1.

[29]   See Ian G. Barbour, *Issues in Science and Religion*, London: SCM Press, 1966, pp. 137 f.

[30]   Cf. Percy S. Cohen, *Modern Social Theory*, London: Heinemann, 1968, ch.9.

First, there are degrees of bias: some omnipresent bias does not legitimate universal great bias; and second, more importantly, does a scholar's position legitimately influence his conclusions in this sphere? In the latter case there has to be some logical or intrinsic connection between his beliefs and his role as explorer of religion. Otherwise, the lament that men are liable to weaknesses and distortions which impede their goals is an old one; we know that men are imperfect, but they can become better at doing things if they set their hearts on it. (One thing they could do is to leave the study of religion to those who are least inclined to bias!) The objection, then, can only hold if there is a logical connection between the scholar's position and the kind of conclusion he ought to arrive at.[31]

Boulard always maintained that his account of religious sociology did have scientific status.[32] On Smart's suggestion, the way to test this claim would be to see whether or not his conclusions could be logically derived from his initial religiously oriented premises. It is insufficient simply to point out that he was a French Roman Catholic priest working for the Catholic Church.

If religious sociology could not be dismissed automatically on the basis that it is value-oriented, it was difficult to see why it should be labelled as 'theologically dependent'. In so far as religious sociologists really did think of themselves as sociologists and not simply as theologians using a certain amount of sociological techniques, they should in principle have been able to relate their findings to sociology as a whole. Granted they should initially have made their value-orientation explicit, they could then have been able to contribute to the sociological enterprise along with other sociologists.

In reality this is exactly what has happened among quite a number of sociologists of religion today. James Beckford is an interesting example. His earlier work on new religious movements[33] and religion and modernity[34] tended to be highly analytical and detached. However, by the late 1990s dispassionate

---

[31]   Ninian Smart, *The Phenomenon of Religion*, London: Macmillan, 1973, p. 17.

[32]   Boulard, p. 73.

[33]   For example James Beckford, *Cult Controversies: The Societal Response to the New Religious Movements*, London: Tavistock, 1985.

[34]   For example James Beckford, *Religion and Advanced Industrial Society*, London: Unwin Hyman, 1989.

analysis was now combined with a moral commitment to social change, as is evident in the subtitle of the study of prison chaplaincy that he wrote with Sophie Gilliat, *Religion in Prison: Equal Rites in a Multi-Faith Society*.[35] The research itself was funded jointly by General Synod of the Church of England and by the Leverhulme Trust and the authors express a wish that their book 'will at least stimulate and inform public debate about the increasingly complex and sensitive relations between the state, the Christian churches and other faith communities'.[36] The theological commitments here are certainly not as explicit as they are in the work of, say, Leslie Francis[37] or Douglas Davies.[38] Nonetheless, Beckford does take explicit church funding for the research *and* makes policy recommendations from this research.

Perhaps it was the third criticism – based on the notion that the sociology of religion pursues knowledge for its own sake, whereas religious sociology is a pragmatic discipline related to the needs of theology and the church – that caused the greatest discontent among sociologists. This appears to be a real distinction between the two disciplines which proponents of each might have accepted.

However, in retrospect the whole idea that the social sciences should not be tainted with pragmatism appears antique. Today social scientists are often keen to demonstrate to research councils and funding charities that their work *is* relevant, applicable and useful. Even in the 1970s there was plenty of evidence that the sociological enterprise as a whole was thoroughly based in pragmatism. Few objected to the use of sociological theory in the fields of industry, education, deviance or race relations. In all these areas sociology was used for pragmatic ends: a need was felt in some way to improve the status quo and the sociologist was unashamedly used to help with this task. Of course, sociologists engaged in any of these four areas might have claimed that they worked simply on the basis of pursuing 'knowledge for its own sake'. Yet, in practice, both the research grants made available by people engaged in these areas and the value-orientations of

---

[35]   Cambridge: Cambridge University Press, 1998.

[36]   p. xiii.

[37]   For example Leslie J. Francis (ed.), *Sociology, Theology and the Curriculum*, London: Cassell, 1999 and (with Philip Richter), *Gone for Good? Church-Leaving and Returning in the 21st Century*, London: Epworth, 2007.

[38]   For example Douglas Davies (with Charles Watkins and Michael Winter) *Church and Religion in Rural England*, Edinburgh: T&T Clark, 1991.

sociologists themselves suggested otherwise. Sociological analysis was already being used extensively on a pragmatic basis.

If this was the case in other areas of sociology, it was difficult to see why it should not be so in the specific area of the sociology of religion. Boulard, too, was aware of this criticism:

> It hardly seems worth replying at length to those who fear that a scientific piece of work is falsified by the intention to make pastoral or missionary use of its results. Has the concern to save human lives ever compromised the scientific quality of medical research? It must, of course, be stressed that only rigorous impartial observation of the facts can produce legitimate conclusions for formulating policy.[39]

Boulard's point remains despite his optimism about 'impartial observation' and 'the facts'. Once it is admitted that the sociology of religion is not value-free and that religious sociology is not necessarily theologically dependent, this final criticism becomes increasingly difficult to maintain. In other areas of sociology it is not usual to make a sharp distinction between sociologists who pursue 'knowledge for its own sake' and those who have some pragmatic orientation – provided that both types of sociologist act within the accepted framework of a sociological perspective. Further, if the distinction between the sociology of religion and religious sociology is to be maintained simply on the basis that the first is concerned with religion 'for its own sake', whereas the second is pragmatically oriented, it is difficult to see that it will hold up in practice. At what point does religious sociology become sociology of religion, and vice versa?

In *The Social Context of Theology* I concluded that from a sociological perspective alone it seems that the traditional distinction between religious sociology and the sociology of religion should be abandoned even if it was useful in the past. It cannot be maintained successfully on the basis of either the supposed value-orientation or the alleged theological dependency of religious sociology. In addition, there seems little point in rigorously distinguishing between those who are concerned about religious phenomena 'for their own sake' and those who are not – even if such a rigorous distinction could be maintained in practice.

---

[39]   Boulard, p. 73.

Doubtless some sociologists will be prepared to work pragmatically for theology or for a church, whereas others will not. But this preparedness will not serve to differentiate them as either religious sociologists or sociologists of religion.

Yet in hindsight the very concept of 'religious sociology' was already beginning to fade into history. However, spurious the sociological arguments against the discipline were, 'religious sociology' was no longer a label that many wished to wear. John Brewer concludes that:

> The existence of religious sociology has been written out of the history of the discipline in Britain, such that when theology and sociology began a more serious engagement in the 1970s in Britain and elsewhere, particularly as biblical studies discovered sociology and as theologians and sociologists first met jointly, this earlier dialogue was entirely overlooked.[40]

Not surprisingly I concluded at the time that there is a non-sociological reason for wishing to abandon the traditional title 'religious sociology'. As a title it is peculiarly unfortunate, since it appears to imply that there are two types of sociology – the one 'religious' and the other presumably 'non-religious'. Doubtless, this implication was not originally intended, but it does appear to be conveyed by the title. By abandoning it this embarrassment was removed.

The objections of the theologian to the use of sociology in the context of theology, however, remain – particularly the claims that the sociologist tends to ignore the transcendent and to provide distressing causal explanations. These will be the subject of the next chapter.

---

[40]   John Brewer, 'Sociology and theology reconsidered', p. 7.

Chapter 3

Explanation in Sociology and Theology

The role and status of 'explanation' in both the sociology of religion and theology are crucial to most theological criticisms of the use of sociology in the context of theology. It is possible, in fact, that many of these criticisms are based on inadequate understandings of sociological 'explanations', particularly as they apply to religious phenomena.

The previous chapter outlined three main theological objections to the use of sociology: it ignores the transcendent, it provides distressing causal explanations, and it moves too easily from sociological descriptions to theological prescriptions. The last of these objections will be examined in the next chapter. It is crucial to the first two objections that those who wish to employ sociology in the context of theology should at least be aware of the difference between analysis, explanation and prediction, on the one hand and prescription, on the other.

Theologians who are prepared to be open to the work of sociologists can, of course, be given no guarantee that they will not at times be confronted with distressing causal explanations. So, for example, the first chapter suggested a number of ways in which theology may act as an independent variable within society. However, neither Weber's nor Glock and Stark's examples of this action may prove particularly congenial to theologians. They may not regard it as welcome news that theology might have contributed to the rise of both Western capitalism and anti-Semitism.

Possibly this is a risk that theologians must take. It is certainly a risk that they have taken in other fields with considerable benefit. The results, for example, of both historical and philosophical criticism, even within theology departments, have at times proved extremely distressing to theologians. Nevertheless, the latter do not usually suggest that these enterprises should on that account be ignored. On balance it might appear that the critical perspectives that both philosophical and historical analysis have contributed to critical theology have proved more beneficial than harmful. A similar case might be advanced for the use of sociology within the context of theology.

This solution, however, may only obscure the central objection of the theologian to sociology. The objection may not be simply that sociology offers distressing causal explanations, but, as John Milbank appears to claim, that its basic methodology is fundamentally opposed to a theological perspective. Framed in this way, the objection comes close to the initial criticism – that is, that sociology tends to ignore the transcendent. It is precisely at this point that the role and status of 'explanation' within both sociology and theology becomes crucial. If 'explanation' within the sociology of religion is to be interpreted in an imperialist and positivist fashion its relevance to the theological perspective becomes doubtful. At best theology must simply ignore sociology: at worst it must be rendered redundant by it.

The sociology of religion does indeed become imperialist when it claims to be *the* way of interpreting religious phenomena. Such a claim would, of course, affect the psychologist, anthropologist and philosopher, as much as the theologian. It becomes positivist when it claims that a behavioural interpretation of the social determinants of religious phenomena expresses the 'true' nature of these phenomena. This claim, if accepted, would, of course, be as damaging to theology today as the philosophical logical positivism of the Vienna Circle was to theology in an earlier generation. If such imperialism and positivism are indeed implicit in sociological method, the prospects of any socio-theological cooperation would be extremely remote.

The Limits of Sociological Explanation

A sophisticated form of this argument appeared in the 1970s in John Bowker's ambitious examination of sociological, psychological and anthropological explanations of the sense of God. He maintained that all of these forms of explanation, as they are usually expounded, are too restrictive. In the conclusion to his study he claimed:

What has emerged quite separately in each of the various disciplines surveyed is an entirely new concern with the differentiating consequences of the responsive objects of encounter. It is this which represents so important a revolution in recent years, because it implies a reversal of the nineteenth century ambition. It now becomes clear that we are not studying massive mechanisms of social process, or of individuation, alone, in which it is virtually irrelevant what objects are or are not encountered – as though the mechanism will in any case run on. It is the contributory effect of the actual objects of encounter which is returning into the analysis of behaviour in all these different disciplines.[1]

The effects of this claim in the specific context of the sense of God are radical. Bowker argued that 'far from the disciplines we have been surveying dissolving the possible reality of reference in the term "God", they actually seem to demand a return to that possibility if sense is to be made of their own evidence'.[2]

Bowker maintained that he was not attempting to produce an argument for the existence of God – in no sense was his claim an implicit ontological argument for divine existence. However, he was determined to show from within the various disciplines that the possibility of the existence of God cannot be excluded and may actually be demanded by the limitations of psychological, sociological and anthropological explanations of the sense of God. This is a discrete claim that he offered, but nevertheless an important and potentially radical one. Further, it was a claim that few social scientists at the time (whether they were themselves 'religious' or not) were prepared to support.

Bowker was not making the sort of crude theological objection noted in the previous chapter, whereby the social sciences are thought to 'explain away' religious phenomena. He was usually aware that, even if the social scientist could provide an adequate social explanation of the sense of God, this would still tell us very little about the reality of its reference. Like most Christians, he was dissatisfied with Freud's account, for example, of the origins of religion, but in general he argued against it on internal, rather than external, grounds. So, he claimed that 'the basic defect of Freud's theory of religion is not that it cannot possibly be right, but that it cannot possibly be wrong: all evidence that superficially appears to

---

[1]   John Bowker, *The Sense of God*, Oxford: Oxford University Press, 1973, p. 181.

[2]   Bowker, pp. 181–182.

contradict the theory is converted to become evidence for the theory'.[3] He did not claim from outside, so to speak, that Freud's theory is inadequate simply because it tends to conflate projection with invalidity.

Bowker's claim was that Freud and others did not take seriously the possibility that God could act as an independent variable within society. For him, an adequate analytical explanation of the sense of God – whether from the psychological, sociological or anthropological perspective – would have to take seriously the proposition that the origins of the sense of God are to be found, to some degree at least, in the relation of God to humankind.

The weakness of Bowker's claim becomes most apparent in his critical interpretation of Berger. He argued that the latter was originally too controlled 'by sociological orthodoxy' in his account of the social construction of religion and societal plausibility structures. He was too determined to interpret 'the social' solely in terms of 'the social':

> In *The Social Reality of Religion*, Berger completely missed this point. He got diverted into sociological orthodoxy – which in itself is not surprising, since sociologists, like all others, have to earn their way in the world, and are thus deeply constrained by norms and conventions of expectation in sociological community. Thus Berger, instead of exploring the possibility that there might be a sufficiency of reality in existence in the external universe for there to be a groundwork of perception on which interpretation can be constructed, suggested that the more important reality is the one which individuals confer on the external universe: individuals 'pour out meaning' into it, on the basis of the language and concepts which they have culturally acquired.[4]

In *A Rumour of Angels*, Bowker argued, Berger changed his mind and was now prepared to examine 'signals of transcendence' contained within the universe. In the original book Berger stated baldy that 'religion is the human enterprise by which a sacred cosmos is established',[5] and claimed in effect that 'God is an

---

[3]   Bowker, pp. 121–122.

[4]   Bowker, p. 34.

[5]   Peter L. Berger, *The Social Reality of Religion*, London: Faber and Faber, 1969, p. 26.

artefact' and 'an end-product of socialization',[6] but now he took seriously the possibility that the sacred cosmos' object could exercise an influence upon the human enterprise.

In fact, this is a misreading of Berger. The latter made it quite plain in a footnote to his claim that 'religion is the human enterprise by which a sacred cosmos is established', that he was well aware of the limitations of this sociological definition of religion:

> Religion is defined here as a human enterprise because this is how it manifests itself as an empirical phenomenon. Within this definition the question as to whether religion may also be something more than that remains bracketed, as, of course, it must be in any attempt at scientific understanding.[7]

In addition, Berger devoted a complete appendix to his book to 'sociological and theological perspectives' – arguing that 'no theological or, for that matter, anti-theological implications are to be sought anywhere in the argument – if anyone should believe such implications to be present sub-rosa, I can only assure him that he is mistaken'.[8] Essentially, the work was concerned with sociological theory, whereas *A Rumour of Angels* had a directly theological orientation. A careful comparison of the two works fails to substantiate Bowker's claim that Berger underwent a process of change between writing them.

The suggestion, however, that Berger was too strictly controlled by 'sociological orthodoxy' in *The Social Reality of Religion* must be taken more seriously. It is precisely at this point that the role and status of 'explanation' within sociology become crucial.

Berger suggested that there are three moments or steps in the process of socialization (the process by which the individual interacts with society). He depicted these three steps as 'externalization', 'objectivation', and 'internalization'. Together these steps form the 'fundamental dialectic process of society':

---

6 Bowker, pp. 35–36.
7 Berger, p. 193 n.34.
8 Berger, p. 181.

Externalization is the ongoing outpouring of human being into the world, both in the physical and mental activity of men. Objectivation is the attainment by the products of this activity (again both physical and mental) of a reality that confronts its original producers as a facticity external to and other than themselves. Internalization is the reappropriation by men of this same reality, transforming it once again from structures of the objective world into structures of the subjective consciousness. It is through externalization that society is a human product. It is through objectivation that society becomes a reality sui generis. It is through internalization that man is a product of society.[9]

In the specific context of religious socialization, these three steps are still apparent. Through externalization the individual 'pours out meaning into reality' – she creates a 'sacred cosmos'. Through objectivation this 'sacred cosmos' assumes an objective identity – the 'sacred cosmos' of a particular society is presented to the child in that society as an objective reality. Through internalization individuals are affected by the 'sacred cosmos' of the particular society in which they live. Thus religion is indeed regarded by Berger in *The Social Reality of Religion* as a thoroughly human enterprise. It is created by society, it is then treated as an objective reality by that society and, in turn, it has an independent influence upon society.

Again, Bowker objected that this account of religious socialization does not take seriously the possibility of the reality of the reference in religious language. The latter, like all language, is regarded simply as a human product, an invention of society, and not as referring to objective reality. Further, at no point does he consider the possibility that the object of religious language – that is, 'God' for Christians – can act as an independent variable in religious socialization.

Writing almost two decades later John Milbank made the same point (albeit without referring back to Bowker):

According to Berger and Luckmann's theory of social genesis, the very first social arrangements do not require 'a sacred canopy', but exist only as conventions which have accidentally grown up through the symbolic interaction between individuals which establish simultaneously the first social rules, and the first

---

[9]   Berger, p. 14.

sense of personal identity. These arrangements are then passed on to the 'second generation', and only at the point of transmission to the 'third generation' do questions start to arise about their *rationale*. Questions arise simply because the circumstances of the genesis of the arrangements have now been forgotten, and instead of the true, forgotten history, a mythical one is substituted, which relates existing social facts to some imagined eternal or natural order. Only at *this* stage does society come to require a 'sacred canopy.'[10]

Milbank used this as a clear example of the sociology of religion 'policing the sublime' and failing to remain 'entirely within a religious grammar'.[11] Berger had distorted his account religious origins by excluding the transcendent.

Bowker and Milbank, however, both missed a vital element in Berger's methodology.

Methodological Atheism

Berger was well aware that he had excluded the transcendent from his sociological account of religious phenomena. He argued, however, that this exclusion is necessary *within* scientific enquiry:

> In all its manifestations, religion constitutes an immense projection of human meanings into the empty vastness of the universe – a projection, to be sure, which comes back as an alien reality to haunt its producers. Needless to say, it is impossible within the frame of reference of scientific theorizing to make any affirmations, positive or negative, about the ultimate ontological status of this alleged reality. Within this frame of reference, the religious projections can be dealt with only as such, as products of human activity and human consciousness, and rigorous brackets have to be placed around the question as to whether these projections may not also be something else than that (or, more accurately, refer to something else than the human world in which they empirically originate).

---

[10] John Milbank, *Theology and Social Theory: Beyond Secular Reason*, Oxford: Blackwell, 1990, 2nd edition 2006, p. 137.

[11] Milbank, *Theology and Social Theory*, p. 139.

In other words, every inquiry into religious matters that limits itself to the empirically available must necessarily be based on a 'methodological atheism'.[12]

Berger's concept of methodological atheism, then, is essentially a methodological, and not an ontological, stance. As a sociologist he believed that he has, quite deliberately, to exclude any reference to transcendent causality – whatever his personal religious beliefs. His whole concept of 'signals of transcendence' lies firmly outside his work as a sociologist of religion, since as a sociologist he is methodologically committed to viewing reality in exclusively empirical terms.

This 'methodological atheism' is different altogether from the sort of imperialist, positivist sociology noted earlier. However, even in the 1970s there were critics of positivism in both sociology and psychology.[13] John Rex, for example, argued that such positivist sociology tends to ignore Hume and suppose that causality is logically based. For him, 'the continued prevalence of purely causal enquiries in sociology is merely an indication of the extreme immaturity of the discipline, and we should expect that, as more adequate theories are developed, such enquiries will become part of a larger and more systematic plan of enquiry'.[14] Berger, however, was no positivist – nor could he have been, unless his methodology were transformed into an ontology.

Ninian Smart, though, was not satisfied at the time with Berger's 'methodological atheism'. He suspected that it *was* imperialist:

> He of course distinguishes this methodological atheism from atheism *tout court*. But one needs to ask what it is in the way of explanations that is excluded by methodological atheism. And further, is it merely a device for operating within 'scientific' sociology? If this be so, then is it assumed that a total account of explanation of religion can be given from a sociological point-of-view? The last is a very bold assumption, but less extravagant perhaps when one realizes that sociological theory tends to subsume other spheres of human enquiry such as psychology within its embrace.[15]

---

[12]   Berger, p. 106.

[13]   Cf. Liam Hudson, *The Cult of the Fact*, London: Jonathan Cape, 1972.

[14]   John Rex, *Key Problems of Sociological Theory*, London: Routledge and Kegan Paul, 1961, p. 25.

[15]   Ninian Smart, *The Phenomenon of Religion*, London: Macmillan, 1973, p. 59.

Smart's three questions can be answered surprisingly simply. Berger made it quite clear that his 'methodological atheism' is intended to exclude anything that is not 'empirically available'. He argued that the sociologist as a sociologist must concentrate solely upon the empirical. Consequently, Bowker's plea for a return within sociology to 'the possible reality of reference in the term "God"', or Milbank's requirement for religion scholars to remain 'entirely within a religious grammar', are clearly excluded. Secondly, it is also clear that Berger proposed 'methodological atheism' precisely for operating within 'scientific sociology': the latter, after all, was his speciality. And finally, there is no reason to believe that Berger ever imagined that 'a total account of explanation of religion can be given from a sociological point-of-view'. On the contrary, even within his description of 'methodological atheism' he deliberately left open the question of the ultimate reference of religious phenomena. If one also takes into account his more specifically theological writings, then it is abundantly clear that he was no sociological imperialist.

Only Smart's final point suggests a certain ambiguity within Berger's stated methodology. Like most sociologists, Berger seldom referred to psychological explanations of religious phenomena, yet these are not specifically excluded by his notion of methodological atheism. Psychological explanations plainly work with the 'empirically available', and, in theory at least, ought to form part of the perspective that Berger was proposing. It is possible, then, that the description of his methodology as 'methodological atheism' only partially depicts the methodology he was proposing.

A second, and less important, criticism might also be suggested. The term 'atheism' may be unfortunate, since it introduces too many extraneous connotations. Certainly it prompted one sociologist at the time to write wittily:

> Berger is determined to surpass, if anything, the sceptics in their scepticism, and to show how cynically and debunkingly sociological a believing sociologist can be, before – just at the very last moment when all seems 'lost' – thrillingly producing an ace from his sleeve and coming out with a starkly absolute confession of faith.[16]

---

[16] Ian Hamnett, 'Sociology of Religion and Sociology of Error', *Religion*, 1973, vol. 3, p. 3.

Obviously this was a caricature of Berger's position, but then the very notion of 'methodological atheism' may have rendered him susceptible to such caricature.

The sociologist Robert Towler's objections at the time to 'methodological atheism' were far more severe. He argued, perhaps unfairly, that it is 'a fail-safe device which protects the sceptical researcher from taking the beliefs of others too seriously, and which protects also the religiously or ideologically committed researcher from allowing his own beliefs to pollute his research'.[17] In contrast, Towler believed that 'the sociologist's task, difficult and uncomfortable though it may be, is to take seriously the beliefs of those whom he studies and to seek to enter into the mentality which they bring to their ritual and to their everyday lives, even if in so doing he runs the risk of "going native"'.[18] This position was closer to Robert Bellah's 'symbolic realism' than to Berger's 'methodological atheism'.

Symbolic Realism

In proposing his research stance of 'symbolic realism', Robert Bellah, also writing in the 1970s, deliberately intended to counter sociological positivists and reductionists. He believed that the position of 'symbolic realism' represents a fundamental break-through for those concerned with the study of religious phenomena – and, in particular, for the sociologist of religion.

Bellah identified two kinds of sociological reductionism. In the first place there is 'consequential reductionism', which is concerned exclusively with 'the explanation of religion in terms of its functional consequences'.[19] This type of reductionism, or positivism, he saw as typical of those eighteenth-century 'secular intellectuals' who opposed the 'historical realism' of contemporary theologians. For 'consequential reductionists' the claims of Christianity were basically fraudulent. During the nineteenth century, however, Bellah argued, 'symbolic reductionism' arose. This type of reductionism no longer regarded religion as fraudulent: rather it was concerned with 'the search for the kernel of truth hidden in the falsity of

---

[17]   Robert Towler, *Homo Religiosus: Sociological Problems in the Study of Religion*, London: Constable, 1974, p. 2.

[18]   Towler, p. 2.

[19]   Robert N. Bellah, *Beyond Belief*, New York: Harper and Row, 1970, p. 247.

religion'.[20] Thus, both Durkheim and Freud 'developed comprehensive formulas for the translation of religious symbols into their real meanings';[21] the latter in terms of the Oedipus complex and the former in terms of society itself.

Bellah maintained, however, that Freud, Durkheim and Weber all encountered difficulties in their interpretations. Freud was confronted with the 'unconscious', Durkheim with the concept of 'collective effervescence' and Weber with that of 'charisma'. In all three instances the pioneer social scientists were faced with irreducible, non-literal concepts. For Bellah this observation was crucial:

> What I am suggesting is that the fact that these three great non-believers, the most seminal minds in modern social science, each in his own way ran up against nonrational, noncognitive factors of central importance to the understanding of human action, but which did not yield readily to any available conceptual resources, is in itself a fact of great significance for religion in the twentieth century. Convinced of the invalidity of traditional religion, each rediscovered the power of the religious consciousness. What could perhaps be suggested on the basis of the work of these men is that when Western religion chose to make its stand purely on the ground of cognitive adequacy, it was forgetting the nature of the reality with which religion has to deal and the kind of symbols religion used.[22]

The new approach that arises from this observation is what Bellah termed 'symbolic realism'. Adopting this approach, he believed the sociology of religion is transformed. In his most modest description of this approach he suggested:

> Some social scientists have come to feel that there are profound depths in the religious symbols that we have scarcely begun to fathom and that we have much to learn from any exchange with other disciplines. While remaining committed to Enlightenment rationalism as the foundation of scientific work and accepting its canons with respect to our research, we nevertheless know that this is only one road to reality. It stands in tension with and under the judgement of other

---

[20]   Bellah, *Beyond Belief*, p. 248.

[21]   Bellah, *Beyond Belief*, p. 249.

[22]   Bellah, *Beyond Belief*, p. 240.

modes of consciousness. And finally we know that the great symbols that justify science itself rest on unprovable assumptions sustained at the deepest levels of our consciousness.[23]

From this account of 'symbolic realism' it would appear that Bellah was offering a number of straightforward methodological proposals. Firstly, he was suggesting that sociologists of religion should take account of the 'profound depths' of the symbols they use. Others too within a number of disciplines at the time – psychology,[24] philosophy,[25] science[26] and theology[27] – had suggested that models or symbols should at times be viewed as irreducible and non-literal. Secondly, he was objecting to sociological imperialism, and maintaining instead that sociology is just 'one road to reality'. Thirdly, he did not intend to abandon the 'scientific' nature of sociology, even in its application to religious phenomena. Fourthly, he appeared to have some implicit notion of the complementary nature of methodologies, whereby sociology is regarded as a separate, but interacting, discipline. And fifthly, he admitted that the symbols which are employed within scientific methodologies are themselves not provable.

All five proposals are important. Taken together they help to present a more sophisticated picture of sociological method than is sometimes offered.

However, Bellah's account of 'symbolic realism' did not conclude here. Only in part is it a methodology: it is also in part an ideology. This becomes plain from his celebrated claim that 'religion is true', or rather, less misleadingly, 'religion is a reality *sui generis*':

> When I say religion is a reality *sui generis* I am certainly not supporting the claims of
> the historical realist theologians, who are still working with a cognitive conception
> of religious belief that makes it parallel to objectivist scientific description. But

---

[23]   Bellah, *Beyond Belief*, pp. 245–246.

[24]   Liam Hudson, *The Cult of the Fact*, London: Jonathan Cape, 1972.

[25]   Max Black, *Models and Metaphors*, Ithaca, NY: Cornell University Press, 1962.

[26]   Ian G. Barbour, *Issues in Science and Religion*, New York: Prentice-Hall and London: SCM Press, 1966; continued in *Religion in an Age of Science*, San Francisco: Harper and London: SCM Press, 1990 and *Religion and Science: Historical and Contemporary Issues*, San Francisco: Harper and London: SCM Press, 1997.

[27]   Ian T. Ramsey, *Religious Language*, London: SCM Press, 1959.

if the theologian comes to his subject with the assumptions of symbolic realism, as many seem to be doing, then we are in a situation where for the first time in centuries theologian and secular intellectual can speak the same language. Their tasks are different but their conceptual framework is shared. What this means for the reintegration of our fragmented culture is almost beyond calculation.[28]

So attractive did he find the work of contemporary theologians such as Paul Tillich that he argued that sociologists must communicate 'the meaning and value of religion along with its analysis' to their students – thereby admitting that 'if this seems to confuse the role of theologian and scientist, of teaching religion and teaching about religion, then so be it'.[29]

Bellah was not proposing anything comparable to Bowker's plea for a return within sociology to 'the possible reality of reference in the term God' or Milbank's later requirement for religion scholars to remain 'entirely within a religious grammar'. He would probably have identified both pleas as 'historical realism'. For Bellah religious symbols 'tell us nothing at all about the universe except insofar as the universe is involved in human experience'.[30] His proposals, though, did face the very real possibility that the methods of 'symbolic realist' sociologists and 'symbolic realist' theologians may eventually become conflated.

It was precisely at this point that the weakness of Bellah's proposals for the sociology of religion became most apparent. Once they became an ideology they may have been of considerable use to the theologian but of distinctly less use to the sociologist, especially if the sociology of religion is to be viewed as a part of the sociological discipline as a whole. If it is too closely conflated with theology it may cease to be relevant to general sociological theory.

An 'As If' Methodology

In *The Social Context of Theology* I argued that a more fruitful account of the basis on which the sociologist in general, and the sociologist of religion in particular,

---

[28]   Bellah, *Beyond Belief*, p. 253.
[29]   Bellah, *Beyond Belief*, p. 257.
[30]   Bellah, *Beyond Belief*, p. 195.

operates, might be found in an 'as if' methodology. Adopting such a methodology the sociologist would work 'as if' there were social determinants of all human interactions – believing as an individual, though, that there may not be. Like Berger's 'methodological atheism' such a stance is methodological, not ontological, and thereby immune from charges of positivism, behaviourism or imperialism. Like Bellah's 'symbolic realism' it recognizes the need for irreducible, non-literal societal models, such as would be necessary, for example, to take into account the complex character of religious symbols and beliefs.

An 'as if' methodology, I still consider, avoids the weaknesses evident in the proposals of both Berger and Bellah. It offers a more generalized theory than Berger's 'methodological atheism': the latter leaves the impression that there is something peculiar about the sociologist of religion, whereas the former allows for an overall theory of methodologies in general, whether or not they are concerned with specifically religious phenomena. Again, an 'as if' methodology deliberately seeks to avoid the sort of socio-theological conflation apparent in Bellah: sociology and theology are regarded as distinct, even if complementary disciplines.

Contemporary anthropology by the 1960s provided an interesting illustration of the use of an 'as if' methodology. At one stage behaviourism and functionalism appeared to be the dominant methodologies within social anthropology. By this stage, however, this dominance no longer appeared to be so evident. The almost biological view of social morphology and structure, for example, that was once so popular, was often questioned by then.[31] Edmund Leach, however, argued that traditional techniques for studying social change should not be abandoned, even if their positivist framework is itself abandoned:

> In practical field work situations the anthropologist must always treat the material of observation as if it were a part of an overall system of equilibrium, otherwise description becomes impossible. All that I am asking is that the fictional nature of this equilibrium be frankly recognised.[32]

---

[31]   Ian Hogbin, *Social Change*, London: C.A. Watts, 1957, pp. 24f.

[32]   Edmund R. Leach, *Political Systems of Highland Burma*, Cambridge, MS: Harvard University Press, 1954, p. 285.

On this understanding of the sociological method, then, sociologists, in their work as sociologists, are obliged to treat religious phenomena as if they were purely social phenomena – whatever their private views about the validity or falsity of religious truth-claims. They are not obliged to *believe* that religious phenomena are purely social phenomena: but they are obliged to take sociological theory sufficiently seriously not to exclude – either a priori or a posteriori – any particular religious phenomenon from their examination.

This understanding will also explain, perhaps, why sociology often appears imperialistic in relation to other disciplines. So, Smart's claim that 'sociological theory tends to subsume other spheres of human enquiry such as psychology within its embrace' becomes explicable, since it is the job of the sociologist to examine human interaction *as if* it were entirely socially determined. This is a deliberate methodological stance, not an act of sociological chauvinism.

It is arguable, for instance, that Berger was wrong when he categorically stated that 'hardly anyone, however, far removed from sociological thinking, is likely to deny that language is a human product', and that 'there are no laws of nature that can be called upon to explain the development of, say, the English language'.[33] Supporters of Chomsky's transformational linguistic theory in the 1970s might have wished to qualify such a claim. However, working as a sociologist, it was arguably still Berger's role to examine human language *as if* it were solely a product of society and nothing at all to do with innate brain structures.

The importance of the deliberate fiction involved in an 'as if' methodology was argued persuasively by Vaihinger in the 1920s. He claimed that 'the object of the world of ideas as a whole is not the portrayal of reality – this would be an utterly impossible task – but rather to provide us with an instrument for finding our way about more easily in this world'.[34] In terms of such an object the methodological fiction plays an important role. So, for example, contemporary science is presumably only possible if one adopts an 'as if' methodology. Individual scientists might well be convinced by David Hume's attack on straightforward logical notions of 'causality' or by Karl Popper's attack on 'verification' as opposed to 'falsification'. Nevertheless, they must still continue their work *as if* there was a logical relationship between cause and effect and *as if* verification

33 Berger, *The Social Reality of Religion*, p. 12.
34 H. Vaihinger, *The Philosophy of 'As If'*, London: Kegan Paul, 1924, p. 15.

were indeed possible. They are not ground to inactivity by their knowledge of Hume and Popper.

If sociologists are committed to a methodology whereby they view human interaction *as if* there were always social determinants of it, theologians will be clearly committed to some other methodology. In contrast to Bellah and Bowker, I would suggest that theologians are committed to a radically different *as if* methodology. They typically view the world *as if* there were transcendent determinants of it. It is the theologian, not the social scientist, who must take seriously 'the possible reality of inference in the term God'. An *as if* methodology in both disciplines, if adopted, might then make them immune to the sort of imperialism and positivism that bedevilled socio-theological correlations in the past.

Nevertheless, there is an additional specifically theological point to make in defence of Bellah's concept of symbolic realism. Disarmingly he admitted early to his own 'lack of competence in intellectual history'[35] and, unlike David Martin, he has not made extensive forays into theology (despite his personal commitment to Anglican worship and his affection for Paul Tillich's theology). However, his fascination with religious symbolism fits well with a theological recognition that all terms used to represent the divine are necessarily symbolic, metaphorical or analogical. In this he stands in a long theological tradition expressed with exceptional clarity by Aquinas. Theological concepts are typically drawn from mundane experience – such as love, compassion and forgiveness – and then extended analogically, elusively and mysteriously in an attempt to depict God.

David Martin, ever sensitive to language, has often explored the metaphorical and multivalent nature of theological concepts. Throughout his writings there is an implicit, and sometimes explicit, tension between the different worlds that he inhabits. Writing in the Preface and Acknowledgements of his highly influential *A Sociology of English Religion*[36] in 1967, he noted his own differences from both sociologists such as Bryan Wilson and theologians such as John Robinson or Harvey Cox writing on the issue of secularization. Yet he concluded:

---

[35]　Bellah, *Beyond Belief*, p. 247.

[36]　David Martin, *A Sociology of English Religion*, London: SCM Press, 1967.

our perspectives must above all be realistic: to take but one example we need to be realistic when we consider ecumenical aspiration in relation to social fissures of nation, colour and status, and to the fundamental and very varied types of religious organization which had found constricted and creative lodgement within them. Theological discussion (like political discussion) must generally take place on a level of high-flown and self-deluding linguistic camouflage. Nevertheless the key word of recent debates has been honesty, and if we are to have the honesty about the Church – that 'wonderful and sacred mystery' as the prayer book very properly calls it – then sociological perspectives and research are not a marginal luxury but an essential.[37]

Many of the ideas here were still present a generation later in his mature collection *Reflections on Sociology and Theology*:[38] his suspicion of easy sentiments about ecumenism (despite his own long-standing ecumenical friendships); his awareness of social fissures in religious organizations; his comparison of theological and political forms of discourse; his isolation of key signs and metaphors (here it is that of honesty); his love of the language and resonances of the 1662 prayer book (in which he had been nourished even as a Methodist child); and his insistence, albeit against the odds, that sociological perspectives are essential to an adequate theological understanding of the church. At the heart of Martin's *Reflections*, as in his earlier work, is a conviction that sociology and theology share a number of characteristics, of which three are particularly important: both disciplines are pattern-seeking forms of enquiry; both return constantly to seminal thinkers; and both depend heavily upon metaphors. The first and third of these characteristics are shared with a number of areas of physical science – notably modern physics at both quantum and cosmological levels – but the second is not. Whereas most forms of physical science keep moving forward, seldom showing much interest, except for historical purposes, in their forebears, sociologists and theologians are profoundly retrospective. Within the sociology of religion the works of Weber and Durkheim (and Marx for more radical forms of sociology) are subject to constant examination and re-examination in a manner very similar to the work

---

[37] Martin, *A* Sociology, pp. 11–12.
[38] David Martin, *Reflections on Sociology and Theology*, Oxford: Clarendon Press, 1996.

of theologians. In both disciplines pattern-seeking and metaphors are constantly tested and retested against the ideas of seminal thinkers:

> Just as the classical foundations of sociology and theology do not go dead and distant so the master metaphors of both are constantly being recovered and reused. These recoveries derive from a more fundamental shared characteristic, which is the inherently metaphorical character of sociological and theological discourse. In sociology, as also in theology, metaphorical language is endemic. Perhaps theology is more metaphorical than sociology but sociology is at least metaphorical. Of course, both subjects devise technical vocabularies, but these remain continuous with ordinary language and with its metaphorical character.[39]

Perhaps the place where he expresses this most lyrically is in the early chapters of *The Breaking of the Image*.[40] Before publication they were delivered as the Gore Lectures given, at that time, in the Jerusalem Chamber at Westminster Abbey. Perhaps it was the extraordinary ambience of that location or perhaps just the challenge of the occasion which inspired the lyricism. Whatever social factors lay behind them, they represent fine examples of his sensitivity to metaphor. However, ever the iconoclast, he combined them in the second half of the book with a polemic against liturgical change within the Church of England. The argument is of a piece – namely that the images used within liturgy and worship profoundly shape Christian identity (the first half) and that liturgical changes, which 'are initiated by clerics and defended by them',[41] are in real danger of distorting this identity (the second half). Now, of course, it is perfectly possible to be convinced by the first of these arguments but not the second. Still swimming against the tide, David Martin remains convinced of both, regarding much liturgical change within the Anglican Church as a secularizing factor imposed by the clergy, rather than as a response to popular piety in a context of widespread rejection of traditional liturgical forms.

Yet, leaving the polemic to one side, liturgical innovators and traditionalists alike can still admire the skilful blend of theological and sociological analysis in

---

[39]   Martin, *Reflections*, p. 23.

[40]   David Martin, *The Breaking of the Image: A Sociology of Christian Theory and Practice*, Oxford: Blackwell, 1980.

[41]   Martin, *Breaking*, p. 100.

the first half of *The Breaking of the Image*. Just to take a single example, he offers an illustration of the way that the cross can become a *double-entendre* within Christianity. He draws, at this point, on his long-standing fascination with the religious symbols and typologies of war and pacifism, which can be found in his earliest and more recent writings.[42] The cross, for him, is at once a symbol of peace and a symbol of war. There is 'a continuous dialectic whereby the sword turns into the cross and the cross into the sword':

> The cross will be carried into the realm of temporal power and will turn into a sword which defends the established order. It will execute the criminals and heretics in the name of God and the King. But temporal kingship will now be defended by reversed arms, that is a sign of reversal and inversion. Another illustrationis provided by the cross which dominates the US Air Force Chapel at Colorado Springs. At the centre of the huge arsenal is a chapel built of stained glass spurs like planes at the point of take-off. The cross is also like a sword. Looked at from another angle the combined cross and sword is a plane and a dove. The plane is poised to deliver death rather than to deliver *from* death and the dove signifies the spirit of peace and concord.[43]

It will be seen in later volumes that a recognition of the analogical, metaphorical and symbolic nature of theological (and often sociological) concepts is crucial to sociological theology. Concepts that are grounded in the mundane (albeit extended to the divine) are clearly open to sociological analysis.

---

[42]   See David Martin, *Pacifism: An Historical and Sociological Study*, London: Routledge and Kegan Paul, 1965; *Does Christianity Cause War?*, Oxford: Clarendon Press, 1997; and *The Future of Christianity: Reflections on Violence, Democracy, Religion and Secularization*, Farnham: Ashgate, 2011.

[43]   Martin, *Breaking*, p. 28.

Chapter 4

Theologians as Amateur Sociologists

An account of the social context of theology presupposes both that a sociological perspective is not necessarily in conflict with a theological perspective, as argued in the previous chapter, and that it is actually relevant to it. Naturally, the latter is not without critics, though the next chapter will argue at length that it is a correct presupposition. More specifically, it will be argued that theologians do need to take note of the social context within which they operate if they are to communicate effectively with each other, let alone with wider society.

This chapter, however, will examine just two theologians both famous in the 1960s – Harvey Cox and John Robinson – who did in fact take contemporary society seriously and attempted to provide an analysis of the social context within which they wrote. Clearly they were both proponents of a fairly radical theology within Britain and the United States at the time and could not be regarded as typical of all shades of theological opinion then. Nevertheless they still represent instructive case studies, serving to uncover some of the pitfalls involved in socio-theological forms of cooperation.

The Secular City

Much of the initial criticism of Harvey Cox's highly successful *The Secular City* centred upon his distinction between the 'secular' and the 'religious'.[1] To a degree he may have been the victim of later theological developments, since increasingly in the latter part of the 1960s the focus of theological debate was on the so-called 'death of God' theologians. Somewhat unfairly, perhaps, they were often seen as identical to theologians such as Cox and Robinson and the latter themselves tended to be classified as 'atheists', or, at least, as 'non-theists'. For

---

[1]   See David B. Harned (ed), *The Ambiguity of Religion*, Louisville, KY: Westminster Press, 1968.

Cox, in particular with his dependence on neo-orthodox theology at the time, such labelling was especially inappropriate. 'Secular' for him was not at all identical with 'non-theistic'. Rather his criticism, both in *The Secular City* and elsewhere,[2] was of the categories of 'religion' and the 'religious'.

However, the feature of *The Secular City* which was particularly discussed in the 1960s was Cox's analysis of, and theological reaction to, the phenomenon of urbanization. The concept of 'anonymity' played an important role within this analysis and reaction and soon proved to be one of the more stimulating features of the study. Possibly it is just here that Cox made his most interesting contribution and it is indeed here that his socio-theological correlation becomes most evident.

By concentrating upon Cox's concept of 'anonymity' within *The Secular City*, I am not, of course, attempting an exhaustive critique of the work. That has been attempted many times before and would, in any case, be irrelevant to the aims of this chapter. Rather, the purpose of examining this particular concept in this particular work is simply to observe how one theologian uses sociological data. Although Cox was naturally not the first writer to claim that contemporary cities tend to be 'anonymous' and 'impersonal', he was one of the first theologians to applaud this aspect of cities. The suggestion that modern cities do possess these characteristics usually implies a negative criticism, since in this context 'anonymous' is often regarded as synonymous with 'soul-less' and 'dehumanised'.

Cox, then, started with the assumption that cities are indeed characterized by 'anonymity':

> Every college sophomore knows that modern man is a face-less cipher. The stock
> in trade of too many humanities courses and religious-emphasis weeks is the
> featureless 'mass man', reduced to a number of a series of holes in an IBM card,
> wandering through T.S. Eliot's 'waste land' starved for a name. 'Loss of identity'
> and 'disappearance of selfhood' have come to play an ever larger role in the popular
> pastime of flagellating urban culture.[3]

---

2   Harvey Cox, 'The Prophetic Purpose of Theology', in Dean Peerman (ed.), *Frontline Theology*, London: SCM Press, 1969.

3   Harvey Cox, *The Secular City*, New York: Macmillan, 1965 and London: Pelican, 1968, p. 52.

He disagreed, however, with contemporary criticisms of this 'anonymity', and particularly with critics of urbanization:

> A writer who becomes essentially anti-urban forfeits his claim to greatness, for what is often left unsaid by the morbid critics of anonymity is, first, that without it life in a modern city would not be human, and second, that anonymity represents for many people a liberating even more than a threatening phenomenon. It serves for a large number of people as the possibility of freedom in contrast to the bondage of the law and convention. The anonymity of city living helps to preserve the privacy essential to human life. Furthermore, anonymity can be understood theologically as Gospel versus Law.[4]

The last sentence in this quotation is crucial. Cox was not simply claiming that urban 'anonymity' can be justified on purely humanitarian grounds, but that it is thoroughly biblical. This becomes more apparent in the following passage:

> How can urban anonymity be understood theologically? Here the traditional distinction between Law and Gospel comes to mind. In using these terms we refer not to religious rules or to fiery preaching, but to the tension between bondage to the past and freedom for the future. In this sense Law means anything that binds us uncritically to inherited conventions, and Gospel is that which frees us to decide for ourselves.[5]

There are, then, three parts to Cox's analysis of urban 'anonymity':

1. Sociological analysis – concluding that anonymity is characteristic of contemporary cities.
2. Humanitarian analysis – concluding that urban anonymity has beneficial features for humankind.
3. Theological analysis – concluding that urban anonymity is an expression of Gospel rather than Law.

---

[4]   Cox, p. 53.
[5]   Cox, p. 59.

Despite the overall appeal of this sociological-humanitarian-theological correlation, each of its parts must face serious criticisms.

1. Sociological Analysis

Urban sociologists at the time were by no means all convinced that 'anonymity' is a characteristic of cities. One of the strongest critics of this notion then was Ray Pahl, who argued that 'the qualitative effects of quantitative changes are hard to assess and are not helpfully described by such terms as "urbanization" which are almost impossible to define precisely'.[6] Pahl pointed out that 'individual autonomy' is typically a feature of the middle classes, rather than the working classes, within cities: the latter are better characterized by 'values of us/them solidarity'. Further, he criticized monochrome treatments of 'urbanization', showing instead that cities differ vastly. So, in one city a Coxian pattern of 'urbanization' might be found, whereas in another an essentially rural culture might still be present among the working classes. Even the much-discussed 'nuclear family' is by no means a feature of all cities. Pahl argued that at the beginning of the industrial revolution poverty and limited housing forced many working-class families to live together in extended families and that contemporary patterns of nuclear-family living might correspond fairly closely to pre-industrial, rural patterns of family life. Interestingly, Pahl later became a key member of the Archbishop of Canterbury's commission that produced the radical and influential report *Faith in the City: A Call for Action by Church and Nation.*[7]

So, it is by no means clear that the first step in Cox's argument was accurate. His whole thesis depended on this step, since his theological interpretation was directly dependent on his sociological analysis. If it is the case that 'anonymity' was an ambiguous characteristic of contemporary cities, then the rest of his argument became problematic.

---

6   R.H. Pahl, *Patterns of Urban Living*, London: Longman, 1970, p. 136.
7   London: Church House Publishing, 1985.

2. Humanitarian Analysis

It is significant, perhaps, that Cox's later writings were more reticent about the merits of contemporary cities. *The Feast of Fools*[8] for example, was less concerned with the merits of contemporary culture and more with its deficiencies. Cox maintained that the features of feasting and celebration were largely absent from contemporary culture.

A number of theologians at the time offered rather different humanitarian analyses. David Harned, for example, argued that it was not so much the 'anonymity' of contemporary culture which he believed to be important, but the 'self-seriousness' of people today. In his criticisms of this 'self-seriousness' Harned repeatedly returned, not to the concepts of feasting and celebration, but to the Dutch historian Johan Huizinga's notion of 'play', which he described as a basic human 'instinct':

> In its pure form, play is, first of all, voluntary, an act of freedom. Since there is no utilitarian motivation for it, play can always be deferred. We never need to do it, except 'to the extent that the enjoyment of it makes it a need'. Secondly, there is always an element of conflict or tension involved in it, a striving either to determine some issue or to win some victory. It can be a contest for something or a representation of something. And sometimes it is both, as when children play at war. Thirdly, play calls us away from ordinary life into a realm with rules all its own and definite boundaries in time and space.[9]

John Ferguson argued that there is a demonic side to 'anonymity', which Cox ignored in his attempt to stress its positive humanitarian aspects:

> But is the anonymity of urban life liberation? Plenty of people flock to the cities as a form of escape. But escape from what? Sometimes from themselves, from personal responsibility. Sometimes from a limited tribal society which they

---

[8]   Cambridge, MS: Harvard University Press, 1969.

[9]   David B. Harned, *Theology and the Arts*, Louisville, KY: Westminster Press, 1966, pp. 24–25.

have found a shackle on their self-fulfilment; these last go to the city with the purpose of finding their true selves. Do they succeed?[10]

Ferguson clearly thought that they do not. Instead he believed that there is an element within every encounter with others which is properly 'personal' and denied the 'impersonality' of Cox's aspirations for society.

David Sheppard, Bishop of Liverpool at the time, argued that an anonymous environment, if indeed it exists, might be desirable only for those who are strong or well enough to choose freedom.[11] Such an environment was not nearly so desirable for those who are hungry, poor, old or lonely.

3. Theological Analysis

Cox's theological analysis, too, was criticized. His interpretation of the distinction between Law and Gospel when applied to cities as 'the tension between bondage to the past and freedom for the future'[12] gained few supporters.

Cox's theological interpretation of urban anonymity was evidently dependent on his sociological assumptions. He began with the sociologist, moved to the humanitarian and finally found that this agreed with what he saw as the biblical evidence. At the time I saw a similar methodology evident in Peter Rudge's analysis of churches in terms of sociological theories of organizations.[13] Of course, it is possible that sociology and theology may correspond so conveniently at times, but it is by no means clear that they always should or will. Both Cox and Rudge, in very different ways, seemed to me to be in danger of jumping straight from the 'is' to the 'ought'. In the process sociological descriptions and theological prescriptions had become thoroughly confused.

This point was crucial to my argument in *The Social Context of Theology*. *The Secular City* offered an important warning precisely because it attempted a socio-theological correlation but raised too many problems in the process. I argued that it is essential that an adequate correlation should distinguish carefully between

---

[10]   John Ferguson, 'The Secular City Revisited', *The Modern Churchman*, April 1973, p. 191.

[11]   David Sheppard, *Built as a City*, London: Hodder & Stoughton, 1974, pp. 18–19.

[12]   Cox, p. 59.

[13]   Peter Rudge, *Ministry and Management*, London: Tavistock, 1969.

analysis, explanation and prediction, on the one hand, and prescription, on the other – that is, between the 'is' and the 'ought'. If Cox had been better aware of this distinction in the material he was handling, he might have been more prepared to admit the obvious demonic aspects of 'anonymity'. The failure of the work at this point suggested that future correlations needed to be considerably more sophisticated. But before such sophisticated socio-theological correlations could be attempted it was obviously important that the sociological analysis adopted was itself sufficiently robust. At the time I was surprised to discover just how often contemporary theologians made assumptions about what 'modern man [*sic*] thinks or does' without any reference to the work of sociologists. Yet it was clear to me then and is still clear to me today that such theologians were and still are already acting as sociologists, albeit as amateur sociologists.

The Human Face of God

John Robinson's *The Human Face of God* provided another example of a theologian-turned-sociologist in his analysis of 'four fundamental shifts' which he believed those studying Christology must take into account. On the basis of this analysis, he argued that theologians needed radically to change their concepts in Christology.

The first of the fundamental shifts which Robinson believed had taken place in the 1960s and early 1970s concerned contemporary attitudes towards 'myths':

> For men today, myth is equated with unreality. The mythical is the fictional. But in fact myth relates to what is deepest in human experience, to something much more primal and potent than the intellect. Psychologically and sociologically myth has been the binding force holding individuals and societies together. Yet today myth cannot be taken as a description of how things did, do or will happen. For us it is an expression of significance, not an explanation for anything.[14]

My primary concern at the time was not, surprisingly perhaps, with Robinson's confident sociological analysis of 'the binding force holding individuals and societies together' – many psychologists and sociologists would indeed be

---

[14]   J.A.T. Robinson, *The Human Face of God*, London: SCM Press, 1973, pp. 20–21.

delighted if they could discover such a force – but rather with his proposal about what contemporary people did or did not believe. Robinson may simply have been making a semantic point – that is, that in popular usage the term 'myth' refers to fictional stories. If that is so, then of course he was correct. But that hardly represented a 'fundamental shift' in contemporary thinking that has taken place in the previous decades – and it is clear from the context of the quotation that Robinson was concerned with just such a shift, albeit without offering significant evidence, or even pointing to sociological research, to suggest that a shift of this nature had occurred.

It was possible, of course, that the 'us' in this quotation referred simply to Robinson's theological colleagues. The footnotes, indeed, referred to the group of theologians who had been concerned to explore and develop Bultmann's concept of 'mythology'. But then, of course, it was open to debate how far this group was representative of contemporary, popular thought.

Robinson's second fundamental shift concerned 'metaphysics':

> What myth is to the imagination, metaphysics is to the intellect. It is the way of trying to state what is most real, most true, ultimate. One cannot, I believe, get away from metaphysics any more than from myth. It is concerned with how things are. Yet the meaningfulness of metaphysical statements in our day is equally problematic. Above all, confidence has gone in the type of supranaturalist ontology to which Christian theology in its classical presentation has been attached. According to this, what is 'really real' … is located in another realm, above, beyond or behind phenomena. Today this language has almost the opposite effect. A child of a friend of mine was heard saying in his prayers 'I'm sorry for you, God, up there while I am in the real world down here'. For we most naturally locate reality, not in another realm, but as the profoundest truth of this one.[15]

Again, it appeared that Robinson had humankind in general or, at least, Western humankind in mind when he wrote about this fundamental shift in thinking. In effect he was presenting a sociological analysis at this point, albeit an 'amateur' sociological analysis, since he was attempting to depict social change. Yet, the only clear piece of evidence that he presented in this passage was the story about the child's prayer,

---

[15]   Robinson, pp. 21–22.

which again may or may not reflect the rest of humankind. Sociologists would surely have required a good deal more evidence before supporting Robinson's thesis. As will be seen much later, among sociologists today there is still considerable debate about cultural secularization. A number of possibilities are open to those who wish to supply a sociological analysis of contemporary attitudes in the West towards metaphysics:

1. That metaphysics is becoming increasingly irrelevant – that is, Robinson's thesis.
2. That metaphysics remains intelligible to most people, with the exception of the academic community.
3. That metaphysics has always been unintelligible to most people in most ages.

Even these three possibilities do not exhaust the list of viable options – particularly if a sharp distinction is made between Western and non-Western peoples, or if it is assumed that no linear, monochrome trends in relation to metaphysics are discernable within any society. Yet they at least show that those who wish to make an adequate analysis of contemporary thought must present serious sociological evidence to support their thesis.

Robinson's third shift concerned 'the demise of the language of the absolute':

> The classic way of expressing ultimate reality has been to use the vocabulary of uniqueness, of finality, of once-and-for-allness, of timeless perfection, of difference not merely of degree but of kind. Truth has been seen as unitary, rising like a Gothic arch and meeting in the One who is the answer to all possible questions. And it is not difficult to see how important a part this has played in Christian theology. Jesus Christ has been presented as *the* Son of God and Son of Man, and Alpha and Omega, in whom all lines meet, unique, perfect and final. Yet we live in a world of what Paul van Buren has called 'the dissolution of the absolute'. The monistic model has lost its power over our thinking, whether about space or time. Ours is a relativistic, pluralistic world in which we are compelled to be more modest about our claims.[16]

---

[16]   Robinson, p. 23.

Here it seems, at first at least, that Robinson was on firmer sociological ground. By introducing the concept of the pluralistic society and by suggesting its possible effects to be a general relativizing of claims to absolutism, Robinson could, at the time, count on the support of a number of sociological theorists.[17] There did seem to be firmer grounds for believing both that contemporary society in the West was becoming increasingly pluralistic and that Christological assertions of 'uniqueness' were consequently becoming more difficult to maintain. A pluralistic society, with a wide variety of competing faiths and claims to the truth, might well create the sort of shift that Robinson suggested.

Nevertheless, even at this point the sociological evidence was by no means unambiguous. Not all sociologists at the time would have agreed that contemporary society in the West had become increasingly pluralistic.[18] Yet, even supposing that the West was becoming increasingly pluralistic, it still remained to be shown that people were becoming correspondingly more modest in their religious truth claims. With hindsight (as Chapter 8 will suggest) the rise of fundamentalism in the 1980s suggested a much more complicated and contradictory picture.

It was, perhaps, only Robinson's final fundamental shift that avoided such sociological difficulties. He argued that traditionally the Incarnation had been thoroughly rooted in history; 'traditional Christology has had a large and fairly crude stake in historicity'.[19] However, many of Robinson's fellow New Testament critics at the time were considerably less confident about the historicity of the Gospels than they were in earlier times: the so-called 'Jesus of history' had become a shadowy figure. At one point Robinson did in fact suggest that this attitude had now spread to 'modern man', but in general his comments were carefully confined to those academics who were concerned with studying the New Testament. It is precisely because he generally avoided statements about what people today think or do, or about how vastly Westerners as a whole had changed in the previous decades, that he was able to avoid in this final point the sort of 'amateur sociology' that was so apparent in his other three points.

---

[17]   For example Peter L. Berger, *A Rumour of Angels*, Garden City, NY: Doubleday, 1969 and Harmondsworth, Middlesex: Penguin, 1970 and Bryan Wilson, *Religion in Secular Society*, London: C.A. Watt, 1966.

[18]   Cf. David Martin, 'The Secularization Question', *Theology*, 76:630, Feb 1973.

[19]   Robinson, p. 27.

An Overview

My two examples – Harvey Cox and John Robinson – might both be described as representatives of fairly radical theology in the 1960s and early 1970s. However, it will become apparent in Chapter 6 that it was not only radical theologians who tended to make rather sweeping and uncritical assumptions about Western society.

The situation in theology at the time had parallels with political analysis. David Martin argued that sociologists could be useful to those concerned with political decision-making in several ways. In the first place, they could provide an analysis of the situation as it actually is, was or will be. In the second place, they could trace both the antecedents of a situation and the possible future consequences of that situation. Of course, they might not tell the politician what 'ought' to be done in a given situation – that, in Martin's view was properly for politicians themselves and ethical commentators to say. But they could analyse the 'is', 'was', 'will be' or 'could be' of that situation – and, indeed, they were best qualified to do just that:

> These services which 'sociology' may provide represent the combined resources of economics, political science, etc., and are only new in that nowadays such services are explicitly sought and are systematically performed. Presumably in the past every politician and ethical commentator was an amateur political scientist and economist, more explicitly perhaps after Machiavelli in the European experience, but implicitly everywhere and at all times. What is now understood in the multi-dimensional perspectives of sociology as systematised, verified propositional knowledge has always been practical knowledge, even if working with a 'Ptolemaic' rather than a 'Copernican' perspective'.[20]

Martin's comments about politics, could, perhaps, be applied to theology. If theologians are to be concerned with the social context of theology – with the way people think within the particular societies in which they are operating – then they must expect to fail in their task if they ignore the critical perspectives offered by sociologists. In the 1960s and 1970s theologians frequently wrote about 'what modern man thinks' or 'what urban man can accept'. Today they would

---

[20]   David Martin, 'Ethical Commentary and Political Decision', *Theology*, Oct. 1973, p. 527.

be likely to change the engendered language here, while remaining suspicious of sociological analysis (assuming it to be inherently reductive) and wedded to their own understanding of social change. However, when they do this, they are in effect acting as 'amateur sociologists'. Too often they ignore the work of professional sociologists and simply assume that they know what their fellow human beings think and how they are changing. Yet it is possible that such theologians are simply dignifying their own thoughts by ascribing them to the rest of society.

Chapter 5

Plausibility Structures and Theology

Harvey Cox and John Robinson shared a common belief. Even though they presented somewhat different analyses of contemporary society, they were both convinced that such analyses are highly relevant to theology. For both men some form of socio-theological correlation was an essential feature of their theological perspective. In this chapter I will defend this basic approach – though not, of course, the specific details of Cox's or Robinson's correlations which I criticized in the previous chapter – and will examine the views of some of its critics.

By no means all theologians in the 1970s considered that the findings of the sociologist were relevant to their enterprise.[1] In his celebrated critique of Paul van Buren, John Knox and John Robinson, Eric Mascall, for example, maintained that all three theologians required that the Christian faith 'should be completely transformed in order to conform' to 'the outlook of contemporary secularised man'.[2] Mascall clearly regarded such a transformation as disastrous for theology. Apparently accepting that a process of secularization is indeed evident within the West, he argued that Christianity should certainly not conform to it:

> It reduces the dialogue between Christianity and contemporary thought to a purely one-way process; there is no question of contemporary thought adapting itself to the Gospel, the Gospel must come into line entirely with contemporary thought ... The contemporary man, they say in effect, is so radically secularised that he simply cannot accept supernatural Christianity; therefore we must completely de-supernaturalise Christianity in order to give him something that he can accept.[3]

---

[1] For example E.L. Mascall, *The Secularisation of Christianity*, Lutterworth, Leics: Libra, 1967, and R. Holloway, *Let God Arise*, Oxford: Mowbrays, 1972.

[2] Mascall, p. 6.

[3] Mascall, p. 7.

Mascall rejected this thesis, since it 'completely capitulates to the outlook of the contemporary world', and, as a result, 'it has no criterion for passing judgement on it'.[4] For him a legitimate role for theology is to pass judgement on, or even effectively ignore, its social context. He was not concerned simply with the tendency of theologians like Cox or Robinson to conflate sociological descriptions with theological prescriptions. Rather, he was offering a critique of socio-theological correlations in general. If modern people cannot accept the claims of the Gospel, then it is they who must change, not the Gospel. Elsewhere Mascall admitted that it may be necessary to review particular theological images at times – though even here he argued that urban dwellers, for example, are still capable of adopting rural images such as the shepherd simply because they are imaginative human beings.[5] The substance of the Gospel, however, must remain unchanged.

A number of crucial issues are involved in this debate. In the first place, there was radical disagreement among contemporary theologians about what does or does not constitute the 'substance of the Gospel'. Secondly, there was disagreement about the extent to which theology should pronounce judgement on contemporary assumptions. Thirdly, there was disagreement about how seriously theology should take its social context. It is the third which is of particular concern here.

From the perspective of this third area of disagreement, it is possible that if Mascall's approach were rigorously followed theologians would largely fail to communicate with each other let alone with the wider public. So, if theologians simply ignore their social context unless they are pronouncing judgement upon it, then they must expect to appear increasingly irrelevant and unintelligible. Later chapters will argue that they may also fall into the ghetto of sectarian fundamentalism. In sociological terms, the relevance and even survival of theology is dependent, in part at least, upon its adaptability to contemporary plausibility structures.

This claim clearly demands an understanding of both the nature of 'plausibility structures' and their relevance to the theological perspective. Peter Berger described 'plausibility structures' as follows:

---

4   Mascall, p. 8.
5   E.L. Mascall, *Theology and Images*, Oxford: Mowbrays, 1963.

One of the fundamental propositions of the sociology of knowledge is that the plausibility, in the sense of what people actually find credible, of views of reality depends upon the social support these receive. Put more simply, we obtain our notions about the world originally from other human beings, and these notions continue to be plausible to us in a very large measure because others continue to affirm them. It is, of course, possible to go against the social consensus that surrounds us, but there are powerful pressures (which manifest themselves as psychological pressures within our own consciousness) to conform to the views and beliefs of our fellow men.[6]

Plausibility Structures

'Plausibility structures', then, are not simply societal assumptions or presuppositions. They are the implicit ways in which particular societies and groups within society distinguish between what is 'true' and what is 'false': they refer to socially structured patterns of verification and falsification. An essential feature of this notion is that societies and groups within society do in fact differ in their appreciation of what is 'plausible' and what is 'implausible'.

Berger did not, of course, specify the extent to which societal plausibility structures are socially determined. He merely suggested that this conditioning is 'in a very large measure'. As argued in Chapter 3, sociologists are committed as sociologists to an 'as if' methodology of social determinism. It is on methodological grounds, then, that they assume that societal plausibility structures are socially determined. Nevertheless, it is possible to demonstrate that plausibility structures do differ from society to society – and to suggest the very real possibility that particular plausibility structures are dependent, to some degree at least, on the social support they receive.

In his innovative account of global Christianity the historian Diarmaid MacCulloch argues that a capacity to mutate in response to changing social contexts has been crucial for the very survival of Christianity over the last 2,000 years:

---

[6] Peter L. Berger, *A Rumour of Angels*, Garden City, NY: Doubleday, 1969 and Harmondsworth: Penguin, 1970, pp. 54–55.

All the world faiths which have known long-term success have shown a remarkable capacity to mutate, and Christianity is no exception, which is why one underlying message of this history is its sheer variety. Many Christians do not like being reminded of Christianity's capacity to develop, particularly those who are in charge of the various religious institutions which call themselves Churches, but that is the reality and has been from the beginning.[7]

As evidence for this strong assertion MacCulloch points to the way that the early church quickly adapted to the realization that the world was not just about to end: 'perhaps one of the greatest turning points in the Christian story':

Since from the beginning, radical change and transmutation were part of the story, the succeeding millennia provide plenty of further examples. After three centuries of tension and confrontation with Roman imperial power, the counter-cultural sect mutated into the agent of settled government and preserved Graeco-Roman civilization in the West when that government collapsed. In nineteenth-century America, marginal Christians created a frontier religion with its own sacred book, the basis of the Church of Jesus Christ of Latter-Day Saints (the Mormons). In Korea, an extraordinarily successful Presbyterian (Reformed Protestant) Church now lectures Reformed Protestants in Europe on how to be true to sixteenth-century European Reformer John Calvin, while this same Korean Church expresses its faith in hymns borrowed from the radically anti-Calvinist Protestantism of Methodism.[8]

In *The Social Context of Theology* I suggested that different plausibility structures could be observed among Christians in radically contrasting cultures. Drawing from my own practical research, I noted how, even in the West, religious attitude questionnaire-surveys had changed in response to social changes. Early surveys often asked a simple question 'Do you believe in God?', without attempting to establish what sort of 'God' people believed in. However, by the 1970s surveys

---

[7]   Diarmaid MacCulloch, *A History of Christianity: The First Three Thousand Years*, London: Allen Lane, 2009, p. 9.

[8]   Ibid., pp. 9–10.

were already becoming more sophisticated. So, one survey at the time,[9] having established whether or not the interviewee believed in God, asked, 'When you think of God, do you see him as "A Person" or "Some kind of impersonal power?"' In this particular British survey, the responses to this question suggested that, whereas 80 per cent of the sample said that they were 'certain there is a God' or that they believed 'there is a God', though they were not certain, only 37 per cent of the sample actually thought that God was 'A Person'.

I noted at the time that even the question in this form was not very sophisticated, since some Christians might have had a problem giving an unequivocal answer to the question 'Do you think God is "A Person"?' Several researchers were beginning to claim that a far more complex series of questions was necessary in a survey to allow for differing types of belief in a context of religious debate.[10] Nevertheless, most of the Western respondents in the sample seemed able to cope with the choice presented in the question.

However, the same question within a different social context produced chaotic results. In a survey that I conducted in the 1970s of Anglican theological students in Papua New Guinea, a highly confused pattern of answers emerged when I employed the question. On analysis it transpired that the students, all of whom were ordinands and spoke English well, found it difficult to distinguish between the alternatives suggested. For them the notion of 'impersonal power' was strange, since they considered that no 'spirit' or 'power' could really be 'impersonal': they typically did not divide phenomena into the 'personal' and the 'impersonal'. A distinction that presented comparatively few problems for the British at the time was highly perplexing for these Papua New Guineans.

The difference between these two sets of thought-forms, though, appeared to be more fundamental than an ability or inability to make certain distinctions. The concept of plausibility structures suggests that the way a Papua New Guinean might test reality could be radically different from the way someone within the West might typically do so. Whereas those living in the West might expect to test technological issues empirically, those living in Papua New Guinea might instead

---

[9]   *Religion in Britain and Northern Ireland*, London: Independent Television Authority, 1970, p. 19.

[10]   Cf. articles on 'The LAM Religiosity Scale', Andrew M. Greeley et al. in *Journal for the Scientific Study of Religion*, 12:1–3, 1973.

test them through 'spirit directed' means. The Papua New Guinean, for example, who became actively involved in a Cargo Cult (which was rife at the time), was clearly working in a different causal system from many Westerners.

In a fascinating book at the time, the Papuan politician Albert Maori Kiki gave this account of his childhood experiences of 'cargo cults':

> Our own version of the cargo cult sprang up after the Second World War, with the return of ex-servicemen from the battlefield or the prisoner of war camps. Of course the notion had long persisted among our people that there was an island somewhere between Australia and Papua where the white man diverted all the cargo that was intended for us. Our own dead were sending us ships with axes, weapons, tinned food and clothes, but the white man had this magic and it enabled him to intercept these boats and change the labels. Thus the cargo intended for Hare, went to Mr Harry instead. The cargo intended for Kave went to Air Cave instead, and so on. In 1945 a man called Larikapu appeared on Orokolo. He told us that when he was carried away by the Japanese into captivity he saw our dead relatives and they had shown him where our cargo was hidden. All that we had to do was raise the money to buy a boat to go and get it. Nobody doubted his word then, and we all contributed money. Of course the boat was never bought and the man disappeared from the village, and although our people knew he was living in Moresby, they never bothered to challenge him seriously and never attempted to recover their money. Nor did this experience make us any wiser.[11]

Two more 'prophets' quickly replaced Larikapu and the villagers again gave money and were deceived. In terms of the sociology of knowledge, it is apparent that the villagers and the 'prophets' were operating with widely differing plausibility structures. The former still lived in a thoroughly spirit-dominated world in which Western 'cargo' could only come from the spirits. The 'prophets', though, seemed to believe that this was not the case.

Kiki also recalled the villagers' attitudes to the Japanese during the war. Although they never actually encountered the Japanese, they were not keen to

---

   [11]   Albert Maori Kiki, *Kiki: Ten Thousand Years in a Lifetime*, Westport, CT: Praeger Press, 1968, p. 52.

help the Allies fight against them. The reason for this is obvious; the villagers were convinced that the Japanese were really their own ancestors' spirits and that the Allies were trying to prevent them from bringing in the 'cargo'. So, by fighting the Japanese, the villagers would in effect be fighting their own ancestors.

For most Western (colonial or even post-colonial) perspectives such explanations will appear deeply implausible. Yet, for the Papuan villagers involved they were clearly plausible. For them it was the Western explanation about tinned meat coming from factories which were implausible. Kiki's own ideas only changed when he actually saw such factories. Equally implausible to the Papuan villager was the Westerner's dismissal of the possibility that the Japanese could be the spirits of ancestors. At both of these points there was a direct confrontation of opposing plausibility structures. Further, the insistence of Westerners that the Papuans were wrong merely tended to confirm in the latter's mind that they had something to hide. Thus, those implicitly assuming one type of plausibility structure naturally found the logic of others assuming a different plausibility structure thoroughly deficient.

Theology and Contemporary Plausibility Structures

Berger argued in the 1970s that contemporary plausibility structures are antagonistic towards Christianity. His overall argument was very similar to that of Mascall: both men believed at the time[12] that the West is characterized by secularization and that the role of theology is to oppose it. For Berger, the contemporary situation could be depicted as follows:

> The proposition of the demise of the supernatural, or at least of its considerable decline, in the modern world is very plausible in terms of the available evidence. It is to be hoped that more plentiful and more precise evidence will yet be produced, and that there will be greater collaboration between social scientists and historians in this undertaking. But even now we have as good an empirical

---

[12]   Berger subsequently changed his mind about secularization, see his *A Far Glory: The Quest for Faith in an Age of Credulity*, New York: Anchor Books, 1992 and *The Desecularization of the World*, Grand Rapids, MI: Eerdmans, 1999.

foundation for the proposition as we do for most generalizations about our world. Whatever the situation may have been in the past, today the supernatural as a meaningful reality is absent or remote from the horizons of everyday life of large numbers, very probably of the majority, of people in modern societies, who seem to manage to get along without it quite well.[13]

It is worth noting an obvious inconsistency in this quotation. Berger (quite unlike Robert Bellah at the time)[14] clearly regarded secularization as a process, that is, a historical process. Further, it is apparent from other contexts,[15] that he believed that it is a process which is likely to continue into the future. Nevertheless, he argued for such a process from a single moment of time – the present. Whatever the weaknesses of this argument, though, it is important to note that Berger, like Mascall, accepted that there is a process of secularization characterizing in the West.

Within this situation of secularization, Berger suggested that Christians inevitably become a 'cognitive minority'. In effect Christians become 'a group of people whose view of the world differs significantly from the one generally taken for granted in their society'.[16] They become a group possessing a body of 'deviant knowledge': that is, a group which no longer shares many of the plausibility structures of society at large.

Berger was aware, of course, that the depiction of Christianity in terms of 'deviance' does not affect its validity.[17] I have already argued in Chapter 2 that it is a mistake to confuse origins and projections with validity. Nevertheless, as a Christian he appeared to be somewhat uneasy about the 'deviant' role he proposed for Christianity within a secularized society. Again this is understandable, perhaps, in the light of my suggestion that, although there is no logical link between origins, projections and validity, there may at times be a psychological link.

His initial solution was to make a somewhat Barthian dichotomy between 'religion' and 'Christianity'.[18] Having made such a dichotomy, the fact that the world rejects 'religious' thinking today is only partially relevant to Christianity. The

---

13 Berger, *A Rumour of Angels*, p. 18.
14 Robert N. Bellah, *Beyond Belief*, New York: Harper and Row, 1970, p. 246.
15 Berger, *A Rumour of Angels*, p. 30.
16 Berger, *A Rumour of Angels*, p. 18.
17 Berger, *A Rumour of Angels*, pp. 18–19.
18 Peter L. Berger, *The Precarious Vision*, New York: Doubleday, 1961.

latter is effectively immunized from trends affecting religious culture in general, including, perhaps, the process of secularization itself.

However, he soon rejected this essentially theological, rather than sociological, dichotomy. In place of this solution to the problem of Christianity's deviant role within contemporary, secularized society, Berger now suggested that the Christian could 'relativize the relativizers'. More specifically, he proposed that Christians should apply the same socio-historical canons to contemporary plausibility structures that they applied to the plausibility structures of past generations:

> It may be conceded that there is in the modern world a certain type of consciousness that has difficulties with the supernatural. The statement remains, however, on the level of the socio-historical diagnosis. The diagnosed condition is not thereupon elevated to the status of an absolute criterion; the contemporary situation is not immune to relativising analysis. We may say that contemporary consciousness is such and such; we are left with the question of whether we will assent to it.[19]

The similarity of Berger's views to those of Mascall can now be clearly seen. Berger suggested that, although Christians should recognize their 'deviant' role within contemporary, secularized society, they should not thereby be deterred from criticizing this society. They are not obliged to conform to contemporary plausibility structures: instead, they may sit in judgement upon them. A generation later that is exactly what John Milbank has sought to do. In *Theology and Social Theory*, having dismissed sociology altogether, he concluded:

> Theology has frequently sought to borrow from elsewhere a fundamental account of society or history, and then to see what theological insights will cohere with it. But it has been shown that no such fundamental account, in the sense of something neutral, rational and universal, is really available. It is theology itself that will have to provide its own account of the final causes at work in human history, on the basis of its own particular, and historically specific faith.[20]

---

[19]   Berger, *A Rumour of Angels*, p. 59.

[20]   John Milbank, *Theology and Social Theory: Beyond Secular Reason*, Oxford: Blackwell, (1990) 2nd edition 2006, p. 382.

Seven years later, encouraged by the acclaim this ambitious book received (along with some fierce criticism as will be seen in Chapter 12), his claims became more strident:

> For all the current talk of a theology that would reflect on practice, the truth is that we remain uncertain as to where today to locate true Christian practice. This would be, as it has always been, a repetition differently, but authentically, of what has always been done. In his or her uncertainty as to where to find this, the theologian feels almost that the entire ecclesial task falls on his own head: in the meagre mode of reflective words he must seek to imagine what a true practical repetition would be like ... the theologian alone who must perpetuate that original making strange which was the divine assumption of human flesh, not to confirm it as it was, but to show it again as it surprising is ... Thus in the following essays, I have hoped to be surprising, since otherwise I should have no chance at all of being authentic. And perhaps the most surprise, the most shock, should arise when what is said is really most orthodox and ancient, since the tradition is so rarely re-performed in practice today. Here rehearsal of ancient formulations (although they sustain an inexhaustible resistance), too often contaminate them by a corrupt context, while on the other hand any 'contemporary garb' for Christian truth is of course the most puerile form of betrayal.[21]

Despite the obvious appeal of Berger's solution to the problem of the church's role as a 'deviant body', it faces certain serious criticisms. Three weaknesses, in particular, might be isolated. The first of these relates to the accuracy of his analysis of contemporary religiosity, the second to the consistency and viability of his theological proposals, and the third to the role he allots to the Christian within contemporary society.

The first of these weaknesses, then, relates to Berger's initial sociological analysis. In *The Social Context of Theology* I argued that the problem of secularization is crucial to any account of the social context of theology in the modern Western world. If there is a process of secularization evident within the West today, then it must have a radical effect on the whole theological enterprise.

---

[21]   John Milbank, *The Word Made Strange: Theology, Language, Culture*, Oxford: Blackwell, 1997, p. 1.

This remains the case whether particular theologians choose to ignore, challenge or accept this process. Even if secularization is viewed, not as a process, but as a perennial condition of humankind, the theologian is still obliged to respond. So, if, as Berger contended at the time, people in the West can no longer make sense of supernatural claims, then this would clearly be a significant finding for theologians since they are typically committed to such claims. Further, it would remain a significant finding even if it could be shown that humankind in general never could make sense of supernatural claims. In the four decades since I made this criticism it has become increasingly apparent that attempts to depict an overarching process (or even permanent state) of cultural secularization face a growing number of sociological critics[22] (including, of course, Berger himself). Indeed, today one of the leading sociologists of religion still defending secularization theory subtitles his latest book on the subject 'In defence of an unfashionable theory'.[23]

The second weakness in Berger's thesis concerns his theological proposals. These have been criticized elsewhere[24] and are not of central importance here. It is sufficient to note, perhaps, that Berger's notion of 'signals of transcendence', which he offered for theology to pursue, were soon confronted with at least two difficulties. On his own argument it was not easy to see why these 'signals' should be viewed as anything other than human projections. They were not, of course, thereby invalidated, but presumably one would require some reason for believing that they were genuinely 'transcendent'. Further, even if he could establish that these 'signals' might be something other than human projections, he still needed to establish the validity of Christianity itself. Berger evidently had an implicit a priori belief in the centrality of Christianity.

However, it is the third criticism which is the most crucial here. If Berger's thoroughgoing secularization model was correct, then it followed that Christians would be forced into a highly 'deviant' role within Western society. If indeed they must refuse to compromise or relativize Christianity in any way – and Berger (at that time), Mascall and Milbank insist upon this – then their own plausibility

---

[22] See Detlef Pollack and Daniel V.A. Olson (eds), *The Role of Religion in Modern Societies*, New York and London: Routledge, 2008 and Bryan S. Turner, *Secularization* (4 volumes), London and New York: Sage, 2010.

[23] Steve Bruce, *Secularization: In Defence of an Unfashionable Theory*, Oxford: Oxford University Press, 2011.

[24] David Cairns, 'Peter Berger', *Scottish Journal of Theology*, 27:2, 1974.

structures will inevitably differ very widely from those of society as a whole. It then becomes difficult to see how the Christian and the non-Christian can communicate effectively with each other. Instead, as Milbank claims (as did the youthful Alasdair MacIntyre 35 years earlier in response to Antony Flew)[25] Christians will somehow need simply to 'out-narrate' non-Christians, although how this can be achieved in the absence of shared plausibility structures remains a mystery.

It is unnecessary, of course, to claim either that theology must be totally dependent upon contemporary plausibility structures, no matter how inhospitable these may be to religious belief, or that it can never sit in judgement upon them. Such claims would amount to an assumption that theology must always act as a dependent, and never as an independent, variable within society. This would thoroughly undermine the interactionist approach to theology that I supported in Chapter 1 and will defend in the final volume. I believe that it is important to see theology as both influenced by, and as an influence upon, society at large.

Nevertheless, my criticism of early Berger, Mascall and Milbank now is that they appear to believe that Christians can effectively ignore contemporary plausibility structures and still expect to communicate with each other let alone other people. If, however, Christians really do reject these plausibility structures in this wholesale manner, they must expect to become largely unintelligible, irrelevant and confined to discreet ghettos. Such indeed would seem to be the fate of some sectarian Christians within the West: communication with introversionist sectarian members can be extraordinarily difficult.[26] In practice, of course, few Christians really do 'relativize the relativizers' in any thoroughgoing manner, no matter how much they may disagree with the 'accepted wisdom' of their age.

Hermeneutics and Plausibility Structures

An adequate understanding of the social context of theology can no longer be viewed as a dispensable luxury. It appears rather to be an essential feature of a theology

---

[25]   In Antony Flew and Alasdair MacIntyre (eds), *New Essays in Philosophical Theology*, London: SCM Press, 1955.

[26]   Cf. Thomas Robbins, Dick Anthony and Thomas E. Curtis, 'The Limits of Symbolic Realism, *Journal for the Scientific Study of Religion*, 12:3, 342–353, 1973.

which communicates effectively within society. Mascall's dismissal of hermeneutics would not seem to have been substantiated by an adequate understanding of plausibility structures even within theology. Some form of hermeneutics, whatever the theological difficulties may be, would appear to be essential in any age of theology. Biblical scholars in fact have been particularly responsive to the historical and present-day challenges of hermeneutics.[27]

I noted at the time in *The Social Context of Theology* that two such different theologians as Leonard Hodgson and Karl Rahner agreed on this issue. In his Gifford Lectures, the former wrote:

> Nowhere within creation is there to be found any attempted statement of truth which is not coloured, and possibly miscoloured, by the outlook of its authors. Those who seek to set up as ultimate rival authorities the words of the Bible, the judgments of the Pope, the decrees of Church Councils or the utterances of saints or scholars, all agree in arguing from the same false premise.[28]

Somewhat similarly Rahner wrote:

> Anyone who takes seriously the 'historicity' of human truth … must see that neither abandonment of a formula nor its preservation in a petrified form does justice to human understanding.[29]

Once theologians take seriously the notion proposed by sociologists of knowledge that 'language', 'knowledge' and 'plausibility structures' are all – in part at least – human products, they are faced with the problem of hermeneutics. Such a sociological perspective does not invalidate the theological pursuit, but it does affect it.

The much-disputed theological methods at the time of both Bultmann and van Buren at least took this point seriously. However, one ultimately assesses

---

[27] See John Barton (ed.), *The Cambridge Companion to Biblical Interpretation*, Cambridge: Cambridge University Press, 1998.

[28] Leonard Hodgson, *For Faith and Freedom*, Oxford: Blackwell, vol. 1, 1956, pp. 13–14.

[29] Karl Rahner, *Theological Investigations*, vol. 1, London: Darton, Longman & Todd, 1961, p. 150.

Bultmann's programme of 'demythologizing', or, however, confused one might feel his concept of 'mythology' to be,[30] it primarily stemmed from a concern that twentieth-century Christians cannot think in the same terms as first-century Christians, and that they would fail to communicate effectively with either 'outsiders' or themselves if they tried to do so.

The hermeneutical context is crucial to an adequate understanding of Bultmann's celebrated claim that 'myth should be interpreted not cosmologically, but anthropologically, or better still, existentially',[31] when he had already defined 'mythology' in a footnote as 'the use of imagery to express the other worldly in terms of this world and the divine in terms of this life'.[32] His early critics at once accused him of theological reductionism – of reducing theology to 'mere philosophy'.[33] However, the fact that Bultmann continued to write about 'acts of God',[34] for example, should have been sufficient to convince his critics that he was no simple reductionist. Instead, he was attempting, albeit inadequately perhaps, to interpret theology within the contemporary social context, that is, he was taking hermeneutics seriously.

Similarly, Paul van Buren's attempt to provide 'the secular meaning of the gospel' was a serious attempt at the time to interpret Christianity in the light of the contemporary social context.[35] It was precisely because he took contemporary philosophical thought seriously, and in particular the problem of verification, that he attempted to re-express Christianity in terms of 'contagious freedom' without reference to God. He argued that this concept both adequately described how Jesus thought about himself and could make sense of doctrines other than just Christology. He admitted later, of course, that he had underestimated the centrality of God-language both in Jesus' own thought and in Christianity as a whole.[36] Nevertheless, at the time he considered the radical experiment of interpreting

---

[30]   Friedrich Schumann, 'Can the Event of Jesus Christ Be Demythologized?', in H.V. Bartsch (ed.), *Kerygma and Myth*, vol. 1, London: SPCK, 1953, and H.P. Owen, *Revelation and Existence*, Cardiff: University of Wales Press, 1957, pp. 6f.

[31]   Rudolf Bultmann in *Kerygma and Myth*, p. 10.

[32]   Bultmann in *Kerygma and Myth*, p. 10.

[33]   For example Helmut Thielicke in *Kerygma and Myth*, pp. 142f., and G. Vaughan Jones, *Christology and Myth in the New Testament*, London: Allen & Unwin, 1956, pp. 6f.

[34]   For example Bultmann in *Kerygma and Myth*, pp. 196f.

[35]   Paul van Buren, *The Secular Meaning of the Gospel*, London: SCM Press, 1963.

[36]   Paul van Buren, interview in *New Christian*, 25 July, 1968, pp. 12–13.

Christianity without reference to God to be necessary in view of the contemporary social context.

It is possible that the greatest problem for both Bultmann and van Buren was not so much their theological interpretations – for which they were both much criticized – as their implicit analyses of their social context. The paramount role that Bultmann assigned to scientific methodology (a thoroughly inductive understanding of this methodology) in contemporary society may have done less than justice to his social context. His programme of 'demythologising' was based in effect on a thoroughgoing secularization model, with all its attendant weaknesses. Paul van Buren, on the other hand, was dependent on logical positivism at a time when it was already giving way to functional analysis within philosophy. In addition, even when logical positivism was at its zenith in philosophy, it may or may not have represented the plausibility structures of society at large. Current philosophical trends may not necessarily be an accurate guide to contemporary social context.

Throughout their history Christians have run the risk of translating the Gospel into different languages, thought-forms and plausibility structures. Doubtless there is always a risk of theological distortion involved in this process of translation – as there was, for example, when Christianity was originally translated from Judaic to Hellenistic thought-forms. Yet this risk may well have been necessary for the survival of Christianity: without translation it would have failed to communicate effectively with, or appeared credible to, even its own members. Theology is likely to become increasingly irrelevant, unintelligible and sectarian if it wholly disavows its social context.

Chapter 6

Societal Assumptions
in a Theological Debate

The previous chapter argued that contemporary plausibility structures are highly relevant to theology and that the latter ignores its social context only at the cost of jeopardizing effective communication and intelligibility. In practice, however, many theologians have made assumptions about the social context within which they pursue their discipline. As an example this chapter will examine some of the societal assumptions that were apparent in the *Honest to God* debate during the 1960s.

This particular debate has attracted sociological interest, partly because of its impact on the theological world at the time, but mainly because of its significance in the non-theological world.[1] A theological debate seldom moves outside the academic community, but, for a variety of reasons, the *Honest to God* debate (whatever its theological merits or demerits) drew an extraordinary number of diverse people into its orbit. Within this debate assumptions about the nature of society's attitudes towards religion played a significant and instructive role. The notion of secularization especially was of central importance,[2] with both defenders and critics of *Honest to God* making assumptions about a supposed process of secularization in the West.

Just suppose for a moment that these theological defenders and critics had actually been reading the work of sociologists of religion at the time. How would their arguments have been judged?

---

[1] Robin Gill, 'British Theology as a Sociological Variable', in Michael Hill (ed.), *A Sociological Yearbook of Religion in Britain*, London: SCM Press, 1974. See also Robert Towler's analysis of the correspondence generated by *Honest to God* in his *The Need for Certainty: A Sociological Study of Conventional Religion*, London: Routledge & Kegan Paul, 1984.

[2] See James F. Childress and David B. Harned (eds), *Secularization and the Protestant Prospect*, New York: Louisville, KY: Westminster Press, 1970.

Preliminary Distinctions

Sociologists of religion in the 1960s – many, perhaps most of whom were committed to the idea that secularization characterized the Western world (David Martin in Britain[3] and Andrew Greeley in the United States[4] were still rather lone dissenting voices) – were already beginning to distinguish between secularization models which refer to various dimensions of individual religiosity and those which refer instead to specifically cultural or socio-structural aspects.

At an individual level, Glock and Stark identified five core dimensions of religiosity.[5] The first is the 'belief dimension'. This 'comprises expectations that the religious person will hold a certain theological outlook, that he will acknowledge the truth of the tenets of the religion'. The second is the dimension of 'religious practice'. This 'includes acts of worship and devotion, the things people do to carry out their religious commitment' and comprises both corporate ritual and solitary prayer. The third is the 'experience dimension'. This 'takes into account the fact that all religions have certain expectations, however imprecisely they may be stated, that the properly religious person will at some time or another achieve a direct, subjective knowledge of ultimate reality; that he will achieve some sense of contact, however fleeting, with a supernatural agency'. The fourth is the 'knowledge dimension'. This 'refers to the expectation that religious persons will possess some minimum of information about the basic tenets of their faith and its rites, scriptures and traditions'. The fifth is the 'consequence dimension'. This 'identifies the effects of religious belief, practice, experience and knowledge in persons' day-to-day lives'.

This analysis of religiosity was not without sociological critics at the time. For example, the sociologist Roland Robertson argued that the experience dimension 'would appear very difficult to handle satisfactorily in the survey context, in so far as the sociologist is seeking to tap the depth and scope of the individual's

---

[3]   David Martin, *The Religious and the Secular*, London: Routledge & Kegan Paul, 1969.

[4]   Andrew M. Greeley, *Unsecular Man: The Persistence of Religion*, New York: Schocken Books, 1972 [English title *The Persistence of Religion*, London: SCM Press, 1973].

[5]   C.Y. Glock and C.R. Stark, *American Piety: The Nature of Religious Commitment*, Berkeley, CA: University of California Press, 1968, pp. 11–19.

religious emotionalism'.[6] On the religious practice dimension, he maintained that, 'important as this theme is, it is difficult to see how in any logical sense one may be permitted to include within a scheme of dimensions of religiosity a dimension which is a consequence of religiosity … something cannot be both an aspect of x and at the same time a consequence of x'.[7] He also pointed out that for Glock and Stark the 'belief dimension' did not take into account 'degrees' of belief.

Nevertheless, the broad framework offered by Glock and Stark does provide a contemporary standard for assessing the adequacy of theologians' assumptions at the time. The 'consequence' dimension of individual religiosity may or may not be a true dimension but it was still relevant to the secularization model. Again, the 'experience' dimension may well be difficult to handle in surveys but it too was still clearly relevant. Finally, the 'belief' dimension was also relevant, whether or not it is susceptible to analysis by 'degrees' – since secularization theorists often claimed at the time that a growing number of people reject whole-heartedly religious beliefs. In any case, Robertson may simply have been wrong in his criticism at this point: Glock and Stark did in fact provide continua of beliefs.[8]

More significantly Robertson argued that, on its own, this framework was inadequate at a socio-structural level:

> We come … to the problem of the relationship between the religiosity of the individual and the religiosity of the system of which the individual is a member. Glock has argued that the 'religiousness of a society is subject to measurement through aggregating indicators of the religiosity of its constituent members'. It is on the other hand widely recognised in the social sciences that this kind of reasoning commits what is often called the individualistic fallacy. It is fallacious because one is viewing the system as no more than the sum or aggregation of the properties of the units within it.[9]

---

[6]   Roland Robertson, *The Sociological Interpretation of Religion*, Oxford: Blackwell, 1969, p. 53.

[7]   Robertson, *Sociological Interpretation*, p. 53.

[8]   See C.Y. Glock and C.R. Stark, *Christian Beliefs and Anti-Semitism*, New York: Harper, 1966.

[9]   Robertson, *Sociological Interpretation*, p. 56.

He pointed out that religiosity was not usually considered to be the same in Soviet Russia as in Britain at the time, 'yet the evidence that we have suggests a broadly similar pattern of commitment at the level of the individual':[10]

> The existence of an 'anti-religious' dominant minority within a country may ensure that the latter does not operate on religious principles. Consequently, in so far as the problem of the relative religiosity of societies is a soluble one, we must pay attention to structural and general characteristics of the system as a whole – the degree of differentiation and autonomy of religious sectors in relation to other social sectors, the strategic location or otherwise of religious leaders, the relationship between religious groups and so on.[11]

At this point, Robertson introduced a further distinction: cultural as distinct from socio-structural religiosity. Here too culture cannot be derived from aggregation:

> Even if we confine our attention to culture, the objection must be made that in estimating the degree of religiosity of a particular culture there is much more to consider than aggregate individual attributes; there is, for example, the religious content in art forms or in language, not to speak of distinctively non-religious culture, such as modern science.[12]

What emerged from this debate within the sociology of religion were important distinctions between individual, socio-structural and cultural forms of religiosity as they relate to secularization. In terms of sociological awareness at the time they offered an analytical framework that might now be used to assess the adequacy of social assumptions of theologians also writing in the 1960s and early 1970s. How did they fare?

---

[10]   Robertson, *Sociological Interpretation*, p. 57.
[11]   Robertson, *Sociological Interpretation*, p. 57.
[12]   Robertson, *Sociological Interpretation*, p. 59.

John Robinson

In *Honest to God*[13] the term secularization appeared very seldom and then mainly in quotations from Bonhoeffer. In *The Honest to God Debate*, however, which followed swiftly afterwards, it featured prominently. In the latter John Robinson disagreed with a definition in terms of 'the great defection from Christianity', arguing instead that secularization was 'essentially a modern phenomenon'.[14] For him 'secularization stands among other things for a revolt against three ways of viewing the world, and probably four, which have been intimately bound up in the past with the presentation of the Christian gospel'; namely, rejections of 'the whole possibility of metaphysics as a meaningful enterprise', 'a supranaturalistic worldview', a 'mythological' world-view, and the notion of 'religion'.[15]

The first three correspond fairly closely to the 'fundamental shifts' depicted in *The Human Face of God* already criticized in Chapter 4. It is clear that they all concern, in particular, the belief dimension of individual religiosity. Robinson believed that there had been a radical change in the beliefs of individuals in the West and even suggested that this had led them to distrust 'any proposition going beyond the empirical evidence'.[16] Nevertheless, he was not personally convinced that 'to be honest as a Christian and as a secular man one must, or indeed can, be shut up to such a complete refusal to speak of "God" or of how things ultimately "are"'.[17] Instead he suggested in effect that there had been a shift away from the belief dimension of individual religiosity and towards the experience dimension. Thus, 'theology is not making affirmations about metaphysical realities per se, but always describes an experienced relationship or engagement to the truth "all theological statements are existential"'.[18]

His fourth contemporary form of rejection, that concerning the notion of 'religion', has implications beyond individual religiosity. He interpreted 'religion' in this context in Bonhoeffer's terms and defined secularization as 'the withdrawal

---

[13] J.A.T. Robinson, *Honest to God*, London: SCM Press, 1963.
[14] Robinson in J.A.T. Robinson and D. Edwards (eds), *The Honest to God Debate*, London: SCM Press, 1963, p. 248.
[15] Robinson in *The Honest to God Debate*, p. 249.
[16] Robinson in *The Honest to God Debate*, p. 253.
[17] Robinson in *The Honest to God Debate*, p. 252.
[18] Robinson in *The Honest to God Debate*, p. 252.

of areas of thought and life from religious – and finally also from metaphysical – control, and the attempt to understand and live in these areas in the terms which they alone offer'.[19] He linked this withdrawal to both decline in ritual practice at the individual level and socio-structural decline, and possibly cultural decline:

> For secularism stands for the conviction that the circle of explanation and control in human affairs can and should be closed – one does not have to 'bring in God' to account for the weather, or the origins of the universe, or the soul, or the foundations of morality, or anything else.[20]

E.L. Mascall

As argued earlier, Eric Mascall, despite his diametrically opposite theological orientation, implicitly accepted a secularization model similar to that of Robinson. He too located the process of secularization primarily at the level of individual religiosity, believing that it signified the 'irreligious' or 'unchristian'. So, for example, he claimed in passing that 'the world is, in its outlook, radically irreligious'[21] and that 'secularism' had 'in effect superseded Christianity as the attitude to life of the greater number of civilised Europeans and Americans'.[22]

There was, however, also a cultural element to Mascall's societal assumptions. In criticizing Paul van Buren's claim that contemporary 'Godlessness' derived from linguistic philosophy, he suggested that 'the main cause is the continual impact upon the senses of a technocratic culture in which all the emphasis falls upon what man can do with things and hardly upon what they really are'.[23] By implication, Mascall apparently linked individual and cultural religiosity and even argued that van Buren and Robinson were themselves a part of the process of secularization in the West.

---

[19]   Robinson in *The Honest to God Debate*, p. 268.

[20]   Robinson in *The Honest to God Debate*, pp. 268–269.

[21]   E.L. Mascall, *The Secularisation of Christianity*, London: Darton, Longman & Todd, 1965, p. 7.

[22]   Mascall, *Secularisation*, p. 35.

[23]   Mascall, *Secularisation*, p. 44.

A.M. Ramsey

One of the clearest definitions of the secularization model in the *Honest to God* debate was provided by Archbishop Michael Ramsey. His initial reaction was somewhat hostile to Robinson's views. However, by 1969 he admitted that these views had been important at the time, suggesting four 'assumptions which are sometimes avowed and sometimes half-consciously present' in 'secularism':

1. The temporal world is the only world which exists. Eternity is irrelevant and meaningless. There can be no ideas of human values which transcend realisation within time and history.

2. Religion is to be dismissed. It involves unscientific superstitions, and can contribute no authentic knowledge about the world. It has encouraged people to resist scientific progress, and the practice of prayer and worship draws into an unreal realm of fantasy energies which should go into the world's proper business.

3. Man's knowledge is based solely upon observable phenomena. Thus 'positivism', though not an inherent part of secularism, is very characteristic of it.

4. Finally, the secularist believes in the autonomous man. Man's own potentialities of knowledge and of the effective use of it will suffice for all man's needs. True, man has his frustrations, but his dignity lies in his power to overcome them, as he can and will through the right application of the sciences to his needs. Religion gives not help but hindrance as it keeps man in a state of puerile dependence and holds him back from his maturity.[24]

Ramsey argued that it was wise to 'avoid exaggeration, for secularism by no means occupies the whole scene' – in both Britain and America 'much from the older traditions still survives and shows creative power'. As evidence he cited the high level of church-going in the States and the 'degree of public interest in religious questions which is reminiscent of middle-class Victorian England', and in Britain the fact that 'very few people would call themselves atheists' at the time and that

---

[24]   A.M. Ramsey, *God, Christ and the World*, London: SCM Press, 1969, p. 16.

the 'ethical tradition as it exists is a pattern derived from earlier Christendom'. Yet, he added that 'the ethos of secularism is strong and contagious, and the efforts of Christian evangelism often meet what can seem to be an almost impenetrable mass of secular-mindedness'.[25]

Clearly, Ramsey too assumed that there was a process of secularization apparent within the West. His first three criteria related to the belief dimension of individual religiosity: in terms of them secularization involves a belief that the temporal world is the only world which matters, a belief that religion involves unscientific superstitions and a belief solely in the empirical. The fourth criterion – 'secular man as autonomous man' – may also have involved the consequence dimension of individual religiosity; for an autonomous person religion was no longer an important factor to be considered in decision-making.

Like Robinson, Ramsey stressed the importance of the experience dimension in contemporary individual religiosity:

> In the modern world the concern about person has had a new kind of prominence. There is a new kind of realisation of the proposition, not in itself of course new, that 'people matter'. One sign of this is the vogue of existential philosophy with its insistence that truth is known not in ontological statements but in terms of personal self-realisation. Another instance of this is the widespread practical concern to help people who are in distress. Another instance, of a totally different kind, is the behaviour of those who, frustrated in the desire for personal fulfilment, are almost compulsively led to try to prove themselves by achievements in sex and violence. Much indeed of the 'people matter' urge is a kind of revolt from the depersonalising of industrial or technological existence, where the secular city fails to satisfy. And movements like the 'hippies' seem to be a revolt from an unsatisfactory established order, perhaps a sort of secular counterpart to the flights of the hermits to the desert in the fourth century. Modern man has built the secular city, and is restless within it.[26]

---

[25] Ramsey, *God, Christ and the World*, p. 16.
[26] Ramsey, *God, Christ and the World*, p. 27.

This correspondence between Ramsey and Robinson is interesting, even though the former restricted his analysis to the level of individual religiosity. He did not consider wider questions of socio-structural or cultural secularization.

Lesslie Newbigin

In complete contrast, Lesslie Newbigin's contribution to the debate was primarily concerned with these wider aspects of the process of secularization. He argued that 'the most significant fact about the time in which we are living is that it is a time in which a single movement of secularization is bringing the peoples of all continents into its sweep'.[27] For him, there were two aspects to this process; unification (today this would be termed globalization) and secularization itself.

On the level of unification, Newbigin argued that a combination of jets and radio 'have put every part of the world into immediate contact with every other'. So, 'even in the most primitive areas the bus, the radio and the bulldozer move inexorably in, and when the necessities of world war or world commerce dictate it, anything from the jungles of Papua to the ice fields of the Antarctic can be swiftly taken over and incorporated in the single entity which is the human civilization of today'. At a more profound level, he claimed that 'thinking men and women in every part of the world are now aware of belonging to a single history … negatively, they are aware of standing under the threat of a single disaster which could destroy human civilization as a whole … positively (but here one can only speak more vaguely), they share increasingly common expectations about the future, about human rights, dignity, technological development – expectations which they know can only be fulfilled if they are sought for all nations together'.[28]

On the level of cultural secularization, he maintained that 'mankind is not being unified on the basis of a common religious faith or even of a common ideology, but on the basis of a shared secular terror and a shared secular hope'. Goals within the 'Third World' today are 'defined in such terms as technical development, industrialization, economic planning, productivity and the more equal distribution of wealth'. Potentially, at least, these goals could draw 'all races into common

---

[27] Lesslie Newbigin, *Religion for Secular Man*, London: SCM Press, 1966, p. 11.
[28] Newbigin, *Religion for Secular Man*, pp. 11–12.

involvement in a single universe of thought as well as a single fabric of economic life':[29]

> Its effect (not recognised at first) is to destroy the cyclical pattern of human thinking which has been characteristic of many ancient societies and to replace it by a linear pattern, a way of thinking about human life which takes change for granted, which encourages the younger generation to think differently from its parents, which looks for satisfaction in an earthly future.[30]

At the socio-structural level, too, Newbigin argued that the process of secularization had deeply affected a country like India. Today, India is no longer 'determined by the traditional ideas of Hindu or Muslim law ... Legislation has been passed which is aimed to destroy completely elements in traditional religious law which are considered incompatible with this intention.'[31] He maintained that in the contemporary secular state of India it had become increasingly irrelevant whether an individual was a Hindu or a Muslim. A similar process was also evident within the West:

> More and more areas of life have been mapped by the research of those who confessed that they did not need the hypothesis of God for this purpose; more and more of the life of society, of the family, of the individual – including the Christian individual; have been organised without any conscious reference to the Christian faith or the Christian Church.[32]

F.R. Barry

Finally, F.R. Barry provided an interesting example of one of the few theologians involved in the *Honest to God* debate who explicitly employed, and showed a real acquaintance with, sociological accounts of secularization. Most theologians

---

[29]   Newbigin, *Religion for Secular Man*, pp. 13–14.
[30]   Newbigin, *Religion for Secular Man*, p. 14.
[31]   Newbigin, *Religion for Secular Man*, p. 15.
[32]   Newbigin, *Religion for Secular Man*, p. 17.

contributing to the debate made assumptions about society and patterns of contemporary religiosity – whether at individual, cultural or socio-structural levels. Some of them, like Ramsey and Newbigin, supported these assumptions with empirical evidence. But few of them actually referred to the work of sociologists of religion. Barry was an exception.

He concentrated on the specific area of the practice and belief dimensions of individual religiosity. He admitted, on the basis of the evidence he reviewed, that there had been some sort of decline in church-going in Britain during the last century. Yet he argued:

> Can it be assumed, for example, that in the Victorian age when social acceptance was bound up with church-going as at least a guarantee of respectability, there were more believers in God than there are today? Or even in the so-called ages of faith? (How Christian, in other words was Christendom?). Can we simply assume that because in the United States church membership embraces 65 per cent of the population, against 22 per cent in Britain, there are more believers in God in the United States than there are in Britain? ... The real influence of a church in the life of its community, and especially such a church as the Church of England, cannot in the nature of the case be assessed by any numerical calculation.[33]

On the basis of the survey-report *Puzzled People*,[34] Barry argued that there is evidence in the belief dimension of individual religiosity of 'the vestigial remainder of confused and muddled Christian tradition in a surprisingly large number of people'.[35] Without adopting a thoroughgoing secularization model, he maintained that people in the West at the time were 'ambivalent'. On the one hand 'the 'modern' mind is indelibly empiricist with a frame of reference almost entirely bounded by facts that lie in the field of natural science, neutral facts which are the same for everybody ... There is no place in the contemporary world-view for transcendent or 'supernatural' realities which do not admit of empirical

---

[33] F.R. Barry, *Secular and Supernatural*, London: SCM Press, 1969, p. 19.

[34] Mass Observation, *Puzzled People*, London, 1948.

[35] Barry, *Secular and Supernatural*, p. 22.

verification or cannot be comprised in equations.'[36] On the other hand, having made what appears to be a bland claim about society, he maintained that there is a 'vestigial remainder' of Christian tradition within the West.

In both of these dimensions of individual religiosity Barry pointed to important ambiguities contained within the available sociological data.

The Debate Assessed

A number of weaknesses emerge from this brief survey of the societal assumptions of five of the theologians involved in the *Honest to God* debate. They all relate to issues which the critical perspective of sociological accounts of secularization, available at the time, might have remedied, since a common factor of all the weaknesses was a tendency on the part of the theologians to make uncritical assumptions about the nature of contemporary society.

The first and most obvious of these weaknesses is that none of the theologians in question supplied a comprehensive secularization model. All of them excluded one or other of the dimensions of secularization that had been suggested by sociologists of religion at the time. Barry concentrated solely on the individual level of secularization and in particular on the dimensions of belief and practice: at no point did he refer to more broadly based understandings of secularization. Ramsey too concentrated on this level of secularization, though he included references to the experience and consequence dimensions of individual religiosity in addition to the two studied by Barry. Both Robinson and Mascall alluded to the socio-structural and cultural levels of secularization, but they too focused upon the process as an individual-oriented phenomenon. Thus, Robinson concentrated upon secularization as a process related to the belief and experience dimensions of individual religiosity, whereas the Mascall was concerned solely with the belief dimension. In contrast to the other theologians, however, Newbigin referred only to the socio-structural and cultural levels of secularization.

Focusing upon certain elements of the secularization model, of course, is not in itself inaccurate. It only becomes so if the focus is taken to constitute the whole. Theologians and sociologists alike may concentrate upon certain features of the

---

[36]   Barry, *Secular and Supernatural*, p. 30.

secularization model, provided they are aware that others have suggested other features too. Yet it would appear that all five theologians were indeed unaware of the sociological framework available at the time.

This lack of awareness may relate to the second weakness apparent from my review – namely, the lack of a critical definition of secularization on the part of the theologians. Only Ramsey provided a systematized definition of secularization and even this lacked the critical perspective that might have been provided by sociologists of religion at the time. Robinson also made four suggestions about the nature of secularization, but these in themselves did not provide a systematized definition, nor again did they contain a critical perspective. Mascall, on the other hand, simply assumed that a process of secularization existed and nowhere attempted to give it a formal definition. Not one of the theologians adopted any of the formal definitions of secularization provided at the time by sociologists of religion.

The final weakness relates to the unwillingness of the theologians to substantiate their claims with empirical data. Admittedly, some of this data became more widely available towards the end of the decade, but it would appear to be the case, as argued earlier, that theologians such as Robinson made societal assumptions without reference to it. Most noticeably, the only data that Mascall employed systematically related to his fellow theologians. For him John Robinson and Paul van Buren were in themselves evidence of a process of secularization. Nowhere, though, did he give the same attention to more obvious empirical evidence for such a process. Ramsey did refer to some of this data, but again he lacked the sort of critical perspective expected by the sociologist. Newbigin too lacked this perspective, though he did allude to a wide range of empirical evidence for socio-structural and cultural types of secularization. Only Barry systematically employed the contemporary data provided by sociologists of religion on individual religiosity.

At each point, then, it would seem that the theologians might have benefited from a greater awareness of the findings of sociologists of religion writing at the time. Yet had they done so an obvious problem emerges. Sociology makes an uneasy bed-fellow for many disciplines since it tends to relativize all disciplines, including its own. This problem must be explored next.

PART II
Sociological Challenges to Theological Assumptions

Chapter 7

Relative Convictions

Sociology, especially when applied to cognitive disciplines, is methodologically inclined towards relativism. Its habitual tendency is to relativize the ideas and cognitive worlds that it seeks to understand. In exploring relationships between ideas and changing social structures and in uncovering the various ways that ideas are relative to these structures, sociology persistently seems to challenge, even threaten, the very basis of knowledge and rationality. It threatens this basis by treating all ideas as culturally specific and thus as culturally relative. Even scientific knowledge is threatened in this way, since it is manifestly controlled by elite, highly socialized communities, which generate culturally specific conventions and 'orthodoxies' that, over time, can be seen to change radically as society at large changes.

As argued in Chapter 3, this relativist tendency of sociology is methodological. Once it assumes ontological, or perhaps more aptly 'credal', status it is easily dismissed. Any sociological claim to the effect that all ideas are socially relative faces obvious problems of coherence. Presumably such a claim is itself subject to social relativism, change and possible revision. Very quickly an endless chain of sociological enquiry ensues; a sociology of sociological claims about social relativism is soon followed by a sociology of that sociology and then by a sociology of the sociology of the sociology ... In retrospect it was a comparatively easy task for Berger to suggest a programme for 'relativizing the relativizers':

> One (perhaps literally) redeeming feature of sociological perspective is that relativizing analysis, in being pushed to its final consequences, bends back upon itself. The relativizers are relativized, the debunkers are debunked – indeed, relativization itself is somewhat liquidated[1]

---

[1] Peter L. Berger, *A Rumour of Angels*, New York: Doubleday, 1969 and London: Penguin, 1970, p. 59.

Once social relativism assumes ontological status it at once becomes vulnerable to such a programme and soon leads to intellectual absurdity.

Methodological social relativism is not so vulnerable. It is an instrument of enquiry – an 'as if' approach as argued earlier– rather than a credal frame. It results from the obvious point that it is not for the sociologist working as sociologist to decide which ideas or forms of knowledge are to be excluded from sociological enquiry. The skill of sociologists in cognitive areas is their ability to suggest possible relationships between ideas and social structures. Some (politicians, religious leaders or academics) may feel threatened by this skill and may seek to confine it to some areas and to protect other areas as inviolate. However, such attempts at control clearly do not belong properly to sociological enquiry itself. The latter knows no bounds and when left unfettered innocently threatens all ideas and forms of knowledge, including its own. It even provides those non-sociologists seeking to control it with some of their strongest ammunition both to undermine its procedures and to exploit these procedures to exercise this control. Unconstrained sociological enquiry does not need to claim that all ideas are socially relative, it merely treats all ideas *as if they are* socially relative. It does this because it does not discriminate between ideas, treating some as socially relative and others not. Its task is to treat all ideas as socially relative. Hence the threat that it presents to other cognitive disciplines.

It is hardly surprising that a method which treats all ideas as if they are socially relative is easily confused with ontological relativism. As has already been noted, sociologists themselves sometimes become imperialistic and contribute to this confusion. Further, a method is usually adopted not simply because it is a useful heuristic device but because it is also thought to have some correspondence with the external reality that is its object. So, scientists study the physical world as if it has an orderly structure, that is as if it is governed by discernible laws. This is clearly a method. Yet since they believe that they are making 'discoveries' and not simply imposing their ordered projections upon a chaotic universe, the method also signals a belief. At least some orderliness is usually presupposed in the very activity of scientists themselves. Similarly, sociologists treat ideas as socially relative because, at least part of the time, they believe that they really are socially relative. Without falling into the trap of thoroughgoing ontological relativism, some degree of relativism is usually presumed about social realities.

This presumption is fostered by the very process of observing how ideas are constructed, propagated and controlled by elite groups. The sociology of knowledge encourages its students to observe cognitive disciplines as socially relative processes. In contrast to those fully engaged in a particular cognitive discipline, the sociology of knowledge encourages detachment and comparison. It soon becomes clear that exponents of cognitive disciplines typically create, and then protect, canons. A number of key founding 'fathers' (and, more rarely 'mothers') are identified and a body of literature is 'canonized' in order to distinguish one cognitive discipline from another. This literature is then used to control the discipline and to criticize rival versions. It is used to identify academic expertise/excellence/'orthodoxy' for 'disciples' and conversely to disparage others. 'Novices' entering a 'discipline' must quickly be disabused of their prior ideas related to the discipline. Works that have been read previously and which do not form part of the 'canon' are dismissed and ridiculed (often without argument) by the 'master'. A new 'rule', usually in the form of an authoritative book-list, tells the 'novices' how they should behave academically in the future. In turn they are enjoined by the 'master' to 'devote' their time to it.

As will be seen later, the religious terms here are no accident. Academic socialization has much in common with more ancient forms of religious socialization. In a religious system the *virtuosi* are typically the theologians, monastics or contemplatives. It is their role to refine, protect and preserve sacred knowledge. Apostolicity, canonical status and credal frames become vital in this process. Just as the religious *virtuosi* are concerned with refining, protecting and preserving 'knowledge', so secular academics too become engaged in these tasks. In observing this across cultures and across disciplines which would normally be regarded as independent from each other, the sociology of knowledge understandably tends to foster relativism.

This process is increasingly observed in many disciplines. If once, for example, it might have been presumed that a course in English literature simply involved the study of what were universally recognized by the educated as classic works of literature, today this is decreasingly the case. There is a growing awareness that 'classic works of literature' are defined by changing elites. In the recent past the judgement of the British intelligentsia was widely accepted by others seeking such a definition. Today, influenced strongly by post-colonial and post-structural theories, other parts of the English-speaking world are breaking away from this cultural hegemony. The list of 'classic works' appears differently in North America, Australia or English-speaking parts of India or Africa. An awareness of these differences soon relativizes assumptions about the appropriateness of any list of 'classic works'.

Again, it is still easy for Western academics to assume that philosophy is properly speaking Western and largely European, philosophy. To study philosophy means to study a number of key Enlightenment (another term with theological roots) thinkers, such as Hume and Kant, and the traditions that they have spawned. At the beginning of the twentieth century much greater emphasis would have been given to classical thinkers, notably Aristotle and Plato. Few would have places, say, for classical Indian thinkers at the centre of philosophical studies. It was readily assumed that the history of philosophy is the history of Western philosophy. Or, more accurately, it was assumed that the history of philosophy is the history of the ideas of a small group of thinkers who have come to be identified as philosophers. On this assumption, not everyone who thinks is a philosopher: not even everyone who thinks deeply about the sort of things that philosophers tend to think about is a philosopher. Rather philosophers are those on the accepted philosophy reading list. Ironically philosophers, who are usually so insistent upon disciplines carefully defining the terms that they use, have failed to agree upon any definition of philosophy itself. So the reading list becomes a crucial determinant of what constitutes the discipline.

Sociologists themselves are also manifestly part of the same process. Founding fathers – Comte, Spencer, Marx, Durkheim, Weber and (for post-structuralists) Foucault and Derrida – are identified and individual reading lists shape how the discipline is to be understood by particular sociologists and their disciples. Since all 'novices' already have many assumptions about society long before they become sociologists, they must be quickly disabused and initiated into the 'orthodox' literature. Much that passes for 'sociology' among the uninitiated must be dismissed and paths must be cut even through literature that other sociologists claim to be properly sociological. The divisions between Marxist and non-Marxist (or between structuralist and post-structuralist) understandings of sociology must be negotiated. To the theologian they may strongly resemble some of the differences between evangelicals and non-evangelicals and, in the

1970s especially, caused as much friction in sociology departments as the latter have done in theology departments. Deep ideological and moral differences have coexisted uneasily within both disciplines. Particular sociologists or theologians have been forced to make choices and then, having made their choices, they have reinforced these choices through the literature they 'recommend' to others.

The process of establishing a discipline through a literature that is sanctified or canonized leads to some curious results. Among these is the practice of continuing to regard a work as seminal long after its methods and contents have been discredited. To the outsider it must seem curious that so many methodological disciplines spend so much of their time discussing works whose deficiencies have been so well established over generations. Those defending this practice might argue that students can be taught more effectively in this manner – since they can read the seminal works for themselves and then learn the art of critical scholarship through reading well-honed criticisms. Up to a point this may well be so. Yet it does not altogether accord with what actually takes place. Academics across methodological disciplines spend a disproportionate amount of their time arguing with one another about the works that are regarded as seminal in their discipline and covering and recovering criticisms that have been made for generations. Again, this is an activity that has much in common with the function of religious *virtuosi* refining, protecting, interpreting and passing on sacred knowledge.

Within sociology this practice is evident among both Marxists and non-Marxists. It is of course immediately evident among the former. Enormous trouble is taken to present 'authentic' texts of Marx and then to exegete and interpret them. The sociologically naive, like the naive biblical user, will quote Marx out of context and will generalize about 'Marxism', producing in effect harmonies of disparate texts. The sophisticated sociologist using Marx, like the hermeneutical theologian, will be careful to use specific works of Marx or specific redactions within those works and distinguish their tenets from those of other works. For the sophisticated Marxist sociologist, just as for the sophisticated biblical theologian, hermeneutics and contextual analysis are prerequisites. Only so can the 'sacred' text be refined and made adequately available to the 'faithful' today (whether or not the faithful themselves are fully appreciative of, or even aware of, this complex and painstaking work).

But the practice is also evident among non-Marxist sociologists. It is instructive, for example, to note how much time and trouble is spent analysing and re-analysing a work such as Emile Durkheim's *The Elementary Forms of the Religious Life*. Careful scholarship has revealed just how many of the criticisms that are now made of this work were first made in the decade following its publication.[2] Yet the criticisms are still made and remade from one account of the sociology of religion to another. Most would agree that Durkheim's method was fundamentally flawed in its secondary use of evidence about the Arunta (which was inaccurate), in its evolutionary assumptions about 'primitive' religion, in its understanding of totemism, and in the tautological nature of its functionalist treatment of the relation between religion and society. Despite this widespread agreement the work is still treated as seminal and its thesis is still vigorously debated. However, once it is realized that the work itself has a canonical function in some approaches to sociology, none of this appears so surprising. This is not simply a way of teaching sociological error. *The Elementary Forms of the Religious Life* is being treated almost as if it is itself a 'sacred' text, or, to use Durkheim's own terms, as something that is 'set apart' and surrounded by interdictions.

One of the features of sacred texts is that frequently they can be appropriated by competing groups and communities. The scriptures of long-surviving religious traditions are usually sufficiently opaque and pluralistic to allow mutually exclusive interpretations and to nurture competing and sometimes mutually hostile communities. This is particularly evident within Judaism, Christianity and Islam, but arguably it is also apparent in many Asian religious traditions that have a more ambiguous relationship to 'sacred texts'. In all of these instances, ancient scriptures themselves are pluralistic and their reception and interpretation through the ages is even more pluralistic. As a result, mutually hostile groups can claim them as their own and anathematize the divergent uses of them by others.

This too can be observed in a number of cognitive disciplines. Durkheim's work is, after all, claimed differently by both sociologists and social anthropologists. In a modern academic world of carefully compartmentalized disciplines, recent works may be less likely to be variously appropriated (although concepts such

---

[2]   See W.S.F. Pickering, *Durkheim on Religion*, London: Routledge & Kegan Paul, 1975, and *Durkheim's Sociology of Religion: Themes and Theories*, London: Routledge & Kegan Paul, 1984.

as 'functionalism', 'structuralism' and more recently 'post-structuralism' clearly cross disciplines). However, founding 'fathers' are in greater demand and are less readily available. Sometimes competing appropriations are largely unknown to modern exponents of the separate disciplines. So both sociologists and theologians until fairly recently used the writings of Ernst Troeltsch and Richard Niebuhr with little apparent awareness of their separate discussions.[3]

By calling attention to this separate and competing appropriation of founding 'fathers' by different disciplines, a sociology of knowledge again tends to foster relativism. Observing this process, by which academic disciplines attempt to establish credibility and to define and then defend boundaries, contributes to this relativism. By noting its similarities to more ancient forms of religious socialization, it raises suspicions that the procedures of disciplines are not as pragmatic as some of their exponents might wish. In effect, it tends to undermine some confidence in the rationality of cognitive disciplines and of the claims that they make. Thus a growing sense of the social relativism of ideas emerges from the very procedures of a sociology of knowledge. In examining 'knowledge' as manufactured and controlled, it threatens in the process the basis of all knowledge, including ironically its own. Without engaging in imperialistic ontological claims, it nonetheless encourages a form of study which is thoroughly iconoclastic. It seems to be methodologically programmed towards total and, in the end, totally incoherent relativism.

Theology too, once subjected to the scrutiny of the sociology of knowledge, feels the winds of relativism. Theologians may initially derive some satisfaction from the discomfiture of other cognitive disciplines from this scrutiny, especially of those disciplines which have sometimes been hostile to theology. But the satisfaction is only short lived. Having observed that other disciplines use processes analogous to religious socialization, theologians soon realize that such observation also tends to relativize their own discipline.

Theology is as pluralistic as philosophy or sociology and theologians adopt procedures comparable to philosophers and sociologists to cope with this pluralism. The founding 'fathers' adopted by one set of theologians are not identical with those of another and, even when they are, their appropriations differ radically.

---

[3] See further my *Theology and Sociology: A Reader*, London: Geoffrey Chapman, 1987, New York: Paulist Press, 1988 (revised edition London: Cassell, 1996).

Theologians use reading lists to control students and are just as dismissive as their secular counterparts of 'unauthorized' literature. They are just as repetitious as others in their use and re-use of seminal works and just as changeable in their convictions. Once the process of doing theology (as distinct from the contents of theology) becomes an object of sociological scrutiny, relativism seems to be inescapable.

And theology *is* increasingly an object of sociological scrutiny. More accurately, sociological methods are increasingly being deployed in various branches of academic theology. If once the bias of many theologians was towards classics or philosophy, today sociology is playing an increasing role within theological studies. Nowhere is this more evident than within New Testament studies.[4] There has been a dramatic growth of New Testament sociology which shows no signs of abating. Approaching New Testament evidence with sociological, rather than just historical or theological, questions has opened the discipline to a new generation of scholars. Not surprisingly it has also heightened a sense of relativism which is seldom entirely absent for the Christian from critical New Testament scholarship. Christian convictions, or the biblical foundations of these convictions, are confronted with what seem to be the corrosive effects of relativism. New Testament sociology appears to be even more corrosive than other methods within the discipline.

Studying competing convictions in recent sectarianism also fosters a sense of relativism. A sociological analysis of those religious groups with the strongest convictions (most evident in the recent resurgence of fundamentalism) heightens this sense of relativism. This resurgence presents a challenge to recent sociological models of secularization. In the next chapter I will look for more satisfactory sociological forms of analysis before raising the specifically theological questions that arise from viewing fundamentalist convictions sociologically. In the chapter beyond I will examine critically the theory of cognitive dissonance as it seeks to explain the predictions of sectarian groups. The theory is particularly challenging for theology because of its possible extension into New Testament studies.

---

[4]   I used some of these in *Theology and Sociology: A Reader*. For a more recent survey see David Horrell, *Social-Scientific Approaches to New Testament Interpretation*, Edinburgh: T&T Clark, 1999 and *After the First Urban Christians: The Social-Scientific Study of Pauline Christianity Twenty-Five Years Later*, London and New York: T&T Clark, 2009.

Although I will finally be critical of the basis on which the theory was established (thus making it less applicable to New Testament studies), it does serve to highlight the way the social sciences can appear threatening to religious convictions.

For the critical theologian the religious subjects of these two chapters will appear somewhat crude. Understanding modern religious fundamentalism is important, but it may not finally challenge a more sophisticated and critical approach to theology. Theologians may feel happy to relativize these particular forms of religious conviction. However, the evidence that I presented, first in *The Myth of the Empty Church*[5] and then in *The 'Empty' Church Revisited,*[6] might seem distinctly more corrosive. While many may be happy to use sociology to account for practices and ideas which they regard as frankly erroneous, they may be less happy to apply sociology to their own foundations. The next Volume will return to this.

It is commonly held that competing convictions among the Victorian churches contributed to their strength, whereas in a more ecumenical age churches compromise on doctrinal issues, are less convinced and indeed convincing to others, and decline accordingly. Church decline is regarded as both a product of secularization and an instrument of further secularization. In contrast, it is only conservative, fundamentalist religious movements, mutually competing from absolutist tenets, that can hope to thrive in a secular age.

The evidence presented at length in these two books calls much of this into question. It suggests, quite oppositely, that competing convictions in the context of rural depopulation were instrumental in church decline. Competing convictions, which may or may not have been responsible for the rise in churchgoing in the first half of the nineteenth century, became a significant factor fostering decline in the second. I argued that demography may actually be more significant than some supposed process of secularization in uncovering factors responsible for rural church decline.

At first this analysis may seem comforting to churches, since it suggests that their decline (at least in rural areas) resulted more from misplaced ideology in the context of depopulation than from some progressive loss of faith. Yet it may soon be realized that churches have not altogether lost their ideological rivalries (of which

---

[5]   London: SPCK, 1993.
[6]   Aldershot, Hants: Ashgate, 2003.

tensions within, say, Pentecostal churches and between them and other churches are a current example). Further, explanations which rely upon demography may eventually prove just as relativistic as those which presume an ineluctable process of secularization.

Returning to biblical studies, it is possibly the sociological study of biblical interpretation that involves a particularly sharp sense of relativism and one of the most serious challenges to the foundations of modern theology. Tracing the path of a key New Testament text or *pericope* through a variety of differing social contexts evidently heightens a sense of relativism. It is not simply that meanings change somewhat over the ages and in differing social contexts. Rather it is that such mutually contradictory and opposite interpretations emerge from this form of study that the whole enterprise of building theology on biblical foundations appears to be challenged. A thoroughly sociological approach proves much more uncomfortable for biblical hermeneutics than is sometimes imagined. Hermeneutics appears to be culture bound and socially relative.

Theologians have often regarded relativism as an enemy, as a corrosive perspective that eats into the subject matter of theology and undercuts its very basis. Relativism and reductionism have frequently been confused and the social sciences, as apparent agents of both, have long been regarded with deep suspicion in some theological circles. A heightened sense of relativism (but not necessarily reductionism) does seem to result from applying sociological methods to various aspects of theology and the churches. Whether all theologians like it or not these methods are increasingly entering the discipline of theology and especially New Testament studies. Theological protests or disdain are hardly likely to halt this trend or to stem the sense of relativism that it bears. Religious convictions do appear more relative after the introduction of sociological method than they did before.

Even those who are most disdainful of social or cultural relativism are changed by a knowledge of its possibility. Someone with strong religious or ideological convictions, who exists wholly within an enclave of others with similar convictions, differs significantly from someone with apparently similar convictions, but who is surrounded by a pluralistic environment of competing convictions. Biblical literalism provides an obvious example of this. In previous ages, when Christians arguably assumed the literal truth of the apparent historical claims of the Bible, it would have been considered to be a perfectly intelligent activity to compute the age of the world from biblical genealogies. Some creationist fundamentalists still make such computations today. Yet they do so in the knowledge that their activity is regarded as eccentric and deviant by many others and they are aware that their very activity constitutes a challenge to prevailing scientific orthodoxies. Their actions appear similar to those of earlier Christians, even though their attitude towards these actions is radically changed. It is changed precisely by their knowledge that such literalistic beliefs are minority beliefs in a pluralistic society. Or to express this epigrammatically, prejudices that are unchallenged are blind prejudices, whereas those which dismiss legitimate challenges are wilful prejudices.

It is possible, then, for theologians to question the propriety of applying a sociological perspective to church structures, to the New Testament or, say, to the history and functions of ordained ministry. It is distinctly more difficult for them to avoid the relativizing effects of these applications. Once they are aware that other theologians are using sociology in this way, the status of their own claims about churches, about the New Testament or about ordained ministry are inevitably changed. So, once Schillebeeckx's socio-historical analysis of *ordo* and *ordinatio* is known,[7] ontological claims about ordained ministry become claims against the analysis as well as claims about ministry. Or, once Graham Shaw's socio-political analysis of Paul's claims to apostolicity are known,[8] a purely theological interpretation of these claims becomes itself an assertion of theology over-and-against this socio-political analysis.

In any case, those theologians who are most dismissive of sociology are apt to make assumptions about social determination when analysing opposing viewpoints. In several places in this book it is noted how often forms of social analysis have been used by theologians past and present as means of discounting opposing views. Thus, those who ostensibly reject a positive use of sociology within theology have still tended to use forms of sociology polemically. Current polemics about ordained ministry/episcopacy for women well illustrate this point.

---

[7] E. Schillebeeckx, *Ministry: A Case for Change*, SCM Press, 1981 and *The Church with a Human Face*, London: SCM Press, 1985.

[8] Graham Shaw, *The Cost of Authority: Manipulation and Freedom in the New Testament*, London: SCM Press, 1983.

It is not simply those challenging ontological claims about ordained ministry who adopt sociological perspectives. Those defending these claims against, for instance, the movement for the ordination/consecration of women are just as likely to use forms of social analysis, typically depicting the movement as a product of secular liberalism.

It will be argued later that these polemical uses of sociology are fundamentally flawed. A greater awareness of the genetic fallacy (outlined in Chapter 3) should persuade theologians that this is so. My point for the moment is only that these uses belie the disdain of sociology by some theologians. Perhaps what the latter really fear is that sociology tends to relativize convictions. And in this respect they are surely correct. Sociology even relativizes the convictions of those who claim certainties to counter the relativism that it fosters. The claiming of certainties does not in itself eliminate suspicions of relativism. It may even serve to reinforce these suspicions, especially when antagonistic theological factions claim differing and competing certainties. In drawing attention to this, sociology again heightens a sense of relativism.

Chapter 8

Fundamentalist Convictions

The rise of religious fundamentalism in the 1980s within both the West and the Middle East provided a curious paradox. In a situation of apparent secularism, or at least of ideological pluralism, it presented a sharp reaffirmation of doctrinal certainty of conviction. In the light of this resurgent and militant fundamentalism any concept of relative convictions might appear as an example of outmoded and epiphenomenal liberalism. The religious and political passion which tends to accompany fundamentalism all too easily overwhelms relativist/liberal religious or political positions. The latter largely failed to predict this resurgence. Many academics at the time (shaped as they were by Western concepts of secularization) found difficulty in understanding or even taking seriously fundamentalist convictions. They all too readily predicted the imminent eclipse of the political and social influence of fundamentalism. Today, a generation later, this eclipse is yet to happen.

Fundamentalism in the 1980s became problematic for both sociologists and theologians. In this chapter I intend to show how the theories of secularization which typified the 1960s seriously misled both sociologists and theologians at the time and reduced their ability to predict or understand the rise of fundamentalism. The demise or privatization of religious thinking, practices and institutions which was thought to characterize some ineluctable process of secularization in urban industrial society gradually began to seem less obvious. A new generation of social historians, sociologists and theologians slowly became more sceptical of such models of secularization. In different ways they started to challenge the premises underlying these models and to treat fundamentalism more seriously. The latter was no longer regarded simply as a temporary aberration which will soon pass. Instead, it began to be seen as evidence that thoroughgoing secularization models might actually be misleading heuristic devices.

To complete the paradox, once fundamentalism was taken seriously by critical scholarship it was also relativized and thereby undermined. If thoroughgoing secularization models now appeared misleading in the context of resurgent fundamentalism, more recent and, apparently more sympathetic, sociological and theological accounts revealed fundamentalist convictions to be themselves pluralistic and relative to specific and changing social contexts. Far from providing counter-evidence to a theory of relative convictions, they actually supplied an illuminating example of the relativist challenge facing all theological certainties in a sociologically conscious world. And, precisely because modern fundamentalists self-consciously attempted to counter this world, it was all the more vulnerable to sociological inspection. Sociologists' insistent probing into the social origins, maintenance, variability and social fragility of fundamentalism was more damaging to fundamentalist convictions than to relative convictions. Sociologists had much success in undermining religious, ideological or political claims to certainty, even the claims to certainty periodically made by sociologists themselves. Since certainty is so crucial to fundamentalists – certainty steadfastly maintained in a manifestly uncertain world – sociological methods appeared all the more damaging to their cause.

In seeking to set out the two sides of this paradox it became important to agree upon a definition of fundamentalism. Unfortunately the term had been used so widely in the media and academic circles that its meaning was far from clear (and three decades later it still remains unclear). In setting out the alternative sociological and theological definitions it soon became apparent that each tends to include some groups which were widely thought to be fundamentalist and to exclude others. Some choice was and remains inevitable. Preferably this choice should find an understanding of fundamentalism which could be adopted both by those who depicted themselves as fundamentalists and by those wishing simply to study fundamentalism. Only so might the sociological practice of imposing labels upon others, which they personally reject, be avoided.

Defining Fundamentalism

The term 'fundamentalism' was first used, according to some scholars, in 1920 by an American Baptist paper to depict 'those ready to do battle royal for the Fundamentals of Protestantism'.[1] It had its origins in the series of 12 booklets entitled *The Fundamentals*[2] published between 1910 and 1915. Although often adopted as a term of abuse by critics of fundamentalism, it continued to be used as a means of self-identification by American (and less frequently British) Protestant 'fundamentalists' themselves. Unusually the term is still used widely by both groups. In contrast, few religious groups identify themselves as 'sects' or 'cults'. The pejorative overtones inherent in the popular usage of these terms seem to preclude them from doing so. For example, although Mormons, Christian Scientists and Jehovah's Witnesses all might be regarded as 'sects' or 'cults' by society at large, members of each of these movements habitually refer to them as 'churches'. Occasionally – as with the Quakers and later the Shakers – a movement will adopt an originally somewhat derisory sobriquet as one way of referring to itself to the outside world. However, the term 'fundamentalism' is very much more than that. In origin it is a term coined in defiance of the perceived 'modernism' of the mainline denominations in the United States and is still used by some American Protestants as a primary means of self-identification in a context of 'modernism' and 'liberalism'. If anything the secular pejorative use of the term 'fundamentalism' has strengthened its use as a primary means of self-identification among fundamentalists. It is thus at once a cultural and a countercultural term in its use in the West.

'Fundamentalism' is also a term used as a cultural and a countercultural term within the social-scientific study of Islam over the last three decades. In an important study, originally made for the United States government in its attempt to understand resurgent Islamic fundamentalism, R. Hrair Dekmejian in 1985 contrasted the various terms used outside and within Islam to depict this phenomenon:

> The heightening of Islamic consciousness has been variously characterized as revivalism, rebirth, puritanism, fundamentalism, reassertion, awakening, reformism, resurgence, renewal, renaissance, revitalization, militancy, activism, millenarianism, messianism, return to Islam, and the march of Islam. Collectively, these terms are useful in describing the complexity of the Islamic phenomenon;

---

[1] See E. Sandeen, *The Roots of Fundamentalism: British and American Millenarianism 1800–1930*, Chicago, IL: University of Chicago Press, 1970, p. 246; see also G. Marsden, *Fundamentalism and American Culture: The Shaping of Twentieth-Century Evangelicalism 1870–1925*, Oxford: Oxford University Press, 1980.

[2] Chicago: Testimony Publishing Company, 1910–15.

yet they impute a certain dormancy to Islam, which does not conform to reality. In point of fact, Islam has successfully resisted the encapsulation imposed upon Christianity in the West – a resistance that is at the core of the ongoing conflict between state and religion in the Islamic world. Thus, it is instructive to review terms and constructs in the original Arabic usage regarding the Islamic revolution. Proponents and sympathizers frequently use the following expressions: *bath al Islami* (Islamic renaissance), *sahwah al-Islamiyyah* (Islamic awakening), *ihya al-Din* (Religious revival) *al-usuliyyah al-Islamiyyah* (Islamic fundamentalism). The most appropriate term is *al-usuliyyah al Islamiyyah* since it connotes a search for the fundamentals of the faith, the foundations of the Islamic polity (*ummah*), and the bases of legitimate authority (*al-shariyyah al-hukm*).[3]

Dekmejian was at pains to emphasize the continuity of the 1980s resurgence of Islamic fundamentalism with periodic Islamic revivals since the Prophet died. Similarly James Barr in his studies of Christian fundamentalism in 1981[4] traced its roots to the eighteenth rather than to the twentieth century. Nonetheless most sociological accounts of recent forms of fundamentalism also stress its specifically modern features. Both Dekmejian and Barr were aware that it is a countercultural phenomenon at odds with modernity. If the latter is emphasized, fundamentalism, however, rooted in past revivalism, is identified as a specifically modern phenomenon. It is seen as a form, or varying forms, of religious response to the 'relativism' and 'liberalism' of modernity. Both Shi'ite fundamentalists in Iran (identifying 'modernity' as 'Westernization') and Southern Baptist fundamentalists in the United States might have been happy in the 1980s (and perhaps still today) to see themselves in these countercultural terms. They would not of course have agreed on the substantive contents of their respective religious responses to modernity. Yet their understandings of modernity and their determinations to oppose its perceived effects through religious means have had many points in common.

---

[3]   R. Hrair Dekmejian, *Islam in Revolution: Fundamentalism in the Arab World*, Syracuse, NY: Syracuse University Press, 1985, p. 4.

[4]   James Barr, *Fundamentalism*, London: SCM Press, 1981.

Writing two decades later scholars such as the veteran Bernard Lewis and Olivier Roy still use the term 'fundamentalism' to depict the more radical (and sometimes violent) forms of recent Islamic resurgence. Lewis is careful to remind readers that Islamic fundamentalism takes many different forms:

> Radical Islamism, to which it has become customary to give the name Islamic fundamentalism, is not a single homogenous movement. There are many types of Islamic fundamentalism in different countries and even sometimes within a single country. Some are state-sponsored – promulgated, used, and promoted by one or other Muslim government for its own purposes; some are genuine population movements from below. The Muslim fundamentalists, unlike the Protestant groups whose name was transferred to them, do not differ from the mainstream on questions of theology and the interpretation of scripture. Their critique is, in the broadest sense, societal. The Islamic world, in their view, has taken a wrong turning. Fundamentalists are anti-Western in the sense that they regard the West as the source of the evil that is corroding Muslim society, but their primary attack is directed against their own rulers and leaders.[5]

Olivier Roy tends to prefer the term 'neo-fundamentalist' (which he distinguishes from Islamist), yet he too sees a variety of different ways that these new Muslim fundamentalists present an exclusivist opposition to those forms of modern society that are shaped by Western precepts and values:

> Neo-fundamentalists advocate the strict implementation of *sharia*, with no concession to man-made law. They consider that there is nothing positive to be borrowed from the West and nothing to discuss with Christians and Jews except calling them to Islam, although mainstream Salafis agree that one should treat non-belligerent infidels leniently. Islam is for neo-fundamentalists an all-encompassing religion, but mainly in so far as the daily life of the individual is concerned.[6]

---

[5] Bernard Lewis, *The Crisis of Islam: Holy War and Unholy Terror*, New York: Random House, 2004, pp. 23–24.

[6] Olivier Roy, *Globalised Islam: The Search for a New Ummah*, London: Hurst, 2004, p. 245.

The concept of 'modernity' here has long generated a considerable debate among sociologists about both its meaning and its relationship to urbanization, industrialization and especially to secularization.[7] Without being sidetracked into this debate, it is still possible to see that the 'modern world' (for convenience 'modernity'), or at least the effects of modernity, are frequently and explicitly the object of attack from self-styled fundamentalists, even when they are expert exponents of modern technology. The irony, for example, of critics of the media using the media to disseminate their criticisms, is certainly not limited to religious fundamentalists. Yet the latter, especially in the United States, have been among the most successful in exploiting deregulated commercial television. In Iran, too, public television has been used extensively as a medium of fundamentalist control. Further, the Iran–Iraq war in the 1980s made protracted use of 'modern' war technology. It even supplied an 'invaluable' source of field information about the strategic capabilities of this technology for those industrialized nations manufacturing it. Despite the rhetoric of many fundamentalists against modernity, their actual opposition to it was and remains selective. Similarly, although anti-evolutionary creationism has typified many American Southern Baptist fundamentalists, they have frequently sought to justify this through scientific means.

In his introduction to a collection of studies on Islamic resurgence, Ernest Gellner sought to depict the relationship between this resurgence and modernity. He argued that 'the introduction of the new and very powerful productive, military and administrative technology has a number of consequences, amongst which the one most relevant for our purposes is the erosion of the small sub-communities which were the essential cells of social life in the traditional situation'.[8] An immediate consequence of the new technology has been a considerable increase in the complexity of the division of labour and a greatly enhanced power of the central state. A tribal society allowing for private vengeance and communal military

---

[7] See Peter. L. Berger, *Facing up to Modernity: Excursions in Society, Politics and Religion*, London: Penguin, 1977, and *The Heretical Imperative: Contemporary Possibilities of Religious Affirmation*, London: Collins, 1980. But see also essays in L. Caplan (ed.), *Studies in Religious Fundamentalism*, Albany, NY: State University of New York Press, 1987.

[8] 'Introduction' in E. Gellner (ed.), *Islamic Dilemmas: Reformers, Nationalists and Industrialization*, The Hague, NL: Mouton, 1985, p. 6.

self-help has given way to a modern, technologically based state. Durkheimian religious communities have lost their central role. Old forms of the sacred 'had once ratified and sustained and oiled social forms which have disappeared or are disappearing. So their function vanishes, only their personnel, and their doctrinal rationale, remains'.[9] Islamic fundamentalism filled this vacuum and was better adapted to the new urban order (while still being deeply rooted in the historic past of the Muslim community):

> The new style enables the recently urbanised rustics simultaneously to disavow their rural past, of which they are openly ashamed, and to express their resentment of their opulent and questionably orthodox rulers, whom they secretly envy. Thus, one and the same style, serves simultaneously to define a new emergent Muslim nationality against the foreigner, to provide a charter for self-disciplining and a disavowal of past weakness, for the elevation of rustics into townsmen, and for a critical stance towards the rulers, one which the latter cannot easily disregard. So is there a mystery about the social bases of the puritanical, scripturalist reformism which has swept Islam?[10]

Gellner clearly believed that there was not. Other Middle East specialists at the time interpreted the situation slightly differently. Dekmejian ignored rural/ urban transitions in the Islamic world and saw the rise of fundamentalism as a result of a combination of a charismatic leadership and political crisis (notably the 1967 Arab defeat). For him military and economic modernization had rather caused a clash of values: 'whilst the modernists are inclined toward the wholesale emulation of Western social theory and practice, most traditionalists advocate the selective borrowing of aspects of Western experience thought to be compatible with Islam, that is, science and technology.'[11] Sami Zubaida's analysis of the social composition of fundamentalists also seemed to differ from that of Gellner:

---

[9] Gellner, p. 7.

[10] Gellner, pp. 7–8.

[11] Dekmejian, *Islam in Revolution*, p. 32. See also Roy Mottahedeh, *The Mantle of the Prophet: Religion and Politics in Iran*, New York: Pantheon, 1985.

The main activists in the Islamic movements in both Egypt and Iran are the young intelligentsia, which may be termed the intellectual proletariat of students, teachers and minor functionaries, together with some elements drawn from the urban working class and 'petty bourgeois' shopkeepers and artisans (these latter elements constituting a numerical minority). These are the same social groups from whom support is drawn for all oppositional politics, left and right, religious and secular. As for the urban poor, the indications are that their participation is sporadic, little organized and probably dependent on bandwagon effect.[12]

Two decades later Olivier Roy's concept of 'globalized Islam'[13] focuses not just upon countercultural Muslim fundamentalists living in living Muslim nations but also upon Muslims settled permanently in non-Muslim countries (mainly in the West). By now, of course, following 9/11, radical Islam has become a contentious issue *within* the West and not just *for* the West.

These varying analyses may not have been mutually exclusive. Most have seen Islamic fundamentalism as a response in some form to modernity, combining an ambivalent attitude towards modern technology and the Western values associated with it. In this respect it has much in common with American Protestant fundamentalism. This, in turn, may or may not have been causally related in both manifestations of fundamentalism to the urbanization of a rural community. In the context of Sunni fundamentalism, Emmanuel Sivan argued that, especially in poorer Arab countries where it was strong, 'the very failure of modernity to deliver upon its promises explains the radical message'.[14] The latter may also have been peculiarly related to the Arab–Israeli political crisis of 1967 (sometimes used within the apocalyptic visions of American fundamentalists, but certainly not a causal agency of them).[15]

---

[12]   Sami Zubaida, 'The Quest for the Islamic State: Islamic Fundamentalism in Egypt and Iran' in Caplan (ed.), *Studies in Religious Fundamentalism*, p. 49.

[13]   See Olivier Roy, *Globalised Islam*, London: Hurst, 2004 and Mark Juergensmeyer (ed), *The Oxford Handbook of Global Religions*, Oxford: Oxford University Press, 2006.

[14]   E. Sivan, *Radical Islam: Medieval Theology and Modern Politics*, New Haven, CT: Yale University Press, 1985, p. 188.

[15]   See Roger Ruston, 'Apocalyptic and the Peace Movement', *New Blackfriars* 67: 791, 204–215, May 1986.

For Ian Lustick it was this crisis which was central to the emergence of Jewish fundamentalism. Lustick related the founding of the militant fundamentalist movement in Israel, *Gush Emunim* (literally 'the Bloc of the Faithful') in 1974, firstly to the territorial aspirations that followed the Six Day War in 1967 and then to the political crisis following the Yom Kippur War in 1973. He argued:

> The Yom Kippur War was the first major conflict in which substantial numbers of Orthodox Jews participated within regular combat units. Famous for their knitted skullcaps, these soldiers came mainly from the recently created Yeshivot Hesder in which young religious Jews were permitted to integrate halftime study of sacred texts with regular service in the army. This participation gave religious Israeli Jews self-confidence and legitimacy within the wider secular society. Amid the psychological confusion of the period following the Yom Kippur War, a generation of young religious idealists, whose pride had always suffered by the honour granted to kibbutzniks and other secular Jews for serving in the army, felt empowered to offer their own analysis of Israel's predicament, and their own solution. But their analysis was not technocratic, it was theological. Their solution was a spiritual rejuvenation of society whose most important expression and source of strength would be settlement on and communion with the greater, liberated Land of Israel.[16]

Lustick maintained in 1988 that *Gush Emunim* consisted primarily of well-educated, middle-class Ashkenazic Israelis and had 10,000–20,000 activists. With the slogan 'The Land of Israel, for the People of Israel, According to the Torah of Israel', they were most visible in their settlements (supported financially by Likud) in the West Bank and Gaza Strip. Indeed, 'the men and women of *Gush Emunim* have made it their life's work to ensure that the occupied West Bank and Gaza Strip are permanently incorporated into the State of Israel. The level and intensity of their commitment, flowing from the fundamental, even cosmic, issues they perceive to be directly at stake, had largely disappeared from Israeli politics. Their operational objective is to accelerate the pace at which the Jewish people

---

[16] Ian S. Lustick, *For the Land and the Lord: Jewish Fundamentalism in Israel*, New York: Council on Foreign Relations, 1988, p. 44. For the effect of the 1967 War on Egyptian Sunni fundamentalists, see Sivan, *Radical Islam*.

fulfils its destiny.'[17] Religious aspirations were predominant with *Gush Emunim*, although Lustick pointed out that an important non-religious minority had also formed settlements and belongs to the movement.

The combination of fundamentalism and territorial claims and actions made *Gush Emunim* particularly potent in the Middle East. Indeed, the juxtaposition of Islamic and Jewish fundamentalism had obvious implications for the peace of the world. Lustick's aims in studying Jewish fundamentalism were overtly political. He maintained that 'virtually no serious observers believe a negotiated solution to the Arab–Israeli conflict is possible unless Jewish fundamentalism's key goal – establishment of permanent Jewish rule of the whole Land of Israel – is thwarted. Yet, for the foreseeable future, the political leverage this movement and its allies can exert will prevent the Israeli political system from responding positively, by normal, peaceful parliamentary means, to opportunities to achieve such an agreement, no matter how attractive its terms.'[18] Most terrifying of all, Lustick outlined the way some within *Gush Emunim* since 1983 had sought to remove Muslim shrines from the Dome of the Rock and to re-establish the Jewish Temple. He even quoted military sources speculating on the possibility of fundamentalists planting explosives within the Dome of the Rock – a possibility that later proved to have real substance.[19]

Gush Emunim continued to be a highly fluid movement and Lustick had some difficulty in reaching a definition of fundamentalism which would cover it adequately. Because its members were not wholly religious and also because his own interests were predominantly political, he rejected specifically religious definitions of the term. He was fully aware of the American Protestant origins of the term, but regarded etymology as finally unsatisfactory, since 'it would apply as well to monastic sects and traditionalist religions whose rigid enforcement of elaborate rules entails complete withdrawal from society as to crusades designed to reorder the world according to the dictates of the Holy Writ'.[20] Instead, he believed that what characterizes fundamentalists is their unwillingness to engage in any form of political pragmatism while seeking to implement radical changes in

---

[17]   Lustick, p. 9.

[18]   Lustick, pp. 177–178.

[19]   See Gershon Gorenberg, *The End of Days: Fundamentalisms and the Struggle for the Temple Mount*, New York: Free Press, 2000.

[20]   Lustick, p. 5.

society. Their political aspirations are uncompromising, dogmatically based and comprehensive. In short, 'a belief system is defined as fundamentalist in so far as its adherents regard its tenets as uncompromizable and direct transcendental imperatives to political action oriented toward the rapid and comprehensive reconstruction of society'.[21]

Lustick was unusual at the time in offering a formal definition of fundamentalism. Others characteristically grouped together features which they regarded as fundamentalist. Frequently this was done by referring to the supposedly five features commended in *The Fundamentals*: namely, biblical inerrancy, the virgin birth, substitutionary atonement, the bodily resurrection, and the historicity of miracles.[22] The difficulty here is that it limited fundamentalism to Christianity and that, even within Christian fundamentalism, it ignored the debate about whether or not other elements (notably apocalypticism) needed to be included. Christian fundamentalism from the outset has been internally divided on this second point. Alternatively, following Barr,[23] more analytic features were sometimes grouped together to depict fundamentalism – namely its exclusivity, oppositional character, its prominent soteriological and eschatological beliefs, its compartmentalization of religion, its ahistoricity, and its rationalistic character (for Barr this last was an important feature distinguishing modern fundamentalism from earlier exclusive systems of Christian belief). Lustick went beyond this by offering a formal definition rather an analytic description.

However, his definition has obvious limitations. It took a term developed in a religious context and removed all religious reference from it. Sometimes this has been done in church-sect typology when political parties are analysed as 'church-like' or 'sect-like'. Although this can be useful, it might more properly be regarded as an analogical use of typology. It alters such typology very considerably if instead politics becomes its primary reference. Perhaps Lustick dismissed etymology too easily. Again, his definition would seem to cover such movements as economic monetarism (if strongly and radically held) and exclude rigid religious groups

---

[21] Lustick, p. 6.

[22] See L. Caplan, 'Fundamentalism as Counter-Culture' in Caplan (ed.), *Studies in Religious Fundamentalism*.

[23] Barr, *Fundamentalism*. See also Richard Tapper and Nancy Tapper, '"Thank God We're Secular!" Aspects of Fundamentalism in a Turkish Town', in Caplan (ed.), *Studies in Religious Fundamentalism*.

which withdraw from society. Indeed, Lustick regarded it as a virtue of his definition that it is able to include secular members of *Gush Emunim* and exclude ultra-orthodox Jewish groups in Israel. Yet, on this understanding, self-styled American Protestant fundamentalists can be regarded as 'fundamentalist' only if they are also politically active – which, in previous generations, they have seldom been. Those who claimed to be fundamentalist, but did not participate in political movements such as Moral Majority in the 1980s, would then be excluded by definition, whereas non-religious but bigoted political activists who made no claim to fundamentalism are to be included. Of course definitions are but tools for analysis, but it is possible that Lustick's was too specifically related to a particular context for wider application.

Before suggesting an alternative definition, it is necessary first to isolate those features which the various groups who refer to themselves as fundamentalists (across religious traditions) seem to have in common. If this is to be achieved these features clearly cannot be specifically related to Christian doctrines. For this reason more general analytic features are to be preferred. Yet they must be sufficiently religious and sufficiently distinct within religious systems if they are meaningfully to depict modern forms of fundamentalism. Ideally they should also have some relationship to the original use of the term: etymology should at least be taken seriously.

Two general features of fundamentalism might be isolated, the first cognitive and the second sociological. At a cognitive level, fundamentalism can be seen as a series of movements committed to sacred text and/or holy law absolutism. And, at a sociological level, it can be seen as a series of countercultures, that is, as movements consciously opposed to the pluralism and relativism that appear to accompany modernity. In fundamentalism these two features are intimately related: sacred text and/or holy law absolutism is upheld as a counter to modernity and defines the varying countercultural forms that fundamentalism assumes.

The notion of sacred text and/or holy law absolutism does not simply involve a high view of scripture which characterizes many evangelical forms of Christianity or of the *Qur'an* and *Shari'a* within Islam or of laws within the *Torah* in orthodox Judaism. Even the notion of scriptural inerrancy is too wide, since it is possible to believe that scripture is inerrant but in need of supplementation and further, but optional, interpretation. Rather a sacred text and/or holy law (and additional, but non-optional, interpretations of either or both) is regarded as *the only* resource to guide the modern world and as *the only* source for imperatives about how the modern world is to be challenged and changed. Such certainty/absolutism typically regards with disdain historical/critical scriptural scholarship and anathematizes any approaches to scripture which are anything less than absolute.

Once again the veteran scholar of Islam, Bernard Lewis, expresses the distinction here clearly:

> There are several forms of Islamic extremism current in the present time. The best known are the subversive radicalism of Al-Qai'da and other groups that resemble it all over the Muslim world; the pre-emptive fundamentalism of the Saudi establishment; and the institutionalized revolution of the ruling Iranian hierarchy. All of these are, in a sense, Islamic in origin, but some of them have deviated very far from their origins. All of these extremist groups sanctify their action through pious references to Islamic texts, notably the Qur'an and the traditions of the Prophet, and all three claim to represent a truer, purer, and more authentic Islam than that currently practiced by the vast majority of Muslims and endorsed by most though not all religious leadership. They are, however, highly selective in their choice and interpretation of sacred texts.[24]

Counterculture is clearly present in this understanding of (selective) sacred text absolutism. Without serious competitors various forms of Christianity, Islam and Judaism have of course been literalistic at times in their understanding of scripture. Yet it would be an anachronism to call this fundamentalism. Self-styled fundamentalism has in addition been characterized by a systematic attempt to counter sacred text and/or holy law relativism. Within American fundamentalism this has taken the form of frequent attacks upon liberal Protestantism and biblical criticism. The latter are viewed as the typical products of a relativist, liberal and permissive society. As Peter Berger frequently claimed,[25] a link can be made between modernity and pluralism: modern technology and systems of

---

[24]   Bernard Lewis, *The Crisis of Islam*, p. 138.

[25]   For example in *Facing up to Modernity*, 1977 and *The Heretical Imperative*, 1980. See also Roland Robertson, 'Anti-global Religion?', in Mark Juergensmeyer (ed), *The Oxford Handbook of Global Religions*, Oxford: Oxford University Press, 2006, pp. 611–623.

communication foster a level of cultural pluralism and consequent relativism hitherto unknown.

Within Islamic fundamentalism an attack upon sacred text relativism and upon pluralistic modernity has been just as apparent. In this respect the attack upon Salman Rushdie's *The Satanic Verses* was not an aberration. Shi'ite fundamentalism in Iran in 1979 very consciously made an attempt to reverse the 'evil' cultural effects of modernity and to place instead a society founded upon Islamic holy law. Sunni fundamentalism in Egypt was also characterized by a sustained attack on 'permissive' modernity and an attempt to replace it with a greater adherence to sacred text and holy law. Within Judaism, too, even the ostensibly non-religious minority of *Gush Emunim* was party to territorial demands based upon scriptural certainty/absolutism. Some analysts in the 1980s also included as fundamentalists militant Sikhs' use of *Guru Granth Sahib* and Sri Lankan Tamil worshippers of Siva's use of Agamic canons.[26] By 2000 Mark Juergensmeyer's list of religious movements involved in the 'global rise of religious violence' was far more extensive[27] and by 2011 a lengthy Blackwell Companion is devoted entirely to the topic of 'religion and violence' across many different cultures and religious traditions.[28]

Counterculture based upon sacred text and/or holy law certainty/absolutism is also a feature of some religious groups – within Christianity, Islam and Judaism – that withdraw from the world. Some of these seek to build the purest form of counterculture which avoids unnecessary contact with the contaminating world. There is no reason why their political quietism should exclude them from being regarded as fundamentalist. On the other hand, purely political groups or even countercultural religious groups which are not characterized by such absolutism can, on this understanding, only be termed 'fundamentalist' by analogy. This may not be a disadvantage since they would not usually use the term to depict themselves. It may not be possible finally to find an exact match between groups

---

[26]   See Caplan (ed.), *Studies in Religious Fundamentalism*, pp. 14–15.

[27]   Mark Juergensmeyer, *Terror in the Mind of God: The Global Rise of Religious Violence*, Berkeley, CA; University of California Press, 2000.

[28]   Andrew R. Murphy (ed.), *The Blackwell Companion to Religion and Violence*, Malden, MA and Oxford: Wiley-Blackwell, 2011.

that can be analytically identified as fundamentalist and groups that regard themselves as fundamentalist,[29] but the closer the match the better.

With all of these points in mind, fundamentalism may be tentatively defined as a system of beliefs and practices which treat sacred text and/or holy law certainty/absolutism as the only way to counter the pluralism and relativism engendered by modernity. And the term militant fundamentalism might be used further to distinguish those forms of fundamentalism which have sought to counter modernity through radical political and, especially, violent means

Resurgences of Fundamentalism

So defined it is hardly surprising that Western social scientists, religionists and theologians in the 1970s largely failed to predict the modern resurgences of fundamentalism and were slow in the 1980s to take them seriously. Countercultural sacred text and/or holy law certainty/absolutism was so antithetical to the presumptions that predominate in Western scholarship that the Shi'ite revolution in Iran in 1979 and the political role of the Moral Majority in the American elections in the 1980s were slow at being adequately assessed. Only gradually was it realized in the scholarly world that they represent a challenge to the consensus about secularization that dominated the 1960s. As noted in earlier chapters, it was a consensus that predominated among historians, sociologists, political theorists, religionists and also theologians. Even those few critics of secularization models in the 1960s largely failed to foresee a resurgence of countercultural scriptural certainty/absolutism.

Dekmejian (writing in 1985) well expressed the situation in the scholarly West:

> The Western practice of placing Islamic fundamentalism under the rubric of 'fanaticism' is singularly dysfunctional to a balanced and dispassionate analysis of the subject. Indeed, to a Western world preoccupied with growing economic problems and security concerns, the Islamic challenge was unexpected and ominous. Few in the non-Islamic sphere were able to anticipate an Islamic

---

[29] See A. Walker, 'Fundamentalism and Modernity: The Restoration Movement in Britain', in Caplan (ed.), *Studies in Religious Fundamentalism*.

resurgence in the modern context. The conceptual myopia induced by Western and Marxist materialism had effectively blindfolded both scholars and statesmen, who tended to dismiss or underestimate the regenerative capacity of Islam.[30]

Of course there was considerable debate among scholars at the time about the durability of this resurgence and about the extent and political importance of militant Protestant fundamentalism within the United States.[31] However, this debate did not detract from Dekmejian's central argument, namely, that the 1979 resurgence of militant fundamentalism was largely unforeseen by scholars at the time.[32] Many had been convinced by the dominant assumption at the time that radical secularization characterizes the modern world (including Iran in the 1970s).

The Italian sociologist S.S. Acquaviva typified this assumption in his influential study of 1966 *The Decline of the Sacred in Industrial Society*.[33] His intention was to examine the religious crisis that he believed accompanies industrialization. To do this he first examined available statistical data from Europe, Britain and the United States and then turned to more cultural considerations. For him the statistical/structural decline of the churches that his data suggested was related, but at a slight distance, to the demise of cognitive form of religiosity in society. Thus, 'as secularization advances in industrial and post-industrial society, the traditional "sacred cosmos" loses its significance as the index of a religiosity bound up with the experience of the sacred. This is because of the high degree of subjectivization of models of belief'.[34] In other words, as the ecclesial basis of religiosity diminishes as an accompaniment of industrialization, religious belief, if it survives at all, becomes more private and idiosyncratic. Further, secularism

---

[30]   Dekmejian, *Islam in Revolution*, pp. 7–8.

[31]   See Steve Bruce, *The Rise and fall of the New Christian Right: Protestant Politics in America 1978–88*, Oxford: Clarendon, 1988 and *Politics and Religion*, Oxford: Polity Press, 2003.

[32]   A very instructive exception that Dekmejian cites is indeed Bernard Lewis' article 'The Return of Islam', *Commentary*, 61, 39–49, 1976. Others have cited predictions published later in Michael M.J. Fischer's *Iran: From Religious Dispute to Revolution*, Cambridge, MS: Harvard University Press 1980, and Hamid Algar's *The Roots of the Islamic Revolution*, London: Open Press, The Muslim Institute, 1983.

[33]   New York: Harper and Row, 1979 [Italian original 1966].

[34]   Acquaviva, *Decline*, p. 48.

grows in such a society, especially among those who are best educated. This represents a radical departure from previous ages:

> In the centuries prior to our own, religiosity – at least externally, and with only marginal exceptions – was universal. The abandonment of religion was then no more than the passage from one religion to another, and not a shift from religion to atheism. Those who never engaged in any sort of religious practice were very few indeed, and locally could usually be picked out by name … To this near unanimity of practice there corresponded a fairly unanimous religiosity on the past of the individual: social life was shot through with religious significance. It is widely accepted that in the early stages of human history the structure of society was thoroughly pervaded by religious conceptions.[35]

Secularization, in Acquaviva's analysis, affects church structures, it affects 'the attribution of sacred significance … to things, persons, spaces, etc.', and it affects 'the attribution of sacred significance to behaviour (moral, etc.)'.[36] It does not necessarily entail the total disappearance of religion, but it has changed religious conviction within society:

> One might maintain the thesis that in industrial society, the sacred and the religious tend more and more to become a sort of unexpressed potentiality instead of the active, manifest elements that they were until relatively recently … Our review of the various levels of inquiry relevant to the problem of religion in contemporary society, do not allow us to say where the process of secularization will terminate, or whether there will be any substantial reversal of the current tendency. All that can be said with certainty is that the decline of the sacred is intimately connected with the changes in society and human psychology. It cannot be considered as merely a contingent fact: it is associated with the collapse, whether temporarily or finally, of traditions, cultures, and values. From the religious point of view, humanity has entered a long night that will become darker and darker with the passing of the generations, and of which no end can yet be seen. It is a night in which there seems to be no place

---

[35] Acquaviva, *Decline*, p. 85.
[36] Acquaviva, *Decline*, p. 35.

for a conception of God, or for a sense of the sacred, and ancient ways of giving significance to our own existence, of confronting life and death, are becoming increasingly untenable. At bottom, the motivation for religious behaviour and for faith persists – the need to explain ourselves and what surrounds us, the anguish, and the sense of precariousness. But man remains uncertain whether somewhere there exists, or ever existed, something different from uncertainty, doubt, and existential insecurity.[37]

Acquaviva's analysis was far from crude. This passage alone shows theological as well as sociological sensitivity. The church statistics that he used are indeed crude by more recent standards (for instance, he frequently drew conclusions about church decline from single decade statistics). Further a sweeping contrast between the modern world and the 'golden age' of religion in the past has been subjected to considerable criticism.[38] Nevertheless, he did not claim that secularization is an ineluctable process: this is not social determinism. Nor did he ignore more privatized forms of religiosity. Yet having conceded that, there was nothing in his analysis which would make imminent resurgences of militant fundamentalism in heavily industrialized societies even remotely feasible. Countercultural sacred text and/or holy law certainty/absolutism should not have been a viable option for people within burgeoning industrial societies if his analysis was correct. And it certainly should not have been a viable option for an educated urban elite in the 1980s within the Arab world.[39]

By the mid-1980s many scholars were beginning to shift away from these assumptions articulated by Acquaviva. Clear examples of this shift can be seen in a number of influential scholarly collections that were made at the time.

Disciplines of Faith: Studies in Religion, Politics and Patriarchy[40] that had its origins in the Religion and Society History Workshop meeting of 1983 in London. In the Introduction the editors were aware that their 'recognition of the

---

[37]   Acquaviva, *Decline*, pp. 200–202.

[38]   See P.E. Glasner, *The Sociology of Secularisation*, London: Routledge & Kegan Paul, 1977 and Bryan S. Turner, *Secularization* (4 volumes), London and New York: Sage, 2010.

[39]   See Sivan, *Radical Islam*, p. 183.

[40]   J. Obelkevich, L. Roper and R. Samuel (eds), *Disciplines of Faith: Studies in Religion, Politics and Patriarchy*, London: Routledge & Kegan Paul, 1987.

power of religion as a shaping force of politics in the contemporary world ... is uncomfortable for socialists who have traditionally anticipated the eventual triumph of reason over superstition, as it is for sociologists with their paradigms of secularization and rationalization, allegedly characteristic of the modern world'.[41] Yet they argued that in a wide variety of situations in the 1980s – Iran, Northern Ireland, Israel, Poland and the United States – this power was evident. They pointed to the remarkable political changes that were taking place then within the Roman Catholic world. In particular, they highlighted the rise of liberation theology in South America, Christian–Marxist dialogue and the shift to the left of much Western Catholicism. All of this, they argued, fits uncomfortably with traditional socialist and sociological interpretations of the demise of religion in modern society.

The Political Role of Religion in the United States,[42] with a mixture of sociologists and political scientists, was similarly convinced that resurgences of religiosity in the modern world now required greater attention from specialists. In similar tones to the first collection, the editors of the second began their introduction as follows:

> To many social scientists the current burst of political activity by religious leaders that we have witnessed in the later 1970s and early 1980s has come as a surprise. A dominant scholarly thesis had been that modern-day society trends, such as the cultural diversity of the American people and the increased use of science to solve today's problems, had brought greater secularization in all of our lives. Secularization is a system of ideas and practices that disregards or rejects any form of religious faith or worship. But despite these long-term secular trends, we have recently seen in the United States, and indeed around the world, the resurgence of religion into the secular sphere of the political arena.[43]

They then proceeded to point to all the same instances of resurgence cited by the editors of *Disciplines of Faith*. These two collections, it should be noted, were

---

[41] *Disciplines of Faith*, pp. 5–6.

[42] S.D. Johnson and J.B. Tamney (eds), *The Political Role of Religion in the United States*, Boulder, CO: Westview Press, 1986.

[43] *The Political Role of Religion in the United States*, p. 1.

written quite independently, the first from Britain and the second from the United States. The editors of the second collection, however, were still convinced that there is apparent a process of secularization. This process was evident for them in the cultural effects of technology and science, in the rise of humanism, in the dominance of economic systems and in the increasing privatization of religion. Without detracting from this they concluded:

> This analysis of secular trends would seem to justify the conclusions that religious influence in modern life is weak and that those who attempt to change this condition will find it to be no easy task. The remarkable feature of the eighties, however, is that churches have increasingly taken up the challenge presented by secularization. The response of the religious institution is twofold. On the one hand, there are those leaders who resist the changes associated with modernity or modern secular trends. These are mainly the Christian Rightists. On the other hand, there are those leaders and institutions that more or less accept modernity and try to adjust, not necessarily accommodate, to the new situation. These are the liberal Catholics, Protestants, and Jews.[44]

The Sacred in a Secular Age[45] brought together a number of leading sociologists of religion. In the light of the dominance of thoroughgoing secularization models in the 1960s, the most remarkable feature of this collection is that only one of its contributors, Bryan Wilson, appeared to hold an unmodified position on secularization. The editor, Phillip Hammond, cited three sets of data which have been responsible for this modification: the resurgences of fundamentalism, the persistence of 'popular', 'folk' or 'unofficial' religion in the modern world,[46] and the continuing role of religion within political/military conflicts in Northern Ireland then and the Middle East.

Perhaps the most surprising group of social scientists at the time to note a resurgence of religiosity in the modern world were geographers. Among them the

---

[44]   *The Political Role of Religion in the United States*, p. 3.

[45]   Phillip E. Hammond (ed.), *The Sacred in a Secular Age*, Berkeley, CA: University of California Press, 1984: see also James A. Beckford and Thomas Luckmann (eds), *The Changing Face of Religion*, London: Sage, 1989.

[46]   See P.H. Vrijhof and J. Waardenburg, *Official and Popular Religion: Analysis of a Theme for Religious Studies*, The Hague, NL: Mouton, 1979.

phenomenon of pilgrimage was attracting increasing attention. A session of the 83rd Annual Meeting of the Association of American Geographers concentrated upon this subject with scholars contributing from both North America and West Germany. In the collection that resulted the editors noted in their introduction:

Pilgrimages to holy places have taken place since early days in the history of mankind. They, however, attained great significance with the emergence and development of the great world religions (Hinduism, Buddhism, Judaism, Christianity and Islam). They may be considered among the oldest forms of circulation based upon non-economic factors, although they were greatly facilitated by the contemporary trade routes ... Despite a general tendency toward secularization in the modern world and other religious changes, pilgrimages have been experiencing a worldwide boom during the last few decades, thanks to the modern means of mass transportation and the increasing use of the automobile. *The World Christian Encyclopaedia* (1982) estimates that altogether about 130 million people take part in pilgrimages every year.[47]

There were, of course, problems in treating all pilgrimages uncritically as manifestations of religious resurgence. For instance it proved extremely difficult to distinguish adequately between pilgrimages and tourism and to be clear about the motivation of all those visiting pilgrim shrines in the modern world (and perhaps the mediaeval world too). Nevertheless, within Europe especially, the very considerable interest in pilgrim shrines seemed to these geographers to point to a resurgence of popular Catholicism. This, they argued, appeared to run counter to 'a general tendency toward secularization in the modern world'.

Among theologians Harvey Cox represented perhaps the most remarkable shift in the 1980s. Two decades after producing *Secular City* (already criticized in Chapter 4 above) he now published its sequel, *Religion in the Secular City*.[48] If the first book offered one of the most forthright defences of the theological opportunities offered by secularization, the second reversed many of his previous

---

[47]   S.M. Bhardwaj and G. Rinschede (eds), *Pilgrimage in World Religions: Geographia Religionum, Interdisziplinare Schriftenreihe zur Religions-geographie*, Band 4, Berlin: Dietrich Reimer Verlag, 1988, p. 11.

[48]   Harvey Cox, *Religion in the Secular City: Toward a Postmodern Theology*, New York: Simon and Schuster, 1984.

arguments about secularization and maintained instead that 'postmodern' theology must come to terms with the resurgences of religion in the modern world apparent in both liberation theology[49] and, perhaps surprisingly, fundamentalism. He argued that there are theological reasons for taking the latter seriously:

> When theologians do pay attention to fundamentalism, they often misunderstand it. They tend to examine it as a somewhat bizarre variant of Protestantism. Most fail to recognize it not only as a theology, but also as the faith of an identifiable subculture and as an ideology. The rudiments of a postmodern theology will emerge from Christian subcultures that have been in touch with the dominant liberal theological consensus of the modern world but have not been absorbed by it. The American fundamentalist movement qualifies as such a subculture.[50]

The theological challenge of fundamentalism for Cox resided in its location as a subculture (perhaps the term 'counterculture' is more accurate) and as an ideology. It is a religious challenge to modernity. Yet, finally preferring the base communities of South American liberation theology, he concluded that fundamentalism is also a flawed challenge to modernity:

> [B]eginning as an intellectual movement that quickly developed a grass-roots following but had articulate scholarly defenders, it has become an elite-led phenomenon which – with some important exceptions – displays relatively little interest in intellectual questions. Starting as a ferociously antimodernist movement, it has recently embraced some of the most questionable features of the modern world its founders despised.[51]

Not all of this theological critique fitted Islamic and Jewish forms of fundamentalism. Indeed, in so far as various forms of Shi'ite and Sunni fundamentalism had grass-root, radical and subcultural support in parts of the Muslim world, it was difficult to see why they should not qualify for Cox's approval. They even successfully

---

[49]   See also Harvey Cox, *The Silencing of Leonardo Boff*, Yorktown Heights, NY: Meyer-Stone, 1988.

[50]   Cox, *Religion in the Secular City*, p. 50.

[51]   Cox, *Religion in the Secular City*, p. 74.

combined a radical rejection of Western materialism (if not armaments) with strong religious commitment. The rejection of elitism among the Sunni also seemed to meet his critique. It is possible that Cox's own critique of modernity and modern theology in *Religion in the Secular City* was more vulnerable to the Islamic fundamentalist examples than he realized at the time.

Nonetheless, Cox's dramatic shift from *The Secular City* in the 1960s to *Religion in the Secular City* in the 1980s was an important indicator of changing attitudes to secularization. If the first book largely applauded modernity and welcomed the opportunities provided by thoroughgoing secularization, the second was deeply critical of modernity and sceptical about the pervasiveness of secularization. In both instances Cox accurately reflected the predominant (but of course mutually contradictory) assumptions among social scientists and historians within these separate decades. Militant fundamentalism (among other signs of religious resurgence) was now being taken more seriously by scholars who would have found many of its tenets distasteful. Even theologians who had been nurtured on scriptural criticism were slowly being forced to pay attention to fundamentalist claims and convictions.

Coping with Fundamentalism

Herein lies the challenge to a theological concept of relative convictions. Resurgent fundamentalism seems to provide a startling counter-demonstration, even within heavily industrialized, urban society, of absolutist convictions. The sacred text certainties/absolutism that characterizes it appears untempered by the relativism of a pluralist society. Indeed, this certainty/absolutism was being used as the means to challenge, judge and change modernity and its accompanying relativism and pluralism. For the millions of fundamentalists worldwide any concept of relative convictions must appear as anathema and as a part of the modernity that is to be countered through absolutist appeals to sacred texts or holy laws.

Yet, even within this expression of the fundamentalist challenge lie the seeds of its scholarly undermining. Because fundamentalism has been widely seen to be a feature not just of parts of Christianity but also of Islam and Judaism (and possibly of other traditions too), it has proved necessary to define it in terms that are not solely Christian. The term 'sacred text and/or holy law' certainty/absolutism has been adopted precisely for this reason. It is not simply the Bible (itself, of course, a contentious term for Christians and Jews) which is the object of this absolutism, it is a number of distinct and mutually exclusive sacred texts and holy laws. By observing this, sociologists will inevitably conclude that the resultant absolutist convictions seem to be similar only in form not in content. Further, by subjecting their differing contents to comparative analysis sociologists appear thereby to relativize them.

This process of sociological relativization is applicable even to the fundamentalism of a single religious tradition. It has already been pointed out that one of the limitations of defining Christian fundamentalism in terms of the supposedly five doctrinal claims of *The Fundamentals* of 1910–15, is that fundamentalists themselves cannot agree on the five. In other words, from the outset pluralism was apparent *within* Christian fundamentalism. It is even more apparent when Christian fundamentalism is also studied in its modern extensions into the non-Western world. This was already abundantly clear in the social anthropologist Lionel Caplan's study of Christian fundamentalism in Madras. In this context, Christian fundamentalism has distinct similarities to Hinduism. Caplan argued:

> Despite what some scholars might regard as a wide ontological chasm between them, and the extremely harsh judgments of Hinduism by Protestant pietists and fundamentalists alike, at the phenomenological level, at least, there would appear to be a wide measure of overlap. For people of both 'faiths' the world is populated by a host of maleficent forces – human or superhuman which must either be avoided, or against which the protection of more powerful, benign beings must be sought. In accord with this conception, both traditions have recourse to a divine hierarchy, though one (the Hindu) consists of a number of subtle gradations, while that of Protestantism is starkly dualistic, with Jesus opposed to all the forces of malignancy. There is, thus, also a place in both for the prophet, the divinely inspired worker of miracles who is set apart from

and may be seen to undermine the authority of the priestly specialist operating within prescribed textual or traditional systems of knowledge.[52]

It will come as no surprise to the critical theologian to discover that Christian scriptural absolutisms result in differing visions of Christianity. Only a unitary understanding of the New Testament would suggest otherwise. Once the New Testament is regarded as itself pluralistic, it becomes evident that Christian fundamentalists must make choices (which they could have made differently) in their particular version of scriptural certainty/absolutism. By observing this process the sociologist tends to relativize the particular scriptural absolutism that is being observed. In turn this undermines the very absolutist convictions of fundamentalists themselves. Sociological analysis thus becomes an arch-enemy of fundamentalism.

Again, as soon as differing versions of fundamentalism are compared, it becomes evident that their countercultural oppositions to modernity differ. In part this doubtless results from their settings in different cultures. By definition countercultures will be affected by cultural change. So, whereas American Protestant fundamentalists in the 1980s made considerable use of privatized media technology, Shi'ite fundamentalists in Iran at the times seemed to have been more attracted to military technology. In themselves these compromises with modernity may affect them quite differently. To use commercial television effectively tele-evangelists needed to be careful not to alienate their major source of revenue (the television audience itself) which was essential to their continuing use of this expensive medium (Shi'ites in Iran were less susceptible since they used publicly funded television). Sociological analysis of the practical implications of this[53] again tends to foster relativization. Indeed, media sociologists sometimes term this process 'mediatization',[54] a term that suggests that organizations or movements that seek to engage with the media, in turn, are themselves changed

---

[52] L. Caplan, *Class and Culture in Urban India: Fundamentalism in a Christian Community*, Oxford: Oxford University Press, 1987, p. 254.

[53] See J.K. Hadden and C.E. Swann, *Prime-time Preachers: the Rising Power of Televangelism*, Reading, MS: Addison-Wesley 1981: see also Steve Bruce, *The Rise and Fall of the New Christian Right: Conservative Protestant Politics in America 1978–88*, Oxford: Oxford University Press, 1988.

[54] See Knut Lundby (ed), *Mediatization, Concept, Changes, Consequences*, New York and Oxford: Peter Lang, 2009.

and shaped by this engagement. Sociological analysis of the countercultural variations within Islamic fundamentalism had a similar effect.[55] There was no single countercultural opposition to modernity apparent within fundamentalism. There were wide variations in political orientation (from the far right to the far left), in the acceptance or non-acceptance of technology, and in the tolerance or intolerance shown to secular art, music or literature.

The sociological observation of these variations within fundamentalism has done much to undermine their absolutist claims. Of course it is still possible for individual fundamentalists to be aware of these variations, yet to continue with the belief that their certainties alone are correct (what else can people with 'certainties' think?). All others, even those claiming uniquely to possess the truth, are quite simply mistaken. However, to maintain this belief, while knowing about fundamentalist variations, is already to change the belief itself. Absolutist conviction, in this instance, becomes not just a countercultural opposition to modernity but also an opposition to competing forms of fundamentalism. In other words, it is a claim to certainty in the context of a knowledge of competing certainties and wider scepticism. Of course fundamentalism has long reacted against the scepticism of the world at large, but now it must also react against an awareness of competing fundamentalist convictions. Steve Bruce expresses the dilemma of the modern fundamentalist epigrammatically: 'in order to resist the incursions of the modern rational world, fundamentalists must act and think like members of that world'.[56]

Sociological method produces 'knowledge' for those who adopt its procedures which is particularly damaging to the absolutist claims of fundamentalists. In the light of this method the dramatic example of resurgent fundamentalism no longer appears as counter-evidence to a theory of relative convictions. Rather it becomes an example (paradoxically) of relative convictions.

---

[55]   See Dekmejian, *Islam in Revolution*, and Ali E. Hillal Dessouki (ed.), *Islamic Resurgence in the Arab World*, New York: Praeger, 1982 and Bernard Lewis, *The Crisis of Islam*.

[56]   Steve Bruce, 'The Moral Majority: the Politics of Fundamentalism in Secular Society', in Caplan (ed.), *Studies in Religious Fundamentalism*, p. 191.

Chapter 9

Impending Convictions

The previous chapter examined the resurgence of fundamentalism in the 1980s as a response to modernity and specifically to the religious and cultural pluralism that modernity tends to engender. Confronted with a social context that seems to relativize all religious and ideological convictions, fundamentalists respond with an attempt to enforce cognitive uniformity. From a perspective within sociological theology, they achieve this uniformity in Christianity only by ignoring the pluralism of the New Testament and by constructing a 'harmony' of biblical and doctrinal resources. From this perspective, they do so by overcoming key moments of dissonance when their cognitive world conflicts with their social context. If fundamentalists are tempted at times to make specific and refutable predictions about the world, they are particularly vulnerable to dissonance.

Their most obvious temptation is to make specific predictions about an impending catastrophe linked to nuclear destruction or perhaps even global climate change. Parts of the fundamentalist religious right have linked human-induced global catastrophe with Armageddon and the dawning of the New Heaven here on earth. Paradoxically their connections may even be prophetic. Tragically it might be religious fundamentalists – Shi'ite or Christian – who finally unleash nuclear weapons upon the world. After all, from their perspective, they have the least reason for fearing the consequences of nuclear war. God is good and will protect or reward them for their courage. Some commentators in the 1980s noted that such fundamentalists, unlike the pragmatic bureaucracies of Russia and the West who invented nuclear deterrence, are largely impervious to the temporal consequential logic upon which it is based.[1] After the tragic events of 9/11 and 7/7 this impervious trait became obvious to many more commentators.

Among North American fundamentalists in the 1980s there appeared to be a framework of ideas which linked confrontation between Russia and the West in

[1] See Roger Ruston, 'Apocalyptic and the Peace Movement', *New Blackfriars* 67: 791, 204–215, 1986.

the Middle East, the final destruction of Israel, nuclear holocaust, the heavenly 'rapture' of born-again Christians and the return of Christ. The exact chronological order of these events varied from one fundamentalist group to another, yet their association together seemed widespread particularly before the collapse of the Soviet Union.

The attractions of Western capitalism, consumerism and permissiveness, were once thought by many Westerners to be so self-evident that few realized that religious fundamentalism could actually reverse them. Yet after the Iranian Revolution of 1979 commentators gradually came to realize that this was not so. Likewise the horrors of nuclear warfare were so self-evident to nuclear strategists and the politicians who relied upon them that it was often regarded as quite unthinkable that anyone could ever use them. Religious fundamentalists may again prove them disastrously wrong. They still have powers once forgotten by secular commentators.

This chapter will examine some of the social and psychological structures undergirding these powers. Within the context of human-induced global catastrophe (however caused), learning to identify these structures may be more important than is sometimes realized. Ignoring them might prove literally disastrous. It is the theory of cognitive dissonance which provides one of the most elegant and influential socio-psychological accounts of sectarian or fundamentalist reactions to impending catastrophe.

First this theory will be set out as it appears in the seminal book of 1956, *When Prophecy Fails*,[2] written jointly by Leon Festinger, Henry Riecken and Stanley Schachter. Then the chapter will briefly indicate some of the ways that this theory has played an influential role in theology and religious studies. Thirdly it will face three of the recurring criticisms that theologians and biblical specialists make of the theory and its uses, based upon fears of reductionism, anachronistic use of modern-world theories, and the availability of sufficient social evidence relating to ancient communities. I will argue that all three fears are exaggerated. However, fourthly, a rather unexpected and damning criticism of my own will be offered: a careful examination of *When Prophecy Fails* reveals awkward questions about the

---

[2]   Leon Festinger, Henry W. Riecken and Stanley Schachter, *When Prophecy Fails: A Social and Psychological Study of a Modern Group that Predicted the Destruction of the World*, New York: Harper Torchbooks, 1956.

accuracy and even veracity of its research. In offering this criticism I realize that I am challenging the very grounds of a theory which seems firmly established in socio-psychological orthodoxy. Finally, I will try to draw out from this discussion some of the key insights that a theologian might offer as remaining constant in our understanding of religious responses to impending disaster.

Cognitive Dissonance Theory

Despite its rather awesome name, cognitive dissonance theory has as at its centre a very straightforward premise, namely that someone with strong convictions is hard to change. On the opening page of *When Prophecy Fails* the authors extend this premise as follows:

> Suppose an individual believes something with his whole heart; suppose further that he has a commitment to this belief, that he has taken irrevocable actions because of it; finally, suppose that he is presented with evidence, unequivocal and undeniable evidence, that his belief is wrong: what will happen? The individual will frequently emerge, not only unshaken, but even more convinced of the truth of his beliefs than ever before. Indeed, he may even show a new fervour about convincing and converting other people to his view.[3]

So, for individuals experiencing the dissonance caused by their beliefs being confronted with falsifying evidence, abandonment of these beliefs may be their logical response, but, in practice, it is not their only response. Some individuals respond to such dissonance by becoming even more aggressively evangelical. Indeed, it is not difficult to observe that many of us become most dogmatic about those values and beliefs that guide us, but for which we have the least objective evidence. Academics may be almost as prone to this tendency as religious fundamentalists. Theologians have long argued that secularism and positivism can be dogmatic, unverifiable, and curiously evangelistic. Cognitive dissonance theory, however, is making a more specific claim than that. It is concerned with situations which confront groups holding strong convictions with clear and undeniable

---

[3] Festinger, *When Prophecy Fails*, p. 3.

disproof of these convictions. Even when this happens, the theory maintains, such groups may paradoxically respond with increased evangelistic fervour. In these circumstances proselytism may be less a sign of religious conviction than an attempt to overcome dissonance.

For this to happen five conditions are necessary:

1. A belief must be held with deep conviction and it must have some relevance to action, that is, to what the believer does or how he behaves.
2. The person holding the belief must have committed himself to it; that is, for the sake of his belief, he must have taken some important action that is difficult to undo.
3. The belief must be sufficiently specific and sufficiently concerned with the real world so that events may unequivocally refute the belief.
4. Such undeniable, disconfirming evidence must occur and must be recognized by the individual holding the belief.
5. The individual believer must have social support.[4]

The ideal people to fit the theory would have deep and committed beliefs that had led them both to give up their jobs to join a community of fellow believers and to make specific predictions about the fate of the world. They would then be confronted with evidence which disproved these predictions. They would acknowledge this evidence. Yet, so the theory claims, they could be expected to respond with a heightened sense of evangelism and a renewed attempt to proselytize others.

All five elements are important. They do not specifically depend upon religious convictions or religious groups or communities. Political groups of the far right or of the far left could well fulfil the requirements, provided that they make specific and refutable claims which they subsequently know to have been refuted. Social support is crucial. It is precisely the mutual support of fellow believers which allows individuals to persist with convictions even when they really know that they have been refuted. Together individuals in deviant groups can support each other and protect themselves from outside scepticism. The twist in the tail of cognitive dissonance theory is that they can be expected to do this by actually

---

4   Festinger, *When Prophecy Fails*, p. 4.

increasing their attempts to convert outside sceptics. It can even be the case that previously non-evangelistic groups become aggressively evangelistic as a result of an experience of dissonance and disconfirmation.

The first 30 pages of *When Prophecy Fails* set out the theory, illustrating it with a number of historical examples. The authors are aware that these examples lack the detailed empirical information which would be needed to demonstrate the theory. This they supply through an extended and very remarkable case study that occupies the rest of the book. Having postulated the theory they noticed a news item in the *Lake City Herald* in late September (the year is not specified) under the dramatic headline: 'Prophecy From Planet. Clarion Call To City: Flee That Flood. It'll Swamp Us On Dec. 21, Outer Space Tells Suburbanite'. The item read as follows:

> Lake City will be destroyed by a flood from Great Lake just before dawn, Dec. 21, according to a suburban housewife. Mrs Marian Keech, of 847 West School street, says the prophecy is not her own. It is the purport of many messages she has received by automatic writing, she says ... The messages, according to Mrs Keech, are sent to her by superior beings from a planet called 'Clarion'. These beings have been visiting the earth, she says, in what we call flying saucers. During their visits, she says, they have observed fault lines in the earth's crust that foretoken the deluge. Mrs Keech reports she was told the flood will spread to form an island sea stretching from the Arctic Circle to the Gulf of Mexico. At the same time, she says, a cataclysm will submerge the West Coast from Seattle, Wash., to Chile in South America.[5]

It was at once clear to the authors that this might supply the crucial empirical test that was necessary to establish their theory. A specific and dated prediction had been made which was amenable to falsification. If there was a group of individuals jointly committed to this prediction it could be studied over the next three months. And if the theory of cognitive dissonance was to be verified, increased proselytism should be the reaction of the group after 21 December. This, indeed, is exactly what the authors and their five research assistants claimed to observe.

---

[5]   Festinger, *When Prophecy Fails*, pp. 30–31.

They visited Mrs Keech and quickly established that she had a long association with religious cults, such as Dianetics (which later became Scientology), as well as with flying saucer groups. She received her messages (through her automatic writing) from a variety of spiritual beings from the planets Clarion and Cerus. Chief among these was Sananda, whom she gradually came to see as the contemporary identity of Jesus. At first the messages offered general warnings about impending catastrophe, some of which were connected with nuclear warfare and others with natural disasters. Gradually they became more specific, culminating with the actual date of the future catastrophe reported in the news item. The authors also established that a group of believers was beginning to gather around Mrs Keech. A campus physician, Dr Armstrong and his wife, were particularly active. It was Dr Armstrong who had informed the newspaper and had written the release and it was he who gathered interested students into a group called the Seekers.

Having concluded that all the constituents necessary for their social experiment were present, the authors hurriedly formed a research team and trained student researchers to investigate and become actively involved in the group surrounding Mrs Keech. They invented identities for the students and even gave them stories of cultic experiences to make them acceptable to the group. Then they waited to see what would happen when the inevitable disconfirmation occurred on 21 December. The long anecdotal account that they give of the group's behaviour leading up to and immediately after this date occupies almost half of the book. It is a very remarkable account and at every point it reinforces the theory that the empirical refutation of the prediction, although at first discouraging to individuals, soon led to vigorous proselytism. And this in a group which had previously been very reluctant to engage in active evangelism.

As the impending disaster drew near the group became increasingly querulous. There was a degree of rivalry between Mrs Keech mediating messages from Sananda and another woman claiming to mediate messages from the Creator. At one point in this competitive revelation the second woman predicted that Mr Keech (not a believer) would die that night and be resurrected. Disconfirmation of this prediction led to a spiritual re-interpretation. Mr Keech had died and risen again, but not in ways that could be observed directly by the group. In the few days and hours leading up to 21 December, Mrs Keech, in turn, made a series of predictions that a flying saucer would arrive to collect members of the group and save them from the impending disaster. Each deadline passed with considerable soul-searching, but eventually with a fresh interpretation (for example, that it had just been a test of faith) and then a new prediction.

At last the day came and passed. The researchers in the group pressed the others for their reactions. Certain individuals were indeed disillusioned, left and never returned. However, most stayed and re-interpreted their experience. The world had been granted a reprieve. Extra time was being allowed for evangelization. A new researcher who joined the group only after the date was treated as a visitor from one of the planets. So they had come after all! Five strangers who came to the house were also regarded as ethereal visitors. Members of the group differed radically from each other about these appearances. The re-interpretations varied. What united the group was their determination to carry on. Previously quiescent members (for example, the Armstrong daughter) became strong in the faith and determined to tell all who would listen about its veracity. Media attention reached a crescendo on the day of prediction. Yet, whereas previously members of the group had been very reluctant to talk to such a sceptical audience, now they used every means open to them to publicize their faith. In short, disconfirmation led to a new-found proselytism.

The media attention also attracted the attention of the police. Neighbours and parents had strongly protested. Soon into the New Year the group disbanded. However, the Armstrongs remained believers. Having lost his medical post he became a touring evangelist. Mrs Keech continued her activities elsewhere and other members of the group also found new missionary zeal. In contrast, the Seekers, who as students had almost mostly gone home for the Christmas vacation, experienced the greatest disillusionment. For the authors of *When Prophecy Fails* this was a clear indication of the need for an active support group. It was this that sustained all but a very few of those intimately involved in the central group. Together they could overcome the obvious dissonance caused by the failure of the prediction of impending disaster to materialize. Together they could re-interpret their experience, encouraging each other to overcome dissonance with vigorous proselytism.

The case study was regarded as a dramatic proof of the theory of cognitive dissonance. The authors had been able to specify its required conditions and their likely outcome. They had been able to unmask the social mechanisms that such deviant groups use to sustain dissonant beliefs. In the process they had shown how educated, if somewhat eccentric, individuals can maintain deviant beliefs and even re-invigorate them in the face of empirical falsification. All of this is highly relevant to understanding how modern fundamentalists can maintain convictions that are at odds with the cultural pluralism that surrounds them.

The Influence of Cognitive Dissonance Theory

When Prophecy Fails has been an immensely influential book. Festinger, this time writing on his own, followed it immediately with *A Theory of Cognitive Dissonance*[6] (it is from this book that the theory properly-speaking derives its name) and for some years the *Journal of Abnormal and Social Psychology* carried many articles on it. It then passed into social psychology and the sociology of religion as an accepted orthodoxy. For an analysis of sects, such as the Jehovah's Witness Movement, which in much of the twentieth century made specific and refutable predictions of impending catastrophe, it was been widely accepted as a convincing and fruitful theory. It was been particularly influential in linking the aggressive proselytism of such sects with the fragility created by their specific predictions.

Gradually it also came to occupy a role in biblical studies too, most obviously in Robert Carroll's *When Prophecy Failed*.[7] He was aware that the Old Testament material which is most amenable to the theory – Isaiah, Jeremiah and the post-exilic prophets – never fully satisfies all five of the conditions already outlined. Yet there are strong predictions of impending disaster in these prophetic writings and it is these that encouraged Carroll to use cognitive dissonance theory. Yet it is difficult to find unequivocal predictions which were both falsified and known to have been falsified by the prophets themselves. Carroll concluded modestly:

---

6   Leon Festinger, *A Theory of Cognitive Dissonance*, Evanston, IL: Row Peterson, 1957.

7   Robert P. Carroll, *When Prophecy Failed: Reactions and Responses to Failure in the Old Testament Prophetic Tradition*, London: SCM Press, 1979.

The main thrust of my argument for the existence of response to dissonance in the prophetic traditions is the amount of reinterpreted material in those traditions. The accumulated growth of the prophetic traditions incorporated numerous responses to problems of failure and seriously modified motifs that had become obsolete. Changes in social and political circumstances destroyed the realization of the hope for a Davidic king but interpretative elements within prophecy transformed the hope into one of the city as the throne for the divine king (for example, Jer. 3.17; cf. Isa. 28.5; 33.17, 21; Ezek. 48.35).[8]

In a supporting article Carroll showed that he was well aware of the implications, and the difficulties, of cognitive dissonance being applied additionally to the New Testament. At one point he even envisaged an ambitious programme analysing 'text plus its interpretation within various communities embracing it as holy scripture or authoritative writ' and using the theory for this analysis. He was aware that 'this means the material available for research is increased to include the fields of biblical exegesis and its history, historical theology and the multiple forms of sects deriving their existence from discrete interpretations of the Bible'.[9]

The New Testament scholar John Gager had in fact already begun this task in his seminal and methodologically sophisticated book *Kingdom and Community*.[10] The aim of this book was to study the way a social world is constructed and maintained in early Christianity: 'to explore … the relationship between religion and social status, the enthusiastic character of the earliest Christian communities, their gradual transformation into a formidable religious and social institution, and the emergence of Christianity as the dominant religion of the later Roman Empire'.[11] Cognitive dissonance was used as a central theory in this exploration. Gager (unlike Carroll) argued that it is not hermeneutics but proselytism that is the major outcome of dissonance within earliest Christianity. He identified two catastrophes that faced the earliest Christians, the death of Jesus and the expectation of the Kingdom of God. In the responses to both he detected signs

---

[8]   Carroll, p. 215.

[9]   Robert P. Carroll, 'Ancient Israelite Prophecy and Dissonance Theory', *Numen*, 24: 2, 135–151, 1977–1978, p. 148.

[10]   John G. Gager, *Kingdom and Community: the Social World of Early Christianity*, Englewood Cliffs, NJ: Prentice Hall, 1975.

[11]   Gager, p. 11.

of dissonance leading to increased proselytism. He did not claim that the theory accounted for all forms of early missionary activity. Like others,[12] he maintained that the theory needs supplementation (for example that public ridicule at the time of disconfirmation is an important factor). Nonetheless, it is the basic theory developed in *When Prophecy Fails* that provided a central plank in his account of the growth of earliest Christianity.

Some theologians may feel uneasy about using cognitive dissonance theory as a way of understanding how religious groups cope with impending catastrophe. It is one thing to apply it to a marginal flying saucer cult, but it is quite another to use it as a means of understanding the missionary zeal of early Christianity. Theologians may be happy to watch sociologists using such theories on groups that they regard as marginal and frankly deluded. They may be less than happy to use sociology in this way to understand Christian origins. Three objections, in particular, are frequently encountered: reductionism, anachronism, and evidence.[13]

At first sight there does appear to be a strong reductionist element in such a sociological account of religious belief. Some sociologists, with religious convictions themselves, have even argued that the sociology of religion is essentially a sociology of error.[14] Cognitive dissonance theory would seem to be no exception. The case study in *When Prophecy Fails* derives much of its force from the fact that we know that the beliefs and predictions of the group are absurd. The research workers did not have to wait until 21 December to discover whether or not the predictions of impending catastrophe would materialize. On the contrary, they picked the group because they knew its predictions would be falsified and they wanted to observe the reactions of the group members when they found this out for themselves.

Again, applying theories derived from data from modern urban society to a first-century rural or semi-urban community does appear to be anachronistic.

---

[12]   Such as J.A. Hardyck and M. Braden, 'Prophecy Fails Again: a Report of a Failure to Replicate', *Journal of Abnormal and Social Psychology*, 65:2, 136–141, 1962.

[13]   See, for example, the discussion in Norman K. Gottwald, *The Tribes of Yahweh: a Sociology of the Religion of Liberated Israel*, 1250–1050 B.C.E., Maryknoll, NY: Orbis Books and London: SCM Press, 1979 and *The Hebrew Bible: A Socio-Literary Introduction*, Minneapolis, MI: Fortress, 1985.

[14]   Ian Hamnett, 'Sociology of Religion and Sociology of Error', *Religion*, 3, 1973: although see his 'A Mistake about Error', *New Blackfriars*, 67:788, 69–78, Feb. 1986.

For example, sociology makes presumptions about social class which are highly dependent upon post-industrial observations. It is far from clear that they apply to ancient communities. The case study in *When Prophecy Fails* related to a community that is not just post-industrial and urban, but also has fantasies derived from twentieth-century science fiction. Like Scientology, it produced a peculiarly post-scientific syncretism of religious symbols and extra-terrestrial accretions, quite beyond the wildest dreams of the earliest Christians.

Thirdly, there is the question of evidence. Sociology depends upon an array of scientific procedures – such as, ethnographic statistics, questionnaire-surveys and structured field observations – none of which are available to those applying sociology to ancient communities. The authors of *When Prophecy Fails* are themselves aware of this deficiency and it is for this reason that they finally decide that evidence about earliest Christianity is insufficient for their theory. Gager and others seem to ignore this warning.

This does seem to be the conclusion that John Milbank draws. Here, for example, he writes specifically about John Gager's *Kingdom and Community*:

> Biblical sociologists consistently fall into [a] trap. Besides the appeals to extra-Biblical evidence to illuminate the social structure of the early Church, they have also, more questionably, tried to reconstruct inner-ecclesial transitions on the basis of universal sociological speculations about group behaviour. So, for example, John Gager suggests that the followers of Jesus after the crucifixion can be considered as an example of a group suffering from 'cognitive dissonance', meaning that they could not reconcile their previous expectations with what was now happening to them. 'Research' apparently suggests that groups in such situations may paradoxically seek to proselytize, to reduce the effects of dissonance, by at least ensuring that all participate in it. The problem with this view, another attempt to 'comprehend', sociologically, the transition from Jesus' life and teachings to the Church, is that it is so condescending about the kinds of groups it describes. Many movements or ideas in such situations just fizzle out, and one can suggest that those that do not, usually make some sort of attempt to bring order into their beliefs, and that proselytization may itself be an aspect of such attempts. In the case of the early Church, Gager's view seems to imply that the Church was left at first *only* with a continuity of beliefs now rendered

discordant, whereas one might want to suggest that one reason for the survival of 'dissonance' was the unbroken continuity of action, the carrying forwards of fellowship, teaching and healing.[15]

An interesting point to note in this paragraph is that John Milbank has himself italicised the world 'only'. Despite clear protestations to the contrary running throughout *Kingdom and Community*, Gager's use of cognitive dissonance theory is criticized for being (at least implicitly) a reductive sociological explanation that allows for no other form of explanation. Several phrases and words that precede this dramatic '*only*' serve to heighten it: 'universal sociological speculations about group behaviour'; '"research" apparently suggests'; 'another attempt to "comprehend"'; 'it is so condescending'. Milbank even offers an alternative (sociological) explanation– 'many movements or ideas in such situations just fizzle out' – that ignores the obvious point that Jehovah's Witnesses have provided the most remarkable example throughout the twentieth century and now into the 21st of a movement that has indeed survived despite making several predictions about impending catastrophe.

In reality the more sophisticated exponents of biblical sociology – such as Meeks, Gottwald and Gager – spend a considerable amount of time discussing the objections that Milbank makes in such a cavalier style. They are well aware of the suspicion of reductionism. Yet they are also aware of the distinction examined in Chapter 3 between 'explaining something' and 'explaining something away'. There have been versions of sociological imperialism which have seemed oblivious to this distinction. However, as noted earlier, more mature sociology soon realized that reductionism is self-defeating. Reductionists themselves can soon be reduced by their own canons. All knowledge, even scientific knowledge, can be viewed in social terms, including the knowledge offered by the sociology of knowledge. Once again, origins and validity are logically distinct. So, if someone tells me that I am a theologian because I had a strong attachment to my clerical grandfather, they are not actually telling me anything about the validity of my views as a theologian. Validity must usually be decided on other grounds. Similarly, even if a connection is made between dissonance and the proselytism of early Christians, we still must

---

[15]   John Milbank, *Theology and Social Theory*, Oxford: Blackwell, revised edn, 2006, p. 121.

decide on other grounds about the latter's validity. In any case, John Gager went out of his way to emphasize in *Kingdom and Community* that cognitive dissonance theory does not account for all early Christian missionary activity. Surely John Milbank must have noticed this. In the interests of his overall thesis, did he simply choose to ignore it?

Again, the more sophisticated biblical sociologists are well aware of the dangers of anachronism and insufficient evidence, agreeing that there is insufficient evidence conclusively to establish the presence of cognitive dissonance within early Christianity. The authors of *When Prophecy Fails* were correct when they realized that they could not properly establish their theory on such a basis. Yet, once the theory was established, it became quite a different matter. Sociology is in fact committed to the idea that there are regularities in human social behaviour. It does attempt to establish theories from specific situations which can then be cautiously applied to other situations. Naturally it is more risky doing this diachronically – across periods of time – and of course the scholar must be cautious when there is also a paucity of empirical evidence. Yet biblical scholars perennially face these difficulties. There is nothing very unusual for them about applying theories which have been developed in the modern world to their own subject matter. They are well used to being tentative when handling evidence that lacks outside corroboration.

Gottwald, for example, argues at length that sociological method does not just bring a fresh perspective to biblical studies, it also brings a spur to further research. He sets out in detail the sort of ethnographic, archaeological and comparative research that could be done on ancient communities once sociological questions are raised.[16] This does not eliminate the need for speculation and imaginative application of theory. How could it ever in biblical studies? It is an important part of what makes such studies academically engaging.

Testing Cognitive Dissonance Theory

But an important question remains. Is cognitive dissonance really an established theory? This question may seem strange since it has already been shown that the theory has been widely accepted in socio-psychological orthodoxy. It has been

---

[16] See especially his *The Hebrew Bible*.

supplemented in a number of ways, but its position seems secure. Further, it has evidently become established in biblical studies and I have argued that its theological critics are not finally persuasive. Perhaps the question ought properly to be, should cognitive dissonance be accepted as an established theory?

The theory itself has been widely discussed. However, the veracity of the case study that was used to establish it has received less attention. For most theologians truthfulness is a prerequisite, but the case study in *When Prophecy Fails* is built upon deceit. The research workers were taught to lie systematically in order to gain entry into the group, to adopt fabricated preternatural experiences to gain the confidence of the group leaders, and to continue to lie for some three months while appearing to be committed members of the group. This systematic and remarkably skilful deceit contrasts sharply with the high ethical standards set by the mentor of most corresponding British research, the late Bryan Wilson.[17] For him it was essential that research workers make their sociological intentions unambiguously clear to a group at the outset.

It is not simply professionalism which is at stake here, although surely for most ethical academics that is important. Rather it is trustworthiness. If people admit to deceit in their methods, how can we trust their findings? Suspicions are raised. A careful analysis of the case study in question does raise suspicions. In the final paragraph the authors admitted that, 'our data, in places, are less complete than we would like, our influence on the group somewhat greater than we would like'. Nevertheless, they insisted that, 'we were able, however, to collect enough information to tell a coherent story and, fortunately, the effects of disconfirmation were striking enough to provide for firm conclusions'.[18]

The word 'story' in this sentence is not the only suspicious note in the book. There is almost an element of spoof about parts of it. They dated their preface 21 December, they depicted members of the group hurriedly cutting out the zips from their trousers or clasps from their bras in case the metal should interfere with the expected flying saucer, and a telephone call from a 'Captain Video' was taken seriously by members of the group. There is even a Passion Narrative structure to the 'story' presented in the case study. There are believers and the

---

[17]   See Bryan Wilson, *Religion in Sociological Perspective*, Oxford: Oxford University Press, 1982.

[18]   *When Prophecy Fails*, p. 249.

occasional doubting disciple, there is the death and resurrection of a man, there is a physician evangelist, there are varying and conflicting accounts of extra-terrestrial appearances after 21 December and there is finally a proselytizing *diaspora*.

Again, readers are asked to believe that the group simply accepted the student research workers as fellow members. There is no indication given at any point over the three months that even the educated members of the group were suspicious. This was despite the hurried training given to the research workers and the prolonged intimacy of the group itself. The research workers together represented about a third of the membership of the central group. Yet their real purpose apparently remained hidden to the genuine group members throughout the time in question. Their clandestine activities, such as making transcripts of entire telephone calls, were seemingly undetected.

An indication that something is desperately wrong emerges from a detailed comparison of the case study with the fictionalized version of it that appears in Alison Lurie's *Imaginary Friends*.[19] The skilled novelist instructively changes those very elements of undetected, prolonged deceit by five partially trained students that seem so incredible in the case study itself. In *Imaginary Friends* it is two, not five, sociologists who penetrate the flying saucer group and they are both fully trained academics (one a full professor with considerable experience). Further, the junior academic has real scruples about deceiving the group and, very early, the cover of both is blown. They then admit to the group that they are sociologists, but insist that they are still interested. They remain within the group only on this basis.

It is clear that *Imaginary Friends* is based upon *When Prophecy Fails*. Not only do some of the characters and much of the story correspond, but so does the early description of the senior sociologist's theory:

> McMann's basic hypothesis was that a certain minimum amount of opposition would actually be good for such a group. For one thing, up to a point the energy which the members would have to expend answering the doubts, or combating the opposition, would unite them and involve them as individuals more deeply. Even a disproof from the natural order (as, for example, the non-appearance of men from outer space) would not necessarily be fatal. His theory was a

---

[19] Alison Lurie, *Imaginary Friends*, London: Heinemann, 1967.

disconfirmation of this sort would not really weaken a well-established group, as long as the members faced it together. They would simply rationalize what had happened, and alter their convictions just as much as was necessary to preserve the belief system and the group – both of which probably existed for non-ideological reasons anyway, and filled important social needs.[20]

Alison Lurie finally turns the story into farce. The professor of sociology apparently becomes one of the group's most ardent believers and himself an object of belief. The parody at the expense of sociology is obvious. But perhaps the original case study deserves such parody.

The authors of *When Prophecy Fails* did admit to an 'influence on the group somewhat greater than we would like'. This admission is remarkable only for its understatement. At the key moment of disconfirmation they reported that the research workers acted as follows:

> During this break, which lasted for about half an hour, everyone in the group was reluctant to talk about the failure of the midnight prediction – everyone, that is, except the five observers who wanted to talk about it very much. They kept asking the others in the house such questions as 'What do you think happened to the man who was supposed to come at midnight?' 'Why didn't he come?' 'What did the miracle have to do with his not coming?' 'Will the saucer still pick us up?' and so on.[21]

Not only did this probing raise no suspicions, but it also apparently played no significant part in shaping the 'striking' reaction of the group to disconfirmation. The research workers were fortunate indeed. Those who are more cautious might have supposed that discreet silence would have been less likely to taint the results and to risk detection.

The more the case study is inspected the less capable it seems of bearing the weight of the theory. It occupies a key role in *When Prophecy Fails*. Much of the book is devoted to it and it is clearly intended to establish cognitive dissonance theory on a firm basis. Yet those who have been so influenced by it seem to have

---

[20]   *Imaginary Friends*, pp. 4–5.
[21]   *When Prophecy Fails*, p. 165.

given most of their attention to the theory itself and failed to subject the case study to rigorous scrutiny. Much of the case study is simply beyond scrutiny, especially since the authors stated at the outset that they had deliberately changed all the names and places within it 'to protect the actual people involved in the movement from the curiosity of an unsympathetic reader'.[22] Or, perhaps, from academic scrutiny.

What, then, can be rescued from cognitive dissonance theory in attempting to understand how fundamentalist groups cope with impending catastrophe? Not the specific link between dissonance and proselytism. It is this link which is the most distinctive part of the theory and for which the case study is most needed. It is also this link which has been particularly subject to the most revision among socio-psychologists. However, if we cannot presume that the link is established in *When Prophecy Fails*, we need not then attempt to revise it to fit awkward counter-examples. So the stimulating use that Gager makes of this distinctive part of the theory must also be questioned.

Other parts of the theory are not so vulnerable, since they are largely dependent upon a wide variety of sociological observations of deviant groups. Studies in the sociology of deviance (the term is used to depict dissent from conformity, not of course moral perversity) well indicate how groups can foster, reinforce and spread convictions that are at odds with society at large. In this respect minority fundamentalist groups have much in common with many other deviant political or youth groups. The transcendental features of religious groups make them particularly impervious to outside scepticism. If a sectarian group (such as the Exclusive Brethren or the Jehovah's Witnesses) builds tight membership barriers against society at large, it can successfully maintain and foster socially deviant beliefs. Self-contained groups can develop their own plausibility structures and protect themselves, if that is necessary, from prevailing 'commonsense'.

Recent studies of fundamentalist groups that have turned to violence are also illuminating. James Jones, for example, concedes that religious terrorism is multidimensional and multi-determined. However, he does detect a number of psychological themes (some already familiar from the previous chapter) that are typical:

---

[22]   *When Prophecy Fails*, p. vi.

These themes seem common to most religiously sponsored terrorists – teaching and texts that evoke shame and humiliation; an apocalyptic vision impatient with ambiguity, which presents a polarized view of the world; a drive for godly rule and complete purification (involving the control of gender relations and sexuality); a ritualization of violence and violent imagery; a deep desire for union with God; and the sanctification of violence.[23]

Once these themes are embedded into a tightly socialized fundamentalist group they can reinforce the violence tragically displayed by Muslim fundamentalists at 9/11 and 7/7 and by Christian fundamentalists arrested in Israel in 2003 for plotting to bomb the Temple Mount and by the Revd. Paul Hill executed in Florida in the same year for murdering a doctor who performed abortions.[24]

In a particularly instructive analysis of the Japanese group Aum Shinrikyô, Ian Reader shows how it started peacefully as a yoga and meditation group in the 1980s but soon began to narrow its vision, making exclusivist claims, enforcing internal hierarchic absolutism, polarizing its relationship with society at large and inflicting violent punishment upon dissident members – culminating in its Tokyo subway attack on 20 March 1995:

There are clear differences here from the ways in which such deeds are viewed in the public domain. While the normal public response to acts of terror and mass public violence is to see the victims as innocent and the deeds as indiscriminate, for those who commit such deeds and who see themselves engaged in a cosmic struggle of good and evil in which violence is spiritualized, there are no neutrals, no non-combatants and no innocents. Hence killing them – as Aum did when releasing nerve gas on subway trains – was not an indiscriminate act. In the context of its conspiracy theories anyone not with Aum was guilty.[25]

---

[23]   James W. Jones, 'Sacred Terror: The Psychology of Contemporary Religious Terrorism' in Andrew R. Murphy (ed.), *The Blackwell Companion to Religion and Violence*, Malden, MA and Oxford: Wiley-Blackwell, 2011, pp. 293–294.

[24]   See also, Joel Olson, 'The Politics of Protestant Violence: Abolitionists and Anti-Abortionists', in Andrew R. Murphy (ed.), *The Blackwell Companion to Religion and Violence*, pp. 485–497.

[25]   Ian Reader, 'The Transformation of Failure and the Spiritualization of Violence', in Andrew R. Murphy (ed.), *The Blackwell Companion to Religion and Violence*, p. 313.

Sociological theology offers a double perspective upon such egregious religiously motivated acts. It offers warnings both to secularists and to religious fundamentalists. To secularists it offers timely warnings about the fundamentalists. The latter's powers are not to be underestimated and their apocalyptic visions are to be feared if they gain access to political power. Secular disdain was remarkably ineffective in tempering Shi'ite fundamentalism and secular analysis, as has been seen, largely failed to foresee its resurgence. Theology offers a quite different vision of the world from secularism. It sees the world as created rather than fortuitous and as the gift of a loving God. From this perspective nuclear or biochemical catastrophe is not simply a human catastrophe but a catastrophe that involves the created order. The theologian offers an additional dimension of seriousness to the secularist. Life is not ours to replicate or destroy at will, but a gift requiring gratitude and responsibility.

Sociological theology also offers warnings to religious fundamentalists. They distort religious beliefs by hypostasizing analogical religious symbols. If theology is indeed seen as a social system, then it is only God's relationship to us, not our analogical symbols seeking to express this relationship, that is constant. Sociological theology increases awareness of the plurality of both Christian and world religious beliefs. As departments of theology become increasingly ecumenical, the varied and rich resources of Christianity become ever more apparent. Fundamentalists seek to overcome this plurality by claiming a monopoly of truth for their own convictions. Such claims may be comparatively harmless if they are made by the politically marginal. However, they become potentially catastrophic if they belong to those with access to nuclear or biochemical weapons.

Bruce Malina suggests an alternative understanding of cognitive dissonance which perhaps makes better theological sense of a fundamentalist response to impending catastrophe. He suggests that dissonance, or some degree of normative inconsistency, is a feature of much of everyday life and religious consciousness. It is the fundamentalist who seeks to reduce this dissonance by insisting upon an unambiguous doctrinal or ethical perspective. Reversing Gager, Malina even argues that 'a model of dissonance and ambivalence ... might explain why earliest

Christianity did in fact avoid extremism and survive, while not a few factions from the same period ended in destruction'.[26]

When Prophecy Fails presumes that dissonance is associated with fragility in marginal groups. Malina agrees rather with those who have argued that fragility is not necessarily a feature of unconventional or fundamentalist beliefs at all. Leaving aside the world of specific and refutable predictions, a perspective from sociological theology might suggest that religious faith surely is elusive and at times dissonant. A somewhat modified version of cognitive dissonance theory offers a sociological account of how fundamentalist groups may 'successfully' bypass relativism. However, for the critical theologian, they achieve this 'success' only by ignoring the cultural relativism that is present even within the earliest phases of Christianity itself.

---

[26]   Bruce J. Malina, 'Normative Dissonance and Christian Origins', *Semeia*, 35, 1986, p. 39.

PART III
Social Context Re-assessed

Chapter 10

Secularization Revisited

As has been seen in earlier chapters, 'secularization' was a key concept within the sociological and theological assessments of the British religious context in the 1970s. I devoted the last three chapters of *The Social Context of Theology* to the debate between Bryan Wilson and David Martin in Britain and Peter Berger and Andrew Greeley in the United States about secularization. 'Debate' is probably the wrong word to use. It was characteristic, especially of Wilson and Martin, to reach radically different and strongly held conclusions about the evidence for or against secularization without responding directly to each other's writings. For example, Bryan Wilson's seminal 1966 study *Religion in Secular Society* noted only in a footnote that 'The concept of secularization is sharply criticized as a "counter-religious" ideology by David Martin'.[1] In turn, David Martin's pioneering study of the following year, *A Sociology of English Religion*, had a number of criticisms throughout of 'the secularization thesis', yet it was only in the Preface that he mentioned his colleague and then just to say politely: 'Nevertheless "secularization" has distinguished and persuasive proponents, notably Bryan Wilson in his *Religion in Secular Society*, which provides a sociological discussion in many ways complementary to the present work.'[2]

In contrast, as a young academic I was more scathing at the time about the debate, arguing that 'neither the proponents of a thorough-going secularization model nor the critics of any secularization model are entirely persuasive.

---

[1]   Bryan Wilson, *Religion in Secular Society*, London: C.A. Watts, 1966, p. 11. His *Contemporary Transformations of Religion*, Oxford: Oxford University Press, 1976, also had just a single similar footnote mentioning Martin (p. 7).

[2]   David Martin, *A Sociology of English Religion*, London: SCM Press, 1967, p. 11. Even in his *A General Theology of Secularization*, Oxford: Blackwell, 1978 and *On Secularization: Towards a Revised General Theory*, Aldershot: Ashgate, 2005, references to Wilson are very slight and largely uncritical.

Weaknesses and ambiguities face sociologists of either persuasion.'[3] Here, for example, was part of my blunt critique of Bryan Wilson:

> Wilson ... uses evidence of both decline in churchgoing and persistence, or even increase, in churchgoing to demonstrate a process of secularization. He argues that 'it would require an ingenious sociological analysis to show that the development of American society was materially affected by its high rate of churchgoing, or that of Sweden by its very low rate.'[4] Yet, having argued this he immediately devotes a whole chapter to statistics of decline in the Church of England during the [twentieth] century. On his own presuppositions it should matter very little whether these statistics demonstrate decline, persistence or increase. Another very obvious weakness concerns his unsubstantiated claim that people today 'assess the world in empirical and rational terms.' He immediately compromises this claim with his subsequent admission that 'non logical behaviour', albeit not related to the dogmas of the Christian Church, may continue 'in unabated measure in human society.'[5] The effect of this admission is to produce doubts as to whether Wilson is really writing about secularization at all. The term 'secularization' presumably refers to 'religious' decline and not simply to a decline in Christianity, and yet Wilson's evidence is related almost entirely to the latter.[6]

To my embarrassment now, I also accused David Martin of 'caricature' in the way that he portrayed thoroughgoing secularization theories, using his own words at the time: 'Once upon a time the Church dominated society as the cathedral of St Hugh dominates Lincoln. The Church presented a massive, articulated, over-arching system of belief which defined the horizon of hope, here and hereafter, just as it cast the shadows of fear. Then, as the story goes, men gradually recovered the spirit of free enquiry and personal choice.'[7] However, I was more critical at the time of Andrew Greeley's attempt to replace secularization theory with strong claims about the persistence of religion. He argued that 'however

---

3   Robin Gill, *The Social Context of Theology*, Oxford: Mowbrays, 1975, pp. 117–118.
4   Wilson, *Religion in Secular Society*, p. 12.
5   Wilson, *Religion in Secular Society*, p. 10.
6   Gill, *The Social Context of Theology*, p. 95.
7   David Martin, 'The Secularization Question', *Theology*, 76:630, Feb 1973, p. 82.

much the context has changed, the basic functions religion plays in human life are essentially the same' as they always have been throughout human history.[8] I will return to Greeley's claims in a moment; however, in *The Social Context of Theology* I wrote:

> Undoubtedly the model of persistence is an important counter-balance to thoroughgoing secularization models. Yet it shares with such models a preparedness to apply a single model to a considerable span of history, even when the empirical data is often weak or absent. At the most superficial level it is obviously true that religion has persisted throughout recorded history. However, Greeley's claims clearly seek to go beyond this platitude, since no secularization theorist would be prepared to deny it. Instead, he argues that society is essentially conservative and that the actual functions of religion have remained unchanged throughout history. Even evidence of apparent disengagement of society from religion does not dissuade him from this claim. He can only achieve consistency at this point by distinguishing between the 'context' and 'function' of religion and by ascribing disengagement to the former and not to the latter.[9]

Clearly I was expressing considerable concern at the time both about sweeping historical claims and about empirical data that was either weak or absent. Too many sociologists of religion seemed to me to be making sweeping historical claims (on both sides of the debate) *and* to be using weak empirical data in contradictory ways. More than that, they were typically making claims about religious change or long-term persistence on the basis of static data. In contrast I became increasingly convinced that *longitudinal* historical data was needed if this debate were really to be improved. As a result of this conviction my own research in the sociology of religion during the 1980s and 1990s focused upon attempting to collect and analyse such data – first in the studies of churchgoing census data (starting in the 1830s) that resulted in my book *The Myth of the Empty Church*[10] and its sequel *The*

---

[8] Andrew Greeley, *The Persistence of Religion*, London: SCM Press, 1973, p. 16 [American title *Unsecular Man: The Persistence of Religion*, New York: Schocken Books, 1972].

[9] Gill, *The Social Context of Theology*, p. 117.

[10] London: SPCK, 1993.

'Empty' Church Revisited[11] and then in the studies of religious attitudes, beliefs and stated behaviour in questionnaire surveys (starting properly in the 1940s) reported first by Kirk Hadaway, Penny Long Marler and myself in 1998[12] and then more fully the following year in my book *Churchgoing and Christian Ethics*.[13]

This data made it possible at last to offer a new way of mapping and evaluating differences among sociologists of religion about secularization. A key question became how they relate the now much richer and more reliable British data on a decline (going back into the nineteenth century) of religious belonging to the data on a decline (in the second half of the twentieth century) of specifically Christian belief. Secularization theorists typically interpret this as a crisis of religious belief that has gradually corroded religious practice. Persistence theorists typically argue that there are other forms of religious belief and practice that compensate for this particular pattern of European (but not American) decline. Separation theorists typically maintain that there is no necessary relationship between these two patterns of decline.

In contrast, after looking carefully at each of these three paradigms – secularization, persistence and separation – I argued that a cultural theory or paradigm of religious transmission best accounts for the data.[14] This challenges the more traditional paradigms and assumes that religious beliefs and values depend heavily for their transmission upon religious practices, families and communities. I argued, focusing upon British data, that a cultural paradigm is more distinctively sociological than its three rivals. It alone takes seriously the role of socialization in the transmission of religious beliefs and values.

The Secularization Paradigm

Among the founders of the sociology of religion the secularization paradigm was dominant. Given the fact that so few of them were themselves religious believers, this was perhaps hardly surprising. At both a personal and an academic level they

---

[11]   Aldershot, Hants: Ashgate, 2006.

[12]   Robin Gill, C. Kirk Hadaway and Penny Long Marler, 'Is Religious Belief Declining in Britain?', *Journal for the Scientific Study of Religion*, 37:3, 507–516, 1998.

[13]   Cambridge: Cambridge University Press, 1999.

[14]   See my *Churchgoing and Christian Ethics*, Chapter 4.

simply assumed that what Weber termed 'demystification' or 'disenchantment' characterized the modern world. Of course there were moments of regret in both Weber and Durkheim's writings (as in the later writings of Bryan Wilson) that secularization also puts in danger values derived from religious traditions. However, the forces of modernity, fostered by the rise of science and the Enlightenment, together with the *anomie* of modern urban existence, ensured that people became increasingly disenchanted with religious faith and practice.

Peter Berger, writing in the 1960s, was unusual among proponents of the secularization paradigm in that he was personally a religious believer. However, whatever his personal beliefs, he was, as seen earlier, convinced that the religiously committed formed a 'deviant cognitive minority' in the modern world as a result of increasing secularization. For him secularization was 'the process by which sectors of society and culture are removed from the domination of religious institutions and symbols ... it affects the totality of cultural life and of ideation, and may be observed in the decline of religious contexts in the arts, in philosophy, in literature and, most important of all, in the rise of science as an autonomous, thoroughly secular perspective on the world ... put simply, this means that the modern West has produced an increasing number of individuals who look upon the world and their own lives without the benefit of religious interpretations'.[15]

Of course Berger was writing long before José Casanova forced sociologists of religion to think more carefully before assuming that these three levels of secularization – social structural, cultural and cognitive – are necessarily linked.[16] Nevertheless, if they are linked together (as they were in Bryan Wilson's writings) they provide a clear account of religious transmission. Individuals become disenchanted in the modern world. As a result religious beliefs and values decline and religious structures, dependent upon these beliefs and values, lose their social and cultural significance.

Steve Bruce pithily summarizes this account in the very title of his book *God is Dead: Secularization in the West*.[17] He insists that the secularization

---

[15] Peter L. Berger, *The Social Reality of Religion*, London: Faber & Faber, 1969, p. 113.

[16] José Casanova, *Public Religions in the Modern World*, Chicago: University of Chicago Press, 1994.

[17] Steve Bruce, *God is Dead: Secularization in the West*, Oxford, UK and Malden, MS: Blackwell Publishers, 2002.

paradigm is not intended to depict some universal or inevitable social process. His concern is emphatically only with the West since the Reformation. Nonetheless within this specific geographical context and historical frame he maintains that industrialization brought with it social changes – cultural and social fragmentation together with bureaucratic rationality – which have made religion less plausible at a social level and less compelling at an individual level. Within the West, he argues, there is empirical evidence that religion is increasingly irrelevant within the public forum and a matter of indifference to an increasing number of individuals. What is more, in countries such as Britain the primary means of religious socialization (such as Sunday schools) are now so attenuated that the survival of many religious organizations in the next generation is questionable.

He is fully aware that such a thoroughgoing secularization paradigm faces many sociological critics. Indeed, as noted earlier, the subtitle of his most recent book *Secularization* is tellingly *in defence of an unfashionable theory*.[18] So he examines the criticism that the paradigm presupposes some golden age of faith, that statistics of religious decline are not uniform even in Britain and that the New Age Movement constitutes a reversal of secularization. He argues that none of these criticisms is fatal to the secularization paradigm: even though there may have been no 'golden age of faith', faith was stronger in the past than in the present; statistics of decline may not be uniform, but they do point to overall decline; and the New Age Movement engages only a minority of the population today. He also attempts to state carefully what he sees as the link between the rise of science and secularization – for him it is more to do with bureaucratic rationality than with particular scientific discoveries.

Most sociologists of religion in Britain today would acknowledge that there is now clear evidence of decline within Christian churches in Britain and in many other Western European countries (together with countries such as Australia, New Zealand and Canada that have experienced considerable immigration from Western Europe), as well as growing scepticism about Christianity especially among the young. Where they will differ from Bruce is whether this constitutes secularization as such, or, if it does, whether secularization is either itself a causal agency or even ubiquitous throughout the West. It is interesting that José

---

[18]   Steve Bruce, *Secularization: In Defence of an Unfashionable Theory*, Oxford: Oxford University Press, 2011.

Casanova is cited in Bruce's bibliography of *God is Dead* but not in the text. In *Secularization* Casanova's work is briefly discussed and Bruce acknowledges that 'it is not inevitable that religion be enduringly excluded from public sphere', but immediately adds:

> Casanova is right, but his point seems more like an illustration of secularization than refutation. Churches, because they can claim to represent social values and because they can mobilize large parts of their membership, can still be political actors, but such action requires that they accept secular rules of engagement. No church in a modern society can plausibly claim that its values should predominate because God is on their side.[19]

Later volumes will need to return to this issue. However, in a modern, pluralist society (not necessarily a secular society) legislation and political decisions are typically framed in generic terms. Religious leaders within a modern, pluralist society can still have influence upon legislation and political decisions and may well deploy generic terms to achieve this influence. Yet it is not at all clear why this makes them secular by doing so or why their actions should be framed in terms of a process of secularization.

Steve Bruce is unconvinced by those who claim that despite the obvious decline of churchgoing in most Western countries religion still retains its social significance. He disagrees with Grace Davie's claim[20] that churches still have a powerful vicarious role in wider society extending well beyond their formal membership. He also disagrees with Paul Heelas and Linda Woodhead's claim[21] that new forms of spirituality are fast filling the vacuum left by declining churches. In contrast Bruce argues in *Secularization* that in Britain the fourfold decline in churchgoing since 1851 is not matched by any clear empirical evidence of a significant rise of alternative religious or spiritual forms. Even a vicarious church is, in his view, a poor cultural substitute for dedicated, regular churchgoing.

---

[19]   Bruce, *Secularization*, p. 39.

[20]   Grace Davie, *The Sociology of Religion*, London: Sage, 2007, pp. 126–128 and 140–143.

[21]   Paul Heelas and Linda Woodhead et al., *The Spiritual Revolution: Why Religion is Giving Way to Spirituality*, Oxford: Blackwell, 2005.

In all three of his books that deal extensively with secularization (*Religion in the Modern World*,[22] *God is Dead* and *Secularization*) he offers lengthy accounts of churchgoing decline, followed by a clarification of how the secularization paradigm has been misunderstood or misrepresented, followed by a lengthy deconstruction of non-secularization paradigms and concluding with a robust defence of the secularization. His use of statistics was sometimes sloppy in his earlier works. In *Secularization* he wisely relies more upon the careful statistical work of David Voas.

Yet in all three books he makes the same error about American churchgoing statistics. He wants to claim (against Grace Davie)[23] that American churches show a similar pattern of decline to churches elsewhere in the West. He has some ground for claiming that there is evidence of an increase in Americans claiming to have 'no religion' over the last 50 years (but this may simply indicate increasing polarization rather than secularization). But he is on much weaker ground relying upon evidence that only half of the 40 per cent of Americans who claim to go to church every Sunday are actually to be found in a church on a typical Sunday, since exactly the same phenomenon occurs in Britain (albeit at much lower levels). Nor does he have rigorously established research evidence for a decline in Christian belief among the American population. There is such evidence in Britain based upon research done on multiple opinion polls.[24] In contrast his American 'evidence' is based on just three polls. His robust assertions that 'there is clear evidence of Christianity in the USA losing power, prestige, and popularity' and that 'Christianity in the USA has become increasingly secular'[25] are not matched by clear evidence. American 'exceptionalism' remains a problem for Bruce's thesis just as it did for Wilson's position. It was awkward evidence such as this that finally persuaded Peter Berger to abandon the secularization paradigm.[26]

---

[22]   Steve Bruce, *Religion in the Modern World: From Cathedrals to Cults*, Oxford: Oxford University Press, 1996.

[23]   Grace Davie, *Europe: The Exceptional Case*, London: Darton, Longman & Todd, 2002.

[24]   See Gill, Hadaway and Marler, 1998, updated in my *The 'Empty' Church Revisited*, Table 20.

[25]   Bruce, *Secularization*, p. 157.

[26]   See Peter Berger (ed.), *The Desecularization of the World*, Grand Rapids, MI: Eerdmans, 1999.

If Berger has now abandoned the secularization paradigm, Callum Brown, once a staunch critic, has now embraced the paradigm with enthusiasm. He states his new thesis dramatically at the outset of his challenging book *The Death of Christian Britain*:

> It took several centuries (in what historians used to call the Dark Ages) to convert Britain to Christianity, but it has taken less than forty years for the country to forsake it. For a thousand years, Christianity penetrated deeply into the lives of the people, enduring Reformation, Enlightenment and industrial revolution by adapting to each new social and cultural context that arose. Then, really quite suddenly in 1963, something very profound ruptured the character of the nation and its people, sending organised Christianity on a downward spiral to the margins of social significance.[27]

Interestingly, it is cultural change – specifically, the culture of the 'swinging sixties' – which Brown believes has brought about this radical secularization. The 'swinging sixties', he argues, acted as a highly significant moral challenge to British Christianity.

But again there are obvious problems facing Brown's use of data. Apparently for him de-Christianization and secularization are one and the same phenomenon and the extensive evidence that he offers (consisting of both church statistics and oral history data) focuses very specifically upon Britain albeit making wider claims about the West. In addition, even as British data, it is extraordinarily selective. For example, he simply ignores the extensive data that I will summarize shortly showing decline in British churchgoing long, long before the 'swinging sixties' and that overall levels of churchgoing in places such as York declined considerably faster in the first half of the twentieth century than in the second half.[28]

---

[27] Callum Brown, *The Death of Christian Britain*, London: Routledge, 2001, p. 1. See also Callum Brown and Michael Snape, 'Introduction' in Callum Brown and Michael Snape (eds), *Secularisation in the Christian World*, Farnham: Ashgate, 2010, pp. 3-11.

[28] See my *The 'Empty' Church Revisited*, chapter 9.

The Persistence Paradigm

Persistence or separation paradigms have sought to give an alternative account of religious transmission. Not persuaded that there is some overall process of secularization, even in the modern West, exponents of each of these paradigms offer a very different sociological perspective. The persistence paradigm has proved especially attractive to American sociologists of religion. It characteristically regards religious belief and practice as constants within human nature. These beliefs and practices (and the institutions that enshrine them) may indeed change over time and culture – at one instance being expressed in one form and at another in a very different form – yet their presence among human beings is deemed to be ubiquitous. To be human is to be *homo religiosus*. It was this claim that Andrew Greeley articulated so forcefully in the 1970s in his book *The Persistence of Religion*. For Greeley religion provides human beings everywhere with:

1. a meaning system to cope with the question of the Ultimate
2. a feeling of belonging with a communal group sharing the same ultimate commitments
3. a means of integrating life with the forces of human sexuality
4. a channel for coming into intimate contact with the sacred
5. leaders whose role is to provide comfort and challenge when human being attempt to wrestle with the Ultimate.[29]

If a sufficiently broad functionalist definition of religion is adopted, then perhaps such sweeping claims could appear plausible. However, it soon becomes apparent that such broad functionalist definitions come with a price – almost any form of ideology or commitment (even those explicitly disavowing religion) can be counted as religion. As a result claims about the functions of religion become wholly circular – a broad definition of religion is adopted showing that the functions of religion are ubiquitous and these functions, in turn, are then used to demonstrate the persistence of religion.

In the 1980s Rodney Stark and William Sims Bainbridge proposed a more focused account of persistence in their book *The Future of Religion*. They argued

---

[29]   Greeley, *Persistence*, p. 16.

that religious organizations respond to universal human aspirations for rewards (such as earthly well-being or life after death) or, at the very least, for eventual compensators. However, over time, particular religious organizations are prone to secularization. Yet, given continuing human aspirations for rewards/compensators, secularization is a time-limited phenomenon. As soon as one religious organization succumbs to secularization another will replace it to meet these aspirations:

> Secularization is nothing new... it is occurring constantly in all religious economies. Through secularization, sects are tamed and transformed into churches. Their initial otherworldliness is reduced and worldliness is accommodated. Secularization also eventually leads to the collapse of religious organizations as their extreme worldliness – their weak and vague conceptions of the supernatural – leaves them without the means to satisfy even the universal dimensions of religious commitment. Thus we regard secularization as the primary dynamic of religious economies, a self-limiting process that engenders revival (sect formation) and innovation (cult formation).[30]

In the 1990s Stark, this time working with Roger Finke and the economist Larry Iannaccone, applied rational choice theory to the persistence paradigm, arguing that a free and competitive religious market can create and sustain a vibrant religious culture even in the modern world.[31] The more religiously diverse an area, the greater will be the vibrancy of its religious culture. In contrast, the greater the religious monopoly in an area – that is, the absence of a religious market – the weaker the religious culture. America, they argued, is typified by religious diversity and vibrancy, whereas Europe is typified more by religious monopoly and decline. Grace Davie helpfully depicts this application of rational choice as follows:

---

[30]   Rodney Stark and William Sims Bainbridge, *The Future of Religion: Secularization, Revival and Cult Formation*, Berkeley, CA: University of California Press, 1985, pp. 429–430.

[31]   Roger Finke and Rodney Stark, *The Churchgoing of America, 1776–1990: Winners and Losers in Our Religious Economy*, New Brunswick, NJ: Rutgers University Press, 1992 and Roger Finke and Laurence A. Iannaccone, 'Supply-Side Explanations for Religious Change', *Annals of the American Academy of Political and Social Science*, 527, 27–39, 1993.

Put very simply, the application of rational choice theory to religion develops along two lines. It assumes on the one hand a purposive rational actor who is looking, amongst other things, for religious satisfaction and, on the other, the existence of a religious market from which the actor makes his or her selections. It follows that for many exponents of rational choice theory, if not for all, the theory works in terms of supply rather than demand: religious activity will increase where there is an abundant supply of religious choices, offered by a wide range of 'firms' (religious organizations of various kinds); it will diminish where such supplies are limited.[32]

Given the comparative resilience of American churchgoing and the wealth and vibrancy of American churches, it is perhaps not surprising that all three of these versions of the persistence paradigm were championed by American sociologists of religion. Grace Davie recognizes that it intuitively fits their experience and may even have resonances for what she sees as an increasing shift from 'obligation' or 'duty' to 'personal choice' among British churchgoers. Yet she is finally cautious about adopting rational choice as a theory that accounts wholly for differences of religious vibrancy between the United States and Britain/Europe. Predictably Steve Bruce has no time for the theory at all. For him the United States is clearly secularizing and, in any case, an increase in religious pluralism (say, in Britain in the mid nineteenth century) did not result in an increase in religious vibrancy.[33]

Separation Paradigm

The separation paradigm, in contrast, tends to point to a more specific set of data, independently fluctuating or persisting patterns of religious belief and religious belonging. Grace Davie has done more to develop this paradigm than anyone else. In her book *Religion in Britain Since 1945: Believing Without Belonging* she pointed out that many people in Britain today hold conventional Christian beliefs

---

[32]   Davie, *The Sociology of Religion*, p. 70.

[33]   See Steve Bruce, *Secularization*, chapter 7 and *Choice and Religion: A Critique of Rational Choice Theory*, Oxford: Oxford University Press, 1999.

but seldom or never go to church, while other people go regularly to church but deny these beliefs:

> Regarding practice or active membership of religious organizations, the findings are unequivocal. Such activities involve a relatively small proportion of the population (just under 15 per cent on average). But it is equally evident that between two-thirds and three-quarters of British people indicate fairly consistently that they believe in some sort of God.[34]

Critics of this widely used phrase 'believing without belonging' argued[35] that this was simply a temporary phenomenon and that over time belief would fade without belonging.

In her more recent writings Davie has taken on board a part of this criticism. In 2000, as a result of working on the European Values Survey, she refined her earlier broad distinction between 'believing' and 'belonging' and identified two types of variable (each with a mixture of indicators of both belief and practice):

> On the one hand, those concerned with feelings, experience, and the more numinous religious beliefs; on the other hand, those which measure religious orthodoxy, ritual participation, and institutional attachment. It is, moreover, the latter (the more orthodox indicators of religious attachment) which display, most obviously, an undeniable degree of secularization throughout Western Europe. In contrast the former (the less institutional indicators) demonstrate considerable persistence in some forms of religious life.[36]

Evidently she now agreed that 'the more orthodox indicators of religious attachment' (including both belief and belonging) were related to each other. More explicitly in her most recent writing she agrees that 'statements of credal religion

---

[34] Grace Davie, *Religion in Britain Since 1945: Believing Without Belonging*, Oxford: Blackwell, 1994, p. 74–5.

[35] See Steve Bruce, *God is Dead*, pp. 71–3 and David Voas and Alasdair Crockett, 'Religion in Britain: Neither Believing nor Belonging', *Sociology*, 39, 11–28, 2005.

[36] Grace Davie, *Religion in Modern Europe: A Memory Mutates*, Oxford: Oxford University Press, 2000, p. 7.

endorsed by the churches' diminish if 'unsupported by regular attendance'. Yet she adds:

> I am much less sure, however, about the looser and more heterodox elements of belief ... here are persuasive data emerging from the most recent European Values Survey enquiries, which indicate that the relationship between certain dimensions of belief and belonging may be inverse rather than direct. Notably here are those aspects of belief which relate to the soul and to life after death ... these appear to rise markedly in *younger* rather than older generations, and in precisely those countries of Europe (mostly but not exclusively in the North) where the institutional capacities of the churches are most diminished.[37]

The Cultural Paradigm

A cultural paradigm of religious transmission shares some of the features of Grace Davie's most recent separation paradigm. It also regards both secularization and persistence paradigms as too monolithic to account adequately for the varied empirical data of religious believing and belonging across the Western world. Proponents of both secularization and persistence paradigms have a tendency to resort to special pleading when confronted with awkward data. Neither paradigm is sufficiently sociological whenever their proponents seem determined to maintain them *whatever the evidence*. Yet there is also something unsociological about a separation paradigm: it is one thing to point to data suggesting differing patterns of religious mutation or non-mutation in Western Europe, but it would be quite another for anyone to claim that these are wholly independent social variables (I am not, of course, insisting that anyone has made this claim). The most that might be claimed sociologically is that so far no plausible connection has been found between these two types of religious believing and belonging.

However, a cultural paradigm does attempt to make such a connection. It starts from an eminently sociological presumption, namely that religious beliefs and values are shaped through religious socialization (formal or informal). Of course they may, in turn, shape religious practices and organizations, but they do need

---

[37]   Grace Davie, *The Sociology of Religion*, p. 140.

initially to be culturally embedded in human beings. Thus a cultural paradigm, unlike Greeley, makes no a priori assumptions about *homo religiosus* or about ubiquitous functions of religion. In contrast, it is more concerned to account for the transmission of particular religious beliefs and values than to speculate about 'religion as a whole'.

There are several pieces of evidence[38] suggesting that there is a causal relationship between forms of religious beliefs and values, on the one hand, and specific types of religious belonging. The first is consistently high levels of Christian orthodoxy found among regular churchgoers diachronically and synchronically within and across different Western countries over many decades. The second is a consistent weakening of Christian beliefs and values in relation to a stage-by-stage decrease in frequency of church attendance. The third is a significant difference of Christian beliefs and values among two groups of adult non-attenders, with significantly higher levels in the group of those who attended regularly as children compared with the group of those who did not. The fourth is British diachronic evidence suggesting that church/Sunday school attendance in the general population declined long before general levels of Christian orthodoxy declined. Taken together these four pieces of evidence suggest that the separation paradigm has tended to underestimate a causal connection, at least within Western Europe (together with Canada and Australia and New Zealand) between a decline of religious practice and a subsequent decline of religious orthodoxy. They also count against a secularization paradigm that regards a decline of religious practice as a product of a prior decline of religious belief.

The first piece of evidence points to consistently high levels of Christian orthodoxy (on belief in a personal God, in life after death and in Jesus as divine) found among regular churchgoers, measured both diachronically and synchronically within and across different Western countries over many decades. For once in *Churchgoing and Christian Ethics* I was able to take British questionnaire survey data right back to 1926 to establish this point. The two large and remarkably early polls carried out on readers of *The Daily News* and *The Nation* in that year are usually regarded as sociologically unusable because they relied upon the self-selection of readers rather than upon a stratified randomized sample. However,

---

[38] For all the data evidence that follows, see my *Churchgoing and Christian Ethics* and *The 'Empty' Church Revisited*.

for once they can be useful. Whether representative or not of the whole English population at the time, the levels of churchgoing (much higher in England then than today) and Christian belief in this group correlate closely with each other and with levels in the general population of Northern Ireland (still with high levels of churchgoing) 75 years later. Similarly, the still higher levels of Christian belief measured exclusively among English regular churchgoers since the 1960s show scant evidence of decline. Just as remarkably, very similar levels of belief among regular churchgoers can be found elsewhere in the Western world. To give a single example, using results from the World Value Survey[39] of the early 1980s, there were close similarities between Canadian and American weekly churchgoers on their beliefs in God (99 per cent+), in life after death (USA 88 per cent and Canada 86 per cent), in the soul (98 per cent and 97 per cent) in heaven (98 per cent and 95 per cent) and in sin (96 per cent and 90 per cent) – and this despite radically different levels of both church attendance and Christian belief in the general populations of the United States and Canada.

Crucially, reported levels of regular churchgoing declined significantly between 1947 and 1964, whereas levels of belief remained comparatively static. However, by the 1990s belief in a personal God had also declined significantly (along with a continuing decline in regular churchgoing).

The second piece of evidence concerns a consistent weakening of Christian beliefs and values in relation to a stage-by-stage decrease in the frequency of claimed church attendance. In *Churchgoing and Christian Ethics* I show that *British Social Attitudes*[40] 1991 data provide clear evidence of this. Most questions show a clear and statistically significant directional relation[41] between the regularity of churchgoing and the strength of Christian beliefs. Thus those claiming to go to church more regularly than others generally have higher levels of Christian belief, whereas those who say they never go tend to have significantly lower levels. Conversely, the less

---

[39]   See Samuel H. Reimer, 'A Look at Cultural Effects on Religiosity: A Comparison Between the United States and Canada', *Journal for the Scientific Study of Religion*, 34:4, 1996, p. 452.

[40]   The data used here were made available through Data Archive. Neither the original collectors of the data nor the Archive bear any responsibility for the analyses or interpretations presented here.

[41]   Somers' ordinal by ordinal directional test in SPSS was used on all directional tests on this BSA data: those referred to as 'significant' all recorded a level of statistical significance at between .000 and .006.

people claim to go to church, the more they seem to be attracted to 'new age' beliefs. Clustering data into four levels of churchgoing – weekly, monthly, seldom and never – there is a clear and statistically significant relation between those claiming to go to church most regularly in Britain and those who agree that there is a God concerned personally with human beings (84 per cent, 62 per cent, 37 per cent, 21 per cent). To the statement, 'The course of our lives is decided by God', BSA 1991 also found that there was a highly significant directional relation, albeit at a lower level of positive responses, among churchgoers/non-churchgoers (53 per cent, 28 per cent, 21 per cent, 12 per cent). A slightly higher, but again significantly directional, level of positive responses was found to the statement, 'To me, life is meaningful only because God exists' (68 per cent, 27 per cent, 20 per cent, 8 per cent).

Summarizing a mass of similar evidence from this source and from the *British Household Panel Survey*, I concluded:

> The mass of new data shows that churchgoers are indeed distinctive in their attitudes and behaviour. Some of their attitudes do change over time, especially on issues such as sexuality, and there are obvious moral disagreements between different groups of churchgoers in a number of areas. Nonetheless, there are broad patterns of Christian beliefs, teleology and altruism which distinguish churchgoers as a whole from nonchurchgoers. It has been seen that churchgoers have, in addition to their distinctive theistic and christocentric beliefs, a strong sense of moral order and concern for other people. They are, for example, more likely than others to be involved in voluntary service and to see overseas charitable giving as important. They are more hesitant about euthanasia and capital punishment and more concerned about the family and civic order than other people.[42]

Although sociologists of religion had long underestimated the social significance of churchgoing, I pointed to a few rather neglected surveys going back to a remarkable 1954 BBC survey which suggested otherwise, as did the work of Gary Bouma and Beverley Dixon in Australia in 1986.[43]

---

[42]   *Churchgoing and Christian Ethics*, p. 197.

[43]   Gary D. Bouma and Beverly R. Dixon, *The Religious Factor in Australian Life*, World Vision and the Zadok Centre: MARC Australia, 1986.

Volume 3 will return to this topic. However, it is worth noting that Robert Putnam's most recent work has highlighted the social significance of churchgoing. Putnam is famous for driving the current debate about social capital, notably through his book *Bowling Alone*.[44] There has been much debate about how 'social capital' might actually be measured and only a certain amount of discussion about its relationship to religious institutions.[45] In his new book, written with David Campbell, *American Grace: How Religion Divides and Unites Us*, Putnam directly links churchgoing with 'good neighbourliness'. On the basis of two large surveys of cohorts measured in 2006 and 2007, Putnam and Campbell compile what they term 'an index of religious social networks'. This is based upon the number of close friends weekly churchgoers have in their congregation, their level of participation in small groups in their congregation and the frequency of their talking about religion with family and friends. Using this index they conclude:

> So important are these religiously based social networks that they alone account for most of the apparent effects of church attendance. Our index of religious social networks ... is virtually the most powerful predictor of every measure of good neighbourliness ... no less a predictor than education, the universal predictor... :volunteering for secular causes, giving to secular causes, membership of civic groups, working on a community project, collaborating on community problems, working for social reform, attending club meetings, serving as organizational leader, voting in local elections, and attending public meetings. In virtually every case, although generic friendship ties are a significant predictor, religious social networks are a stronger, more robust predictor.[46]

The third piece of evidence involves a significant difference of Christian beliefs and values among two groups of adult non-attenders, measured again in BSA

---

[44]   Robert D. Putnam, *Bowling Alone: The Collapse and Revival of American Community*, New York: Simon & Schuster, 2000.

[45]   For example Stephen Baron, John Field and Tom Schuller (eds), *Social Capital: Critical Perspectives*, Oxford: Oxford University Press, 2000; David Halpern, *Social Capital*, Cambridge: Polity, 2005; and Chris Baker and Jonathan Miles-Watson, 'Faith and Traditional Capitals: Defining the Public Scope of Spiritual and Religious Capital – a Literature Review', *Implicit Religion*, 13:1, 17–69, 2010.

[46]   Robert D. Putnam and David E. Campbell, *American Grace: How Religion Divides and Unites Us*, New York: Simon & Schuster, 2010, p. 472.

1991, with significantly higher levels in the group of those who attended regularly as children compared with the group of those who did not. For example, the group of adult non-attenders who had been weekly churchgoers as children were twice as likely to believe in God (with or without doubts) as adult non-attenders who had never been churchgoers as children. Conversely, 40 per cent of the latter agreed with the statement 'I don't believe in God now and I never have', but only 6 per cent of the former. Those who never went to church as children were also much less likely to agree that the Bible is 'the inspired word of God', to pray, to believe in religious miracles or to agree that 'There is a God who concerns Himself personally with every human being.

The final piece of evidence is the British diachronic evidence suggesting that church/Sunday school attendance declined in the general population long before general levels of Christian orthodoxy declined. The detailed British evidence, stretching over almost two centuries, is reviewed at length in *The 'Empty' Church Revisited* and summarized in a series of bullet points (the statistics in this area are too complicated to summarize accurately here):

- **By 1900** urban adult Anglican and Free Church churchgoing was already in decline.
    - However, there were still pockets of suburban and rural resilience.
    - Sunday schools were still very strong.
    - However, rural churches were already facing radical problems of overbuilding and depopulation.
- **By 1918** most soldiers in the First World War had been as children to Sunday school, had residual Christian beliefs, but had not been regular churchgoers at home.
    - Chapels and mission halls in rural and central urban areas were already closing.
- **By 1950** Catholics had become a major force among churchgoers.
    - Sunday school attendances and confirmations were still relatively high albeit declining.
    - There were still pockets of resilient churchgoing in some deeply rural areas.
    - There was a slight rise in churchgoing in middle-class suburban areas.
    - Generalized Christian belief was still relatively strong.
    - But otherwise decline continued.

- **By 1970** Catholic decline had started.
  - – Sunday school attendances and confirmations were declining fast.
  - – Christian belief had started to decline.
  - – Independent Free Churches were growing in urban areas.
  - – But older Free Churches were declining fast in rural and urban areas.
- **By 1999** there were no longer pockets of rural resilience and urban resilience was almost entirely confined to Black (but not White) Pentecostals (and Muslims).

From this it can be seen that overall adult churchgoing decline in much of England and Wales (and possibly Scotland too) started in the 19th and not the twentieth century, whereas measurable decline in Christian belief started in the second half of the twentieth century.

It is not possible to rehearse here all of the factors that I suggest in *The 'Empty' Church Revisited* precipitated the long decline of British churchgoing. They include intense, but unequal, rivalry between an established church and free denominations; an extraordinary over-provision of church buildings and then the subsidy of largely empty rural and central urban churches; and the gradual erosions caused by the death of elderly churchgoers accompanied by the disaffection of the young. It is even possible to argue that it is church growth that needs to be explained sociologically rather than church decline. Left to their own devices congregations tend to decline over time simply because elderly churchgoers die and young people need some persuasion to replace them. Church growth, on the other hand, may require both considerable energy from churches and a period of population mobility, such as occurred in the first half of the nineteenth century in Britain or in the second half of the twentieth century in South Korea. Similarly, churches in the United States benefited very significantly in the twentieth century from influxes of immigrants (most recently with Catholics benefiting from Hispanic immigration and Presbyterians from South Korean immigration). Static populations, on the other hand, find church growth much more elusive. So to view British and West European twentieth-century church decline as resulting simply from 'secularization' (whatever that is) would appear too simplistic. Nevertheless, in terms of a cultural paradigm of religious transmission, one of the effects of this decline has been to produce a population that is now increasingly untouched by Christian socialization. A gradual erosion of Christian orthodoxy within the British and West European populations is now sociologically unsurprising.

What emerges from all of this is complex and sometimes confusing. Secularization theory can no longer be trusted to provide a single causal explanation of religious change. Yet forms of secularization are still likely to characterize at least some groups in Britain today. Christian socialization does appear to be declining, but it may not always be replaced simply with secularism. The statistics of belief and belonging do help to bring some clarity, but perhaps other forms of enquiry can contribute as well. The next chapter will suggest that changing and varied patterns of response to religious issues in English newspapers over the last 42 years can also offer useful hints about social context.

Chapter 11

Social Context: Evidence from Newspapers

In 1969 I undertook a survey of the religious content of eight English national newspapers. For four weeks in August I recorded daily the proportion of total page space (including advertisements) given to religious issues in the following newspapers: *The Times*, *The Daily Telegraph*, *The Guardian*, *The Daily Express*, *The Daily Mail*, *The Mirror*, *The Sun* and *The Sketch*. On the first two days of that month Pope Paul VI made his historic Peace Mission to Uganda which received quite an amount of attention in all of the newspaper except *The Telegraph*. In proportional terms *The Mail* had the highest level of coverage (2.5 per cent of overall space) with an overall mean for all the newspapers of 1.5 per cent, but only 0.7 per cent for *The Telegraph*. For the most part the newspapers appeared to welcome the Peace Mission.

I struggled at the time to find a satisfactory way of defining the term 'religious content', aware that Thomas Luckmann's study *The Invisible Religion*[1] had made this task immensely more complex. How wide a definition of 'religion' might be adopted in a survey of this nature? In the end I decided that the sort of wide definition adopted by Luckmann raised the issue discussed earlier in Chapter 7, namely the doubtful sociological practice of imposing labels upon others which they personally reject. So I concluded that a narrow, conventional definition would be more appropriate in this context – namely 'items referring explicitly to religious institutions, their functionaries, or their central transcendent beliefs.' More difficult still was the attempt to distinguish between hostile and non-hostile religious content. Finally I adopted a perceptual definition of the notion of 'deemed hostile': namely, 'items which mainstream religious institutions might themselves deem to be hostile – for example, reports about clergy or their families involved in sex scandals or crime.'

From the work of the sociologist J.D. Halloran at Leicester University I was aware at the time that it was exceedingly difficult to measure the social significance

---

[1]   Thomas Luckmann, *The Invisible Religion*, London: Macmillan, 1967.

of different forms of mass communication.[2] Instead what I sought to produce was a snapshot of the different ways that national newspapers perceived religious institutions, their functionaries and their central transcendent beliefs. My survey was clearly not going to establish whether these perceptions were accurate mirrors of these institutions, functionaries or beliefs in contemporary British society, let alone whether they significantly shaped popular perceptions and attitudes towards them. It was argued by some at the time (perhaps somewhat disingenuously) that even advertising in the media probably reflected public tastes rather than shaped them. Instead what I hoped to achieve was a fresh and largely unexplored way of recording this particular form of public perception.

The exercise did generate a number of insights. The overall mean of deemed hostile material was 18 per cent of all religious content of the newspapers, but was considerably higher within the populist newspapers *The Sun* (28 per cent) and *The Sketch* (35 per cent). In contrast *The Guardian* had the highest overall proportion of religious content (1.1 per cent) of which only 13 per cent was deemed hostile. Another important insight was that, with the exception of *The Express*, readers appeared in their letters to be much more interested in religious issues than were the news and feature editors. If the overall mean of the religious content of the newspapers was 0.8 per cent, among all the letters they carried, 4.5 per cent were concerned with religious issues. Finally within the popular newspapers (that is, not *The Times*, *The Telegraph* or *The Guardian*) horoscopes were given as much space proportionately as the total religious content (given my definition *above* horoscopes were not deemed to be 'religious').

All of this suggested that the different newspapers' perceptions of religion in British society in the late 1960s varied very considerably. They expressed different levels of hostility, scope and interest, just as sociologists of religion were doing at the time. The radically differing perspective of Bryan Wilson, David Martin and others found echoes within the different newspapers.

However, none of this gave any clear indication of change. This survey was a static snapshot and did not provide the sort of longitudinal evidence needed to test rival theories of secularization or persistence. So when I was doing the longitudinal

---

[2]   J.D. Halloran, *The Effects of Mass Communications*, Leicester: Leicester University Press, 1964. For recent studies on the social effects of the media, see Knut Lundby (ed.), *Mediatization, Concept, Changes, Consequences*, New York and Oxford: Peter Lang, 2009.

research needed for *The Myth of the Empty Church* I decided to repeat the survey for four weeks in July 1990.[3] Since I was looking for longitudinal evidence I realized that, whatever the limitations of my original definitions of 'religious content' and material 'deemed hostile', it was methodologically imperative that these definitions were not altered (longitudinal research depends upon like being compared with like over different points of time). However, inevitably the peak religious event was different. This time around it occurred on 26 July 1990 when it was announced that the relatively unknown Bishop George Carey was to become the next Archbishop of Canterbury.

Comparing the evidence from these two surveys it soon became clear that the relative proportion of space given to religious items in national newspapers had declined overall (from 0.8 per cent of total space to 0.6 per cent) between 1969 and 1990 and in all the newspapers except *The Telegraph*. Most dramatically, it had more than halved in *The Guardian*. Now it was a new newspaper, *The Independent*, which had the highest proportion of religious items and percentage of letters with religious content. However, material perceived as 'hostile' had also declined over all (from 18 per cent to 16 per cent of all space given to religious items in the newspapers). Only *The Mail* (in which 'deemed hostile' material had risen from 18 per cent in 1969 to 30 per cent now), *The Sun* (in which it had risen from 28 per cent to 47 per cent) and the new popular newspaper, *The Star* (25 per cent: *The Sketch* was now defunct) were by then noticeably hostile. In those papers that still published general letters from readers, there was always a far higher religious content than in the paper as a whole.

In so far as newspapers might give some indication of contemporary popular sentiments, a shift away from mainstream religious institutions, but with little outright hostility, was apparent. Both of these pieces of evidence, if interpreted as indicating decline and popular indifference, were consonant with a secularization theory. In addition, there also appeared to be a decline in the percentage of readers' letters concerned with religious topics (from 4.5 per cent to 3.2 per cent of overall letters).

However, less consonant with Bryan Wilson's understanding of secularization – which explicitly linked secularization with a general increase in 'rational ... cause-and-effect thinking'[4] – was the evidence that horoscopes seemed to be more popular

---

[3]   See Table 17 in Robin Gill, *The Myth of the Empty Church*, London: SPCK, 1993, p. 322.

[4]   Bryan Wilson, *Religion in Secular Society*, London: C.A. Watts, 1966, p. 17.

than ever. In the tabloids (including *The Daily Express* and *The Daily Mail*) the space given to horoscopes in 1969 was, as just mentioned, approximately equal to that given to religious items, but in 1990 it was half as much again. In addition, letter writers were still decidedly more interested in religious issues than the newspapers themselves. Finally the peak religious event in 1990 attracted far more attention (with an overall mean of 2.5 per cent) than it did in 1969 (1.5 per cent). Of course this peak event in 1990 was home-grown, but even *The Star* (3.0 per cent) and *The Sun* (2.4 per cent) gave it considerable attention. *The Telegraph*, perhaps not surprisingly given that a relatively conservative evangelical was appointed as Archbishop, had the highest proportion of coverage of any the newspapers (3.6 per cent).

What patterns can be observed in 2011? Eight out of nine of the newspapers included in 1990 (only *The Mirror* was absent) were surveyed for four weeks during January and February 2011: *The Times*, *The Daily Telegraph*, *The Guardian*, *The Independent*, *The Daily Express*, *The Daily Mail*, *The Sun* and *The Star*. In order to provide longitudinal evidence, once again the 1969 definitions were used, but percentages were adjusted for overall means for 1990 (that is, by removing data for *The Mirror*) when comparisons were made with 2011.

Overall Changes

A word of caution is necessary at the outset. In the last 21 years newspapers have changed immensely. Ironically they have become both physically larger and less widely read. Many newspapers have supplements in 2011 both at the weekend and during the week. In order to maintain a valid comparison with newspapers published in 1969 and 1990 the religious content of these supplements was noted but not included in the 2011 statistics. However, these supplements still create some ambiguity, since sport or television, for example, are sometimes placed in them and sometimes not. In addition, there are now online versions of many newspapers (some subscription only and others not). For *The Guardian*, for example, the online version in 2011 appears to be used much more widely by the general public than the printed version. So any assessment of the social significance of *The Guardian* today would need to take full account of both the online as well as the printed versions.

My purpose again is emphatically *not* to assess social significance here but only social context. That makes an important sociological difference. By focusing on the continuing printed versions of the main body of each newspaper, the question is whether it is possible to detect *within them* different perceptions of religion in England over the last 42 years? The issue here is whether the approach of *newspapers* (whatever their role in an online age) to religion changes over time and then whether this offers an independent and relatively unexplored clue about different perceptions of social context.

Two striking differences are apparent immediately. This time around the overall religious content has increased slightly (to 0.7 per cent of total space from 0.6 per cent in 1990) rather than declined (as happened between 1969 and 1990) and the material deemed hostile has almost doubled (to 29 per cent of all space given to religious items). Evidently the perception of journalists is that religion is somewhat more newsworthy than it was 21 years ago (although not quite as newsworthy as it was 42 years ago), but that, in some of its manifestations at least, religion is to be regarded with considerable suspicion. In particular, Muslim extremists are given considerable attention in all of the tabloids and in some of the broadsheets.

Chapter 8 puzzled about why, with the important exception of Bernard Lewis,[5] religious fundamentalism was given so little serious attention before the 1979 Iranian Revolution. Even after this crucial event it was possible for academics to argue that it would be a short-term phenomenon and for newspapers to assume an ongoing process of declining interest in religious issues in the modern world. Once religious extremism linked to violence became a reality *within* the West – most dramatically with the shocking events of 9/11 and 7/7 – then it seems that religious coverage in newspapers has both increased and become distinctly more hostile. Academics such as Bernard Lewis,[6] Olivier Roy,[7] and Mark Juergensmeyer[8] also found a new and more attentive audience.

---

[5] Bernard Lewis 'The Return of Islam', *Commentary*, 61 (Jan. 1976), pp. 39–49.

[6] Bernard Lewis, *The Crisis of Islam: Holy War and Unholy Terror*, New York, NY: Random House, 2004.

[7] Olivier Roy, *Globalised Islam: The Search for a New Ummah*, London: Hurst, 2004.

[8] Mark Juergensmeyer, *Terror in the Mind of God: The Global Rise of Religious Violence*, Berkelely, CA: University of California Press, 2000 and *The Oxford Handbook of Global Religions*, Oxford: Oxford University Press, 2006.

Of course these two striking differences are in part related. Precisely because Muslim extremism is being given more attention so the religious content of the newspaper rises. Yet, as will be seen in a moment, the rise in overall religious content is not accounted for wholly by the rise of material deemed hostile (nor is the latter always about Muslims). Much of the peak religious content in 2011 (at least in the broadsheets) was concerned with the announcement by the Dalai Lama that he is to retire from active politics, an announcement that caused little hostile comment. If the overall (adjusted) peak was 2.7 per cent in 1990, it is still 2.6 per cent in 2011. Furthermore, the overall (adjusted) percentage of letters concerned with religious issues has also remained static (3.6 per cent in both surveys). Seemingly readers are still more interested in religious issues than are news or feature editors. The latter, on this reading, are simply catching up slightly with the former.

None of this suggests a straightforward process of secularization (especially if secularization is understood as indifference to religion) in the way that the differences between 1969 and 1990 might have done. A more complicated pattern is present. Four distinct sets of perceptions emerge when the newspapers are grouped together in pairs: general persistence (*The Times* and *Independent*); considerably increased interest and hostility (*The Telegraph* and *Guardian*); marginally increased interest with New Age tendencies and greatly increased hostility (*The Express* and *Mail*); and static low level interest of any kind and very considerable hostility (*The Sun* and *Star*). If these papers accurately represent different sections of English society, then persistence, secularization, hostility to Islam, indifference to Christianity, interest in New Age religion and occasional interest in peak (frequently worldwide) religious events all can have some claim to be depicted now as the social context of theology. A thoroughly confusing set of trends emerges. Perhaps *that* is why British sociologists of religion remain so at odds with each on the issue of secularization.

Pattern 1: General Persistence

The Times shows remarkable continuity over the 42-year period. Overall space given to items with an explicit religious content was 0.8 per cent in 1969 and 0.7 per cent in both 1990 and 2011. Letters with an explicitly religious content amounted to 5 per cent in 1969 and 1990 and to 6 per cent in 2011. The peak religious content changed little between 1990 and 2011 (1.9 and 2.1 per cent respectively). The only striking change was the reduction of religious items deemed hostile. In 1969 this amounted to 17 per cent, but in 1990 it reduced to 6 per cent and in 2011 to just 4 per cent. *The Independent*, as already mentioned, did not exist in 1969, but in 2011 it is the only other newspaper surveyed that has a similarly low level of hostile material (amounting to just 3 per cent in 2011 and 2 per cent in 1990).

Compared with the other six newspapers it is evident that both *The Times* and *The Independent* go to considerable lengths to avoid identifying extremists as being 'Muslim' in their headlines and photo captions. Attention was given in many newspapers to the trial of extremists who had publicly burned poppies on Remembrance Day. *The Times* reported the trial but avoided headlining the fact that they were 'Muslims'. *The Independent* did identify them as Muslims on one occasion but gave the item little space, as did *The Times* when reporting that some Muslim schools were teaching hate and violence. *The Times* also had occasional, but very fleeting, mentions of Christian priests who had been suspended or jailed for sexual acts.

In its 2011 religious coverage *The Times* gave considerable space to the murder of the Catholic politician, Shabaz Bhatti, in Pakistan, including a full-page article by the Archbishop of Canterbury on this issue. Again it was careful to avoid religiously hostile comments. *The Times* was also the only newspaper to cover at length Anglicans becoming Roman Catholics under the new papal dispensation. It had a full-page interview with Dame Julia Neuberger who had recently been appointed Senior Rabbi of the West London Synagogue. Every Saturday it also has a *Credo* piece. Letters in *The Times* in 2011 included items debating gay marriages being conducted in churches, Jewish women being able to say the Kaddish, St George's Day, and George Fox. None were about Muslim extremism. Nor were they in *The Independent*. Here 2011 letters included, instead, discussions of the merits and demerits of hospital chaplains, Catholic schools, the religious question in the Population Census, the cost of the Pope's recent visit, women bishops, and bishops in the House of Lords.

The main difference between *The Times* and *The Independent* was that overall religious content and letters declined in the latter between 1990 and 2011. However, as already noted, the levels in both were exceptionally high in 1990 compared with other newspapers. Overall religious content in *The Independent* declined to 0.9 per cent in 2011(from 1.4 per cent in 1990) and letters with religious content declined to 3 per cent in 2011 (from 8 per cent in 1990). But the unusually high levels in 1990 may possibly reflect the fact the first editor of *The Independent* (1986–1993), Andreas Whittam Smith, is the son of an Anglican priest and himself a committed Anglican who was appointed First Church Estates Commissioner in 2002. Whether or not this had an influence, this paper retains remarkably low levels of religious material deemed hostile and overall religious content well above the mean (0.7 per cent) for all eight newspapers in 2011. Like *The Times* it suggests general persistence.

Pattern 2: Considerably Increased Interest and Hostility

Space given to religious items continued to rise proportionately in *The Daily Telegraph*. In 1969 it represented 0.5 per cent of total space in the main body of the newspaper, rising in 1990 to 0.7 per cent. With the elapse of another 21 years it has now just over 1 per cent. So within 42 years it has doubled proportionately. Since the actual size of the newspaper has expanded very considerably during this period, the volume of religious news within it has also increased significantly.

However, there still remains a very considerable gap between the interests of readers as reflected in the proportion of letters with a religious theme that are published and the overall contents of the newspaper. In 1969 letters with a religious theme represented some 6 per cent of all letters and in 1990 they represented 4 per cent. By 2011 they once more represented 6 per cent.

All of this suggests remarkable resurgence in overall interest in religious issues in *The Daily Telegraph* readers and editors. But there is a sharper point to note as well. In both 1969 and 1990 some 11 per cent of the overall religious content was deemed hostile, whereas in 2011 this had risen significantly to 23 per cent. Even if this hostile material is removed altogether from the overall religious content, there has still been a slight rise in 2011. So the increase in interest is not entirely hostile. Indeed, among 2011 letter writers it is for the most part not. They express differences of view on, say, whether gays should be allowed to be married in church or whether Christians objecting to homosexuality should be allowed to foster children, but they are also just as inclined to debate the merits of having pipe rather than electronic organs in church.

Within the body of the newspaper just over a third of the material deemed hostile was concerned with Muslim extremists. For example, considerable space was given to the trial of the poppy burners. Headlines and photographs in *The Telegraph* explicitly identified them as 'Muslims'. Prominence was also given to one of the 7/7 bombers who had apparently attempted to convert boys to Islam and to an 'abusive' Muslim who had murdered his 'converted' wife and children.

Yet it was not just Islamic fundamentalists who were highlighted by *The Telegraph*. A Northern Irish former policeman, who had murdered his wife and the husband of his lover, was explicitly identified as 'Baptist' in the headline. Similarly a mother who murdered her children was again explicitly identified in the headline as 'a churchgoer' at an evangelical congregation. Evangelical fundamentalism appears to be regarded by *The Telegraph* as a threat to social order alongside that posed by Islamic fundamentalism.

The attention given to both of these 'threats' in 2011 represents a significant change from 1969 and 1990. In the earlier years of *The Telegraph* material deemed hostile was much more likely to consist of stories about adulterous clergy. A Queen's Chaplain who had left his wife was still reported in 2011, as well as a Roman lay chaplain who had apparently made a false accusation of rape, but neither story was given as much space as that on stories about fundamentalists. Even a short item on Scientology was more satirical than critical and only a brief mention was made of evidence that the Pope's visit to Britain in 2010 was going to cost 'taxpayers' 7 million pounds.

The Guardian also showed a pattern both of increased overall interest in religion and of increased hostility. Yet there were differences on both of these points as well. The overall religious content of *The Guardian* had more than halved from 1.1 per cent in 1969 to 0.5 per cent in 1990, before returning to 1.1 per cent in 2011. And the proportion of material deemed hostile had dropped from 13 per cent in 1969 to just 1 per cent in 1990, but now had jumped to 21 per cent.

A clear difference between *The Telegraph* and *The Guardian* in 2011 is that material deemed hostile in the latter is concerned almost entirely with radical Islam. As might be expected in a left-wing newspaper, adulterous clergy went largely unnoticed. In addition, the 'Baptist' or 'churchgoing' identity of particular family killers was not remarked upon. Apart from an item about 'the leader of seaside sex cult', all of the other items deemed hostile were about the actions of individuals identified in headlines as being radical 'Islamists', Muslim 'hate preachers' or a 7/7 bomber who had attempted to 'convert' pupils. If anything more attention was paid in the general/political news of *The Guardian* than of *The Telegraph* to the effects and implications of Arab/Asian terrorists. The main difference between the two newspapers was that *The Guardian* did not always identify them explicitly as Islamists or Muslims whereas *The Telegraph* habitually did so.

As in *The Telegraph*, the letter writers to *The Guardian* appeared to express more interest in religious issues than the journalists/editors. The 1.1 per cent proportion of overall religious content did not match the 3 per cent of letters published that were concerned with religious issues. Nonetheless, this 3 per cent in *The Guardian* in 2011 actually represented a continuing slight decline from 6 per cent in 1969 and then 4 per cent in 1990.

Another contrast between the two newspapers was in their peak religious content. In 1969 *The Guardian* gave more space to the Pope's Peace Mission (1.8 per cent) than *The Telegraph* (0.7 per cent). In 1990 on George Carey's appointment they were more equal, with *The Telegraph* giving this 3.6 per cent of space and *The Guardian* 3.1 per cent. In 2011 *The Telegraph* gave 2 per cent of space to the announcement by the Dalai Lama and *The Guardian* 2.4 per cent. However, the latter also had on the same day a lengthy obituary of Shabaz Bhatti, bringing the overall religious content that day to a remarkably high 4.5 per cent.

If it appeared by 1990 that *The Guardian* was becoming a purely secular newspaper with neither much interest in religious issues (compared with other broadsheets) nor even active antipathy to certain forms of religion, in 2011 it seems very different. *The Guardian Online* might campaign against *Thought for the Day* on Radio 4, but its printed paper on a Saturday still has a regular column *Face to Faith*. It ran a three-page feature in its *Review* (not counted of course in the overall religious content here) on the anniversary of the first publication of *the King James Bible* and it had several (perhaps over-optimistic) articles on the possibility of the Church of England authorities agreeing to allow gay partnerships to be conducted in churches. Like *The Telegraph* it also had an extended and sympathetic obituary of the Anglican Canon Donald Allchin, even though, less surprisingly, it ignored the death of the Conservative Life Peer Canon Peter Pilkington. *The Guardian*, it seems, can no longer be accurately depicted as being simply disinterested in religious issues.

Coming from radically different political positions both *The Telegraph* and *The Guardian* now show a fascinating combination of increased interest in and hostility towards (at least some aspects of) religion.

Pattern 3: Marginally Increased Interest with New Age Tendencies and Greatly Increased Hostility

The Express and *The Mail* display another pattern again. They both have an overall religious content (0.6 per cent) in 2011 that is slightly below the mean for all eight papers, yet both have increased slightly since 1990 (from 0.4 per cent for *The Express* and 0.5 per cent for *The Mail*). Neither of them displays anything like the resurgent interest of *The Telegraph* or *The Guardian*.

However, like *The Telegraph*, both *The Express* and *The Mail* now have considerable amounts of material deemed hostile concerned with Muslim extremists, Christian fundamentalists and the sexual misbehaviour of Catholic clergy. In *The Express* this hostile material has risen sharply in the last 21 years (it represented 11 per cent of overall religious materials in 1969, 12 per cent in 1990 and 31 per cent in 2011). 2011 headlines explicitly identify the poppy burners as 'Muslim extremists', schools of hatred are 'Muslim', it is a 'religious teacher' who commits a mortgage fraud and a 'royal chaplain' who leaves his wife, and the dentist who murders his wife has 'church guilt'. All of the 2011 letters with religious content in *The Express* were concerned with Muslims.

Levels of hostile material in *The Mail* have always been higher in every survey (18 per cent in 1969, 30 per cent in 1990 and 35 per cent in 2011). The 2011 headlines here are 'Muslim mob burned poppies', a female, lay Catholic 'chaplain cried rape after the priest finished their affair', 'Life for killer Sunday School teacher', and ' 'Rot in hell' fanatics told the UK's Muslim Miss Universe girl'. Unlike the letters in *The Express*, only one letter here was about Islam. With a higher proportion of letters with a religious content (here 5 per cent of all letters but only 2 per cent in *The Express*) their topics were more varied, including the date of

Easter, life after death, funerals, whether or not Lincoln was a Christian, and about a Christian bed-and-breakfast husband and wife who refused to accommodate a gay couple.

Unlike the broadsheets, there is also a New Age element in both *The Mail* and *Express*. *The Mail* gave considerable (hostile) space in 2011 both to 'Satanists of Ash Tree Close' and to the rituals of a Wiccan warlock. It also had a full-page (non-hostile) feature on 'Wild child found God (and lost 10 stone)' and another on evidence that belief in God makes people happier and healthier. *The Express* had a two-page feature with the headline 'We've been visited by the spirits of our dear dead pets', as well as a half-page feature on 'The Zen way to sleep soundly' and a third on 'Angels and Ghosts'. Both *The Mail* and *Express* in 2011 also continue to have a daily (non-hostile) astrology column almost rivalling in space their overall religious content (0.4 per cent for *The Express* and 0.5 per cent for *The Mail*).

Evidently interest in Christianity in 2011 was much lower in both of these newspapers than in the broadsheets. In 1969 it was quite low in *The Express*. However, in *The Mail* then it was almost double the present rate of interest and less concerned with either Islam or New Age religion. The marginal increase in interest in religion since 1990 does not reflect any raised interest specifically in Christianity within either of these family tabloids.

Pattern 4: Static Low Level Interest of Any Kind and Very Considerable Hostility

Trends evident in the family tabloids are enhanced strongly in the popular tabloids, *The Sun* and *The Star*. Their low level of overall interest in religion remains from 1990. *The Star* stays at 0.4 per cent overall religious content (the lowest for any of the newspapers surveyed) and *The Sun* has moved only from 0.5 to 0.6 per cent.

The Star was first published in 1978. It is possible to see the former *Sketch* as occupying a similar niche in 1969 (even though it was taken over by *The Mail*, whereas *The Star* was launched as a popular tabloid by the owners of *The Express*). On this assumption *The Sketch* had an overall religious content of 1 per cent in 1969, together with the highest proportion at the time of material deemed hostile (35 per cent). In *The Star* this overall level was less than half in 1990, while the material deemed hostile was a comparatively high 25 per cent. By 2011 the latter has raised very sharply indeed to 65 per cent (once more the highest level of any of the newspapers surveyed). Hostile material in *The Sun* changed more sharply in the earlier period (from 28 per cent in 1969 to 47 per cent in 1990) maintaining this high level today (49 per cent).

Both *The Sun* and *The Star* direct a considerable amount of hostility explicitly at Muslims. *The Star* headlines depict poppy burners as 'Muslim fanatics', 'shameless' and even 'vile Muslims'. In *The Sun* poppy burners are 'Muslim fanatics' and 'Muslim extremists', and it is a 'Muslim' who kills US airmen. Every letter published with religious content in either newspaper (1 per cent in *The Sun* and 3 per cent in *The Star*) is also about Muslims.

However, in common with *The Express* and *The Mail*, *The Sun* in 2011 also extends hostility to the Catholic, lay chaplain ('Jail "Rev" romp rap') and identifies the 'night stalker' as a Jehovah's Witness. In each of these popular tabloid newspapers it is not the largely ignored announcement of the Dalai Lama that causes its peak religious content, but rather long articles and editorials on the poppy burners, accompanied on the same day in *The Sun* by an article by Archbishop John Sentamu defending St George (a religious peak amounting to 3.2 per cent for *The Sun* and 2.2 per cent for *The Star*). This defence of St George, together with a comparison of Cardinal Keith O'Brien with Baroness Warsi and a mention of Cliff Richard's Christian faith is most of what a reader of *The Sun* would discover about Christianity during this period. Readers of *The Star* would similarly learn that David Beckham has angel tattoos and that there is a book claiming that 'Jesus can cure gays'.

Even New Age material is largely confined to the daily astrology columns in both newspapers. In terms of overall space these astrology columns represent 0.5 per cent in *The Sun* and a remarkable 0.9 per cent in *The Star*. So the newspaper with the lowest overall religious content, the highest percentage of material deemed hostile to religion, and a tendency to ignore most items of news relating to Christianity (hostile or non-hostile), now gives more than twice as much space to astrology as it does to religious issues in any form.

Tensions between these Four Patterns

It is worth emphasizing again that this is not an attempt to assess the social significance of newspapers – for example, trying to assess whether they facilitate or deflect some process of secularization. Nor it is it an attempt to measure secularization or persistence. It is an attempt instead to offer under-explored clues about differing perceptions of social context. Journalists act as professional filters of particular perceptions aimed at different markets. Manifestly the perceptions emerging from these four patterns in the way that different printed newspapers represent religion in the world today have radical and unresolved internal tensions. Is religion a threat or a comfort in the modern world? Is Christianity worth reporting? If it is not, is this because it is fast disappearing in England or because it is simply part of the wallpaper? Is Islam to be demonized or integrated? Is New Age religion to be treated with any credence?

It is probably impossible to get widespread agreement on any of these questions. As a cultural paradigm predicts, with the long-term demise of religious socialization and belonging in Britain over the past century, it is only to be expected that religious believing is becoming increasingly fragmented. In this context the four patterns emerging from this newspaper survey may represent four distinctive paths in tension with each other. The newspapers themselves are consciously targeted at differing socio-economic, gender and even age groups. This of course is related to the density and level of language, the depth of analysis that they offer, the political bias they adopt and the pictures they use. Yet behind all of this, the different assumptions about religion in the modern world that they make may have much wider resonance.

As we have seen, four distinct religious types seem to be present: general persistence; considerably increased interest and hostility; marginally increased interest with New Age tendencies and greatly increased hostility; static low level interest of any kind and very considerable hostility. Hostility is present in three out of four of these types. This appears to be consonant with the rhetoric of the so-called 'new atheism' expressed particularly in Richard Dawkins' *The God Delusion*,[9]

---

[9]   Richard Dawkins, *The God Delusion*, London: Bantam Press, 2006 and Boston: Houghton Mifflin, 2008.

Christopher Hitchens' *God is Not Great: How Religion Poisons Everything*,[10] Sam Harris' *The End of Faith: Religion, Terror and the Future of Reason*[11] and (in more scholarly terms) Daniel Dennett's *The Breaking of the Spell: Religion as a Natural Phenomenon*.[12] The use of words such as 'delusion', 'poisons', 'spell' and 'terror' in the titles of these books clearly signals hostility. In sociological terms it represents an important shift from secularization theory more typical of the 1960s and 1970s. The latter was more akin to the assumptions about secularization, noted in the previous chapter, that characterized Weber and Durkheim – a regretful acceptance that religion (with its beneficial features of social cohesion and moral values) is simply disappearing from the modern world. In contrast, the new atheists more typically argue that religion, far from disappearing quietly, is still far too dominant and pernicious in the modern world. This latter perspective might more accurately be depicted as polemical secularism rather than secularization. Rather than regretting or simply noting the disappearance of religion, it strongly resents its persistence.

So is polemical secularism now the dominant culture in modern Britain? Is this what is reflected in the sort of hostility found in six out of eight of the 2011 newspapers surveyed? If a positive answer is given to both of these questions, then that would have very profound implications for the social context of theology in Britain today. It might well mean that those theologians today who construe their central task in terms of so-called 'culture wars' are justified. In the next chapter I will indeed analyse the work of Stanley Hauerwas and John Milbank in terms of a paradigm of culture wars.

However, before reaching this conclusion too readily, it is worth noting an important difference between the hostility found in the six newspapers and the hostility that is more typical of the new atheism. In stylised form the new atheism may be depicted in terms of a series of propositions:

1. We should govern our lives by reason (exemplified by science) not by faith.

---

[10] Christopher Hitchens, *God is Not Great: How Religion Poisons Everything*, London: Atlantic and New York: Warner, 2007.

[11] Sam Harris, *The End of Faith: Religion, Terror and the Future of Reason*, New York: Norton, 2004.

[12] Daniel Dennett, *The Breaking of the Spell: Religion as a Natural Phenomenon*, New York: Viking and London: Pelican, 2006.

2. Belief in God depends upon (blind) faith not reason.
3. Belief in God is a delusion.
4. All religion is a delusion.
5. Religion can be explained away by science.
6. Religion, since it is a demonstrable delusion, results in irrational behaviour.
7. Religion is especially dangerous because it causes war.
8. Religion poisons everything.
9. Humanity would be better off without religion.
10. Religion should be eliminated.

Of course this stylised form is much too crude to capture the arguments of all of the new atheists. Few might actually reach proposition 10. And Daniel Dennett, unlike Christopher Hitchens, would be unlikely to subscribe to proposition 8, since he concedes that 'there is growing evidence that many religions have succeeded remarkably well ... improving both the health and the morale of their members, quite independently of the good works that they have accomplished to benefit others'.[13] He does still wish to balance these benefits against harms caused by religions and to explore purely secular means of achieving the same benefits, but generally he avoids the more dogmatic negative claims made by other new atheists.

That point conceded, it is characteristic of all the new atheists (including Dennett) that they draw conclusions about religion or religions as a whole, whereas the six newspapers are predominantly hostile towards radical Islam (and, more occasionally, towards fundamentalist forms of Christianity). The 2011 survey of newspapers detected little or no hostility towards mainstream Christianity or to the Church of England in particular. If anything hostility in this form was more characteristic of the 1969 and 1990 surveys (although the coverage in 1990 of George Carey's appointment was largely benign). Nor were the 2011 newspapers hostile to the Dalai Lama and his form of Mahayana Buddhism. In terms of the 10 stylised propositions only a modified version of proposition 7 might resonate strongly in the six newspapers that expressed hostility – that is, hostility specifically directed at those forms of religion that promote acts of terrorism and violence.

---

[13]   Dennett, *The Breaking of the Spell*, p. 272.

Mark Juergensmeyer, with an early background in religious activism and journalism, approaches religiously inspired terrorism and violence in a manner more in line with the broadsheet newspapers than the new atheists. It has been seen that *The Times* and *The Independent*, especially, were both careful in 2011 not to express even this more specific form of hostility. Terrorists were typically depicted as 'terrorists' not as 'Muslim terrorists'. It was the broadsheets on the political left and right – *The Guardian* and *The Telegraph* – which characteristically and with apparent hostility identified this as a specifically Muslim issue. Juergensmeyer does discuss 'the global rise of religious violence' at length, interviewing in the process many of its perpetrators. However, he finally distances himself from confrontational and bellicose policies towards these perpetrators:

> The … scenario for peace is one in which the absolutism of the struggle is defused, and the religious aspects are taken out of politics and retired to the moral and metaphysical planes. As long as images of spiritual warfare remain strong in the minds of the religious activists and are linked with struggles in the social world around them, the scenarios we have just discussed – achieving an easy victory over religious activists, intimidating them into submission, or forging a compromise with them – are problematic at best. A more moderate view of the image of religious warfare has been conceived, one that is deflected away from political and social confrontation.[14]

He argues that this 'more moderate' view involves a recognition both that religion can contribute positively to public life (as the broadsheets generally acknowledge) and that religion should be tempered by the 'rationality and fair play' of the Enlightenment: 'religious violence cannot end until some accommodation can be forged between the two – some assertion of moderation in religion's passion, and some acknowledgement of religion in elevating the spiritual and moral values of public life'.[15]

---

[14]   Mark Juergensmeyer, *Terror in the Mind of God: The Global Rise of Religious Violence*, Berkeley, CA: University of California Press, 2000, pp. 240–241.

[15]   Juergensmeyer, *Terror*, p. 249. See also Andrew R. Murphy (ed.), *The Blackwell Companion to Religion and Violence*, Malden, MA and Oxford: Wiley-Blackwell, 2011, Part 5.

Another tension between the newspapers was between those that showed a renewed or ongoing interest in (non-Muslim) religious issues and those instead that were or remained largely indifferent to them. This was mainly a tension between the broadsheets and the tabloids. *The Times*, *The Independent*, *The Telegraph* and (unexpectedly) *The Guardian* all showed strong patterns of persisting or renewed interest. Only in *The Independent* did the proportional coverage drop between 1990 and 2011, but even after this drop the level was still comparatively high. In contrast, readers of *The Express*, *The Mail*, *The Sun* and *The Star* would have been hard pressed to have learned anything much about mainstream Christianity during the period surveyed in 2011. All were characterized by indifference. But again, this was not exactly the sort of *religious* indifference premised by secularization theory, since New Age issues were still in evidence alongside regular horoscopes. In 1990 and 2011 *The Star* showed itself to have the lowest level of interest in religious issues, allied to the highest level of hostility expressed on the few issues it actually reported, compared with any of the other newspapers surveyed. Yet, as has been seen, it also almost doubled the proportionate size of its astrology column in that same period of time. Here too this hardly fits the assumptions of the new atheists.

With the slow demise of Sunday schools in Britain following the first decade of the twentieth century (when they had involved a majority of children even in impoverished urban areas) and their widespread collapse in the 1960s, it may be guessed that many readers of *The Star* are several generations away from any formal religious socialization. The sociologist Christie Davies dramatically links this collapse with rising crime figures, prison populations, drug addiction and illegitimacy in Britain.[16] Whether or not all of these particular correlations can be sustained sociologically, it does seem plausible (given a cultural theory of religious change) that an erosion of religious socialization would be followed by increasing estrangement from mainstream religious institutions. Yet, unless this erosion is interpreted simply as being *caused by* some process of secularization, then it is possible that it would result not simply in secularity but also in non-

---

[16]   Christie Davies, *The Strange Death of Moral Britain*, London: Transaction Publishers, 2007.

institutionalized New Age forms of spirituality.[17] In addition, given the atrocities of 9/11 and 7/7 it may not be too surprising that a religiously unsocialized section of the population would increasingly view the religiously fervent with deep suspicion if not hostility. If that were the only social context of religion remaining in Britain today, the present social and theological assumptions of Stanley Hauerwas and John Milbank would be entirely understandable.

The next chapter will turn to them.

---

[17] Cf. Paul Heelas and Linda Woodhead et al., *The Spiritual Revolution: Why Religion is Giving Way to Spirituality*, Oxford: Blackwell, 2005.

Chapter 12

The Social Context of Virtue Ethics

The rise and growing dominance of virtue ethics within Christian ethics is particularly important for sociological theology as later volumes will seek to show. Church communities, together with the stories, beliefs and virtues that they contain within their worship and life, have received renewed attention. However, this interest in church communities has frequently been accompanied by a paradoxical bias – a bias towards idealized rather than actual church communities. Perhaps this bias was to be expected given such an emphasis upon communities that, in both the past and the present, have often appeared fragile and ambiguous. Yet idealized communities ill fit a virtue ethic whether Christian or secular. Such an ethic requires actual communities to mediate virtues and to shape moral character. Moreover, idealizing church communities generates a sharply polarized understanding of social context – an understanding that, in turn, fuels so-called culture wars.

The present chapter will set out these claims by taking an overview of the work of Stanley Hauerwas before turning once again to John Milbank. Among Christian ethicists in North America today Hauerwas is outstanding. He has had more influence and polarizes more opinions than any other Christian ethicist of his generation. Within the discipline, Alasdair MacIntyre and Charles Taylor[1] have both been highly influential as sympathetic philosophers. Yet, first in North America and now in Britain, it is the work of Hauerwas which is most widely read and discussed. In meetings of the American *Society of Christian Ethics* it is quite usual to find several papers analysing his work, with only occasional references to MacIntyre and Taylor. Even in Britain, as early as 1985 the American James Gustafson was surprised to find so much enthusiasm for his work among theologians from the Church of Scotland, the Church of England and the Roman Catholic Church. At the time he suggested to them that 'some thought be given to

---

[1]   See my *Health Care and Christian Ethics*, Cambridge: Cambridge University Press, 2006, ch. 1.

possible incongruities between the ecclesiology that is necessary for the sectarian ethics and ecclesiologies of these churches'.[2]

At the heart of Hauerwas' recent work there is a changing understanding of social context. There is a shift from actual to idealized Christian communities and an increasing sense of Christian distinctiveness over and against worldly secularity. In a careful and, in part, sympathetic critique of his contribution to Christian ethics, David Fergusson argues for 'a more ambivalent reading of the relationship between church and civil society than is suggested in Hauerwas'.[3] He is finally not convinced that churches are as distinctive as Hauerwas maintains or that all of the inheritance of secular liberalism and the Enlightenment is to be so thoroughly discarded:

> It is one thing to recognize the shortcoming and effects of liberalism, however, and another to appear to enter into wholesale condemnation. It is worth recalling in this context that the Enlightenment project did not simply spring from a misconceived epistemological programme but had its historical context in the religious wars of the seventeenth century. Liberalism was thus borne of a desire to establish a civil order which could unite competing religious factions on a moral ground which everyone could assent to independently of particular traditions.[4]

There seem to be at least three phases in Stanley Hauerwas' assumptions about the social context of Christian ethics. In his earliest work the emphasis is upon individual vision and character with a strong and acknowledged debt to the novelist and philosopher Iris Murdoch. This phase fits well the sort of continuities between the religious and secular apparent in *The Times* and *The Independent* today. In the middle phase of his work church communities become the primary carriers of Christian virtues, albeit with a recognition that secular communities may sometimes embed these virtues more clearly than actual churches. The sort

---

[2]   James Gustafson, 'The Sectarian Temptation', *Proceedings of the Catholic Theological Society of America*, 40, 1985, p. 84.

[3]   David A.S. Fergusson, *Community, Liberalism and Christian Ethics*, Cambridge: Cambridge University Press, 1998, p. 78.

[4]   Fergusson, p. 76. For a finely nuanced theological account of liberalism see Robert Song's *Christianity and Liberal Society*, Oxford: Clarendon Press, 1997.

of polarization detected in *The Telegraph* and *The Guardian* today fit this phase better. In his more recent work, churches (idealized if not actual) are seen as the sole repositories of Christian virtues and Christians are depicted as 'aliens' in what is now seen as a hostile world – a world akin, perhaps, to that typified by the tabloids today.

The earliest phase is seen clearly in Hauerwas' first book *Vision and Virtue*, published in 1974. There he depicts the task of Christian ethics as follows:

> Once ethics is focused on the nature and moral determination of the self, vision and virtue again become morally significant categories. We are as we come to see and as that seeing becomes enduring in our intentionality. We do not come to see, however, just by looking but by training our vision through the metaphors and symbols that constitute our central convictions. How we come to see therefore is a function of how we come to be since our seeing necessarily is determined by how our basic images are embodied by the self – that is, in our character. Christian ethics is the conceptual discipline that analyses and imaginatively tests the images most appropriate to score the Christian life in accordance with the central conviction that the world has been redeemed by the work and person of Christ.[5]

He sets out this understanding of Christian ethics more fully the following year in *Character and the Christian Life*.[6] It already contains some of the enduring features of his thought, as well as some clear elements which he later modifies. Enduring features include an emphasis upon virtue, character and moral training as crucial for Christian ethics rather than upon moral decision-making as such. There is a stress upon the Christian life and the centrality of Christology and Atonement for this life. The concept of moral vision does not altogether disappear in his later work, but it does receive less emphasis. At this stage the influence of Iris Murdoch is openly acknowledged and, indeed, some of her Platonism may be evident in his language. Writing at the time I noted that Hauerwas tended to use philosophy in addition to theology to illuminate his understanding of the task of Christian ethics, but that he might also have used sociology since 'the latter could

---

[5]   Stanley Hauerwas, *Vision and Virtue*, Notre Dame, IN: Fides Press, 1974, p. 2.

[6]   San Antonio, TX: Trinity University Press, 1975.

analyse the images actually used by Christians in their moral lives and suggest ways in which these images are determined or determinative'.[7]

A decade later Hauerwas recognizes that 'though I had stressed the relational character of the self, this is not sufficient to indicate the centrality of a particular community called the church for the development of the kind of character required of Christians'.[8] From this point onwards in his writings he repeatedly makes reference to the church as the Christian community from which individual Christians learn and are shaped by Christian virtues. So at the outset of his important theoretical book *A Community of Character: Toward a Constructive Christian Social Ethic* he now depicts Christian ethics as follows:

> The justification for calling this book 'social ethics' is that I wish to show why any consideration of the truth of Christian convictions cannot be divorced from the kind of community the church is and should be ... my primary interest is to challenge the church to regain a sense of the significance of the polity that derives from convictions peculiar to Christians ... if the church is to serve our liberal society or any society, it is crucial for Christians to regain an appropriate sense of separateness from that society ... such a 'separateness' may involve nothing more nor less than the Christian community's willingness to provide hospitality for the stranger – particularly when that stranger so often comes in the form of our own children.[9]

With the focus evident here upon the role of the church in Christian ethics, there is also a conviction that church polity should derive from distinctively Christian beliefs. In turn, this suggests that the church should have a sense of 'separateness' from the world. It is precisely this new element of 'separateness' in his thought which soon gave rise to the charge of 'sectarianism', evident in the quotation from Gustafson. David Fergusson is not convinced about this charge, pointing out that Hauerwas, unlike a radical sectarian, is still concerned 'to serve our

---

[7]   See my *Theology and Social Structure*, Oxford: Mowbrays, 1977, p. 117.

[8]   From the introduction to the 1985 re-issue of *Character and the Christian Life*, p. xxxi.

[9]   Stanley Hauerwas, *A Community of Character: Toward a Constructive Christian Social Ethic*, Notre Dame, IN: University of Notre Dame, 1981, pp. 1–2.

liberal society'.[10] Hauerwas is not, for example, suggesting that the church should simply withdraw wholly from the world as the Exclusive Brethren have done or even denounce the world totally as the Jehovah's Witnesses have done. At this stage 'separateness' seems to require a resolute distinctiveness but not the radical exclusivity of some sects (although, even here, many sociologists have followed Bryan Wilson's influential classification of sects[11] which includes many less radical positions). The fact that Hauerwas continues to write in such areas as medical ethics and to speak to professionals within these areas might support Fergusson.

Nonetheless, the language of 'the stranger' now emerges in his writings, as well as an increasing dichotomy between the church and what he views (and decries) as 'liberal society'. Accompanying this dichotomy is also an ambivalence about whether or not he is talking about the church as it is or the church as it ought to be. Sometimes it does appear to be the former. This allows him to suggest what almost looks like an empirical test of his understanding of Christian ethics. So he writes:

> All politics should be judged by the character of the people it produces. The depth and variety of character which a polity sustains is a correlative of the narrative that provides its identity and purpose. The contention and witness of the church is that the story of Jesus provides a flourishing of gifts which other politics cannot know. It does so because Christians have been nourished on the story of a savior who insisted on being nothing else than what he was. By being the son of God he provided us with the confidence that insofar as we become his disciples our particularity and our regard for the particularity of our brothers and sisters in Christ contribute to his Kingdom. Our stories become part of the story of the Kingdom.[12]

---

[10] Fergusson, *Community*, p. 76f. See also Oliver O'Donovan, *The Desire of Nations: Rediscovering the Roots of Political Theology*, Cambridge: Cambridge University Press, 1996, pp. 215–217, who depicts Hauerwas' position as 'a kind of return to the catacombs' rather than 'sectarianism'.

[11] For example Bryan Wilson, *Religion in Sociological Perspective*, Oxford: Clarendon Press, 1982, and *The Social Dimension of Sectarianism*, Oxford: Clarendon Press, 1990.

[12] Hauerwas, *A Community of Character*, p. 51.

Only the words 'insofar as we become his disciples' in this quotation raise doubts. Otherwise this does seem to be a statement about the empirical church. It is this church which carries the Christian narrative which, in turn, can nourish Christians and provide evidence to the world at large of the Christian character. Sociology might well have an important role in assessing the fruits of such nourishing. Yet even here Hauerwas leaves this escape clause. It could just be that an analysis of actual churchgoers would be flawed because some of them had not truly 'become his disciples'.

Herein lies the problem for Hauerwas now. He sees the church as the locus of Christian community, as the bearer of the unique Christian story, and thus as the agent of Christian socialization. It should, then, be possible for others outside the church to see clearly the fruits of this socialization. Yet he is aware of the obvious limitations and fragilities of actual church congregations:

> But we must admit the church has not been a society of trust and virtue. At most, people identify the church as a place where the young learn 'morals', but the 'morals' often prove to be little more than conventional pieties coupled with a few unintelligible 'don'ts'. Therefore any radical critique of our secular polity requires an equally radical critique of the church.[13]

In *The Peaceable Kingdom*, written two years later, his criticisms of the church as it is are far more trenchant. Here he insists that 'what makes the church the church is its faithful manifestation of the peaceable kingdom in the world ... the church must never cease from being a community of peace and truth in a world of mendacity and fear'.[14] Given such a high understanding of the church, it is hardly surprising that Hauerwas immediately sees that the empirical church, past or present, can hardly be depicted in such terms. Instead he adds:

> The scandal of the disunity of the church is even more painful when we recognize this social task. For we who have been called to be the foretaste of the peaceable

---

    [13]   Hauerwas, *A Community of Character*, p. 86.

    [14]   Stanley Hauerwas, *The Peaceable Kingdom: A Primer of Christian Ethics*, Notre Dame, IN: University of Notre Dame Press, 1983, and London: SCM Press, 1984, pp. 99–100.

kingdom cannot, it seems, maintain unity among ourselves ... And the divisions I speak of in the church are not just those based on doctrine, history, or practices important though they are. No, the deep and most painful divisions afflicting the church are those based on class, race, and nationality that we have sinfully accepted as written into the nature of things.[15]

It would seem from this quotation that the church (as it is) is quite a long way away from the 'peaceable kingdom' which he regards as essential to the church (as it ought to be). He even adds that we may 'find that people who are not Christians manifest God's peace better than ourselves'.[16] Confusingly, though, in terms of virtue ethics it is presumably communities as they are which actually nourish their members. People may, of course, be inspired by depictions of how their particular community ought to be. Yet, as I argued in Chapter 10, it is actual, existing communities that are their primary means of socialization. At one point in *The Peaceable Kingdom* Hauerwas himself seems to recognize this when he argues that 'people in a community must learn to trust one another as well as trust the community itself ... all communities require a sense of hope in the future and they witness to the necessity of love for sustaining relationships'. He adds that 'there is a profound sense in which the traditional "theological virtues" of faith, hope, and love are "natural"'. He even believes that 'as much as any institution the church is sustained by these "natural virtues"', even though it is not the case that 'what is meant by faith, hope, and love is the same for Christians as for other people'.[17]

Hauerwas again faces an obvious dilemma. The church as it ought to be can enshrine Christian virtues properly, but unfortunately it cannot socialize Christians in the actual world. The church as it is can indeed socialize Christians, but sadly it does not enshrine Christian virtues properly. Of course there could be a church just around the corner which manages to do both ... but after 2,000 years this has yet to happen.

At times Hauerwas is painfully honest. In the introduction to *A Community of Character* he acknowledges that 'perhaps the reason I stress so strongly the significance of the church for social ethics is that I am currently not disciplined

---

[15]   Hauerwas, *The Peaceable Kingdom*, p. 100.

[16]   Hauerwas, *The Peaceable Kingdom*, p. 101.

[17]   Hauerwas, *The Peaceable Kingdom*, p. 103.

by, nor do I feel the ambiguity of, any concrete church. I find I must think and write not only for the church that does exist but for the church that should exist if we were more courageous and faithful'.[18] Two years later in *The Peaceable Kingdom* he makes a point of noting that this issue has been resolved – dedicating the book to his new-found Methodist congregation. Despite this new community, it is difficult to imagine that even it provided him with an adequate empirical basis for his notion of the 'peaceable kingdom'. Methodists have seldom been able to unite behind the sort of radical pacifism espoused by Hauerwas. Even the ideas expressed in some of his medically related books, such as the finely nuanced *Suffering Presence*[19] or *Naming the Silences*,[20] still seem to imply a more alienated church context than Methodism typically provides.

By the time the third phase of his writing is reached it is difficult to avoid David Fergusson's suggestion that:

> ... this church advocated by Hauerwas nowhere exists. It is a fantasy community, the conception of which fails to reflect the ways in which the members of the church are also positioned within civil society. It does not correspond to any visible communities within the *oekumene*.[21]

The publication, with William Willimon, of *Resident Aliens: Life in the Christian Colony*[22] in 1989 decisively marks the start of this phase. Subsequent publications, including *Against the Nations*,[23] *Dispatches from the Front*[24] and *Where Resident Aliens Live*,[25] have re-enforced it. Characteristic of this phase is an increase in hyperbole in Hauerwas' writing. Even the titles of these books reflect this hyperbole – a feature which is only very occasionally acknowledged by Hauerwas himself.[26]

---

[18] Hauerwas, *A Community of Character*, p. 6.

[19] Notre Dame, IN: University of Notre Dame Press, 1986, and Edinburgh: T&T Clark, 1988.

[20] Grand Rapids, MI: Eerdmans, 1990.

[21] Fergusson, p. 66.

[22] Nashville, TN: Abingdon Press, 1989.

[23] Notre Dame, IN: University of Notre Press, 1992.

[24] Durham, NC: Duke University Press, 1995.

[25] Nashville, TN: Abingdon Press, 1996 (again with William H. Willimon).

[26] For example Hauerwas, *Resident Aliens*, p. 165.

It is this increase in hyperbole which may tend to polarize other Christian ethicists. It coincided with Hauerwas' move from the Catholic University of Notre Dame to the Methodist Duke University. Perhaps he felt less constrained within this new environment or perhaps he had fewer colleagues to remind him of continuities between Christian and secular communities (as a natural law approach would suggest). Perhaps his increasing fame encouraged him to heighten his theories. Or perhaps it was a natural, polemical response to the criticism of sectarianism that was gaining currency.[27] Whatever the reason, his theories become increasingly exaggerated and distorted and less subject to any kind of empirical check. He also became a player in what has sometimes been termed 'culture wars'.

A careful reading of *Resident Aliens* makes this clear. Of course it is written in a more popular format than his other books and it is also co-authored. Nevertheless it accurately represents Hauerwas' views in this third phase. The dichotomy between the church and the world has become sharper, with the church increasingly idealized and the world demonized. Liberal theologians are reminded at length about the liberal accommodation with the Nazis, with strong warnings to 'those who take the same path, hoping to update the church, to recover some of the scandal of Jesus by identifying the church with the newest secular solution: Marxism, Feminism, the Sexual Revolution'.[28] In earlier books Hauerwas praises the work of H. Richard Niebuhr,[29] but now *Resident Aliens* states that 'we have come to believe that few books have been a greater hindrance to an accurate assessment of our situation than *Christ and Culture*'.[30] Pastors are told that 'if we live as a colony of resident aliens within a hostile environment, which, in the most subtle but deadly of ways, corrupts and co-opts us as Christians, then the pastor is called to help us gather the resources we need to be the colony of God's righteousness'.[31] The dichotomy is indeed sharp:

> Life in the colony is not a settled affair. Subject to constant attacks upon and
> sedition against its most cherished virtues, always in danger of losing its young,
> regarded as a threat by an atheistic culture, which in the name of freedom and

---

[27] For example see the introduction to *Against the Nations*.

[28] Hauerwas, *Resident Aliens*, p. 27.

[29] For example in Hauerwas, *The Peaceable Kingdom*.

[30] Hauerwas, *Resident Aliens*, p. 40.

[31] Hauerwas, *Resident Aliens*, pp. 139–140.

equality subjugates everyone – the Christian colony can be appreciated by its members as a challenge.[32]

The image of 'resident aliens' was doubtless chosen for its impact and may have been responsible more than anything else for its sales. Yet it is an image which effectively removes the church from reality. By the time of his Gifford Lectures, *With the Grain of the Universe*, Stanley Hauerwas tends to use the term 'witness' rather than 'resident aliens'. Although this new term appears less provocative, it is still framed by hyperbole when he reaches the concluding lecture 'The Necessity of Witness':

> Does the truth of Christian convictions depend on the faithfulness of the church and, if so, how do we determine what would constitute faithfulness? Am I suggesting that the ability of the church to be or not to be nonviolent is constitutive for understanding what it might mean to claim that Christian convictions are true? Do I think the truthfulness of Christian witness is compromised when Christians accept the practices of the 'culture of death' – abortion, suicide, capital punishment, and war? Yes! On every count, the answer is 'Yes'.[33]

He consciously borrows the term 'culture of death' here from Pope John Paul II but adds 'war' (without any qualification) and omits hormonal and barrier contraception as his examples of this culture. Nevertheless he identifies with Pope John Paul II as someone who is a 'witness' against 'the death that grips the life of the world'.[34] Once again this is viewed as a deeply hostile world.

Augustine's image of the 'pilgrim' church would have been distinctly less sensational than either 'resident alien' or 'witness' (in the way that Hauerwas uses the term) and would have allowed some check against the church as it is. It would also have allowed an understanding of social context that is not confined to the narrowly hostile types noted in the previous chapter – whether they are the

---

[32] Hauerwas, *Resident Aliens*, p. 51.

[33] Stanley Hauerwas, *With the Grain of the Universe: The Church's Witness and Natural Theology*, Grand Rapids, MI: Brazos Press, 2001 and London: SCM Press, 2002, p. 231.

[34] Hauerwas, *With the Grain*, p. 230.

particular hostilities detected in a number of newspapers today or the more radical hostilities of the new atheists.

On a broader theological understanding of social context there is still a sense in which a church is properly seen as being in this world but not of this world. Pilgrims are clearly still part of this world, yet they have their sight set steadily beyond this world. At certain periods of history pilgrims have even dressed distinctively and travelled to dangerous and distant places, leaving home and work for long periods of time. Even then they have typically relied upon the charity and hospitality of those who are not pilgrims. However, 'aliens', especially, whether in the older American form of resident foreigners or in the newer film form of visitors from other galaxies, are radical outsiders in a hostile world. They may take our guise but this is just a veneer since, in reality, they are unlike us.

In *Churchgoing and Christian Ethics*[35] I argued that a radically polarized depiction simply does not match detailed empirical data about churchgoers as they are. Churchgoers do have distinctive beliefs, values and practices, but their distinctiveness is relative not absolute. Many non-churchgoers share their beliefs, values and practices (apart from churchgoing itself), even though these are found more among churchgoers than among non-churchgoers. This detailed empirical data helps to settle a theoretical debate which I have outlined elsewhere[36] and to which I will return in the next volumes. I suggested that three distinct positions that have been adopted, within both philosophical and theological discussions, about the status of moral communities in relation to postmodernism.

The first is the most radical. It argues that legitimation is only possible within cultural-linguistic communities and that such communities are incapable of mutual communication. Precisely because the independent 'planks' offered by modernity (notably autonomous rational thought and empirical demonstration) have now been deconstructed, moral values or virtues can only be known within specific communities. We live in polarized communities that can either ignore each other or else fight culture wars. This seems to be the position now taken by Stanley Hauerwas.

---

[35] Cambridge: Cambridge University Press, 1999.

[36] See my *Moral Leadership in a Postmodern Age*, Edinburgh: T&T Clark, 1997, pp. 67f.

The second maintains that communities can communicate with each other precisely because individuals in the West today typically belong to more than one community. In his writings since *After Virtue*[37] Alasdair MacIntyre has sought to trace ways in which communities overlap and in which legitimation may sometimes decline in one at the expense of another. Jonathan Sacks is also an able theological exponent of the moral implications of simultaneously belonging to two communities – in his case those of a pluralist society and a traditional Jewish community.[38]

A third response to postmodernism accepts the general position that moral values and virtues are shaped, sustained and carried in communities, but argues that there *are* some moral 'planks' that apply across cultures.

Whether the second or third position is finally adopted, the first does seem to run contrary to the churchgoing data.

The combination of hyperbole, an idealized church and a demonized secular culture – all of which feature strongly in the first position – can be found in the writings of a number of theologians influenced by Hauerwas' writing. It is now quite common to hear theologians talking with disdain about 'the Enlightenment project' or about 'liberal culture' and contrasting this with '*the* radical Christian alternative'. As has been noted at several points already, such a perspective received powerful expression in John Milbank's *Theology and Social Theory*, especially in his hyperbolic claim: 'I am going to show how all twentieth-century sociology of religion can be exposed as a secular policing of the sublime … deconstructed in this fashion, the entire subject evaporates into the pure ether of the secular will-to-power'.[39] A number of critics have objected to such polarization.[40] Richard Roberts, for example, argues:

---

[37]   Alasdair MacIntyre, *After Virtue: a Study in Moral Theory*, London: Duckworth, 2nd edition, 1985 and 'A Partial Response to my Critics', in John Horton and Susan Mendus (eds), *After MacIntyre: Critical Perspectives on the Work of Alasdair MacIntyre*, Oxford: Polity Press and Notre Dame, IN: University of Notre Dame Press, 283–304, 1994.

[38]   Jonathan Sacks, *The Persistence of Faith*, London: Weidenfeld & Nicholson, 1992 and *Faith in the Future*, London: Darton, Longman & Todd, 1995.

[39]   John Milbank, *Theology and Social Theory: Beyond Secular Reason*, Oxford: Blackwell, 1990, p. 106.

[40]   For example David Martin's *Reflections on Sociology and Theology*, Oxford: Clarendon Press, 1996, p. 8f.

Milbank posits an abstract, quasi-mechanical (yet mutually involuted) opposition of false alternatives which entails abuse of both 'theology' and 'social theory'. In effect, both 'theology' and 'social theory' (equivalent for present purposes to the social sciences) are reduced to the *rhetorics* embedded in and expressive of cultural practices in a way that universalizes Nietzschian perspectivism... The tasks of theology and sociology are mutual in at least as much as they address the human condition in exploratory and interpretative terms, and do not subsume (in however virtuoso a fashion) *everything* into the dance of death and totalitarian logic of Western secular reason. Moreover, sociology and theology which embody concerns for the other cannot afford to neglect or express contempt for ethnography, that is, the effective representation and interpretation of what is actually happening in human lives. Both theology and the social sciences should be concerned in their distinctive ways with life and with how things are.[41]

Others have criticized Milbank's *Theology and Social Theory* precisely because the central picture of the church that it presents is idealized and even misleading. So, Rowan Williams recognizes the power of Milbank's book while regarding its idealization as less than helpful. For Williams 'the insistence on thinking Christ in inseparable relation with the Church is … one of the most important constructive elements of the book', while at the same time 'the risk Milbank's exposition runs is, rather paradoxically, of slipping into a picture of history as the battlefield of ideal types.'[42] Williams is, perhaps, too polite to call this 'culture wars' but the word 'battlefield' hints in this direction. More specifically, he believes that Milbank's account of the 'peace of the Church' (sharing many similarities with Hauerwas' *The Peaceable Kingdom*) pays too little attention to how this peace is historically and socially constructed.'[43]

Aidan Nichols is less polite in his criticism:

---

[41]   Richard H. Roberts, 'Theology and the Social Sciences', in David F. Ford and Rachel Muers (eds), *The Modern Theologians*, Oxford: Blackwell, 3rd edition, 2005, pp. 380–381.

[42]   Rowan Williams, 'Saving Time: Thoughts on Practice, Patience and Vision', *New Blackfriars*, 73:861, 319–326, June 1992.

[43]   See also Duncan B. Forrester, *Christian Justice and Public Policy*, Cambridge: Cambridge University Press, 1997, p. 244 and *Forrester on Christian Ethics and Practical Theology: Collected Writings on Christianity, India, and the Social Order*, Farnham: Ashgate, 2010, pp. 187, 207 and 276.

Despite the numerous true judgments, good maxims and beautiful insights to be found scattered through this book, its overall message is deplorable. My objections can be summed up in two words: 'hermeticism' and 'theocracy'. By 'hermeticism' I mean the enclosure of Christian discourse and practice within a wholly separate universe of thought and action, a universe constituted by the prior 'mythos' of Christianity. For Milbank there can be no such thing as an intellectual indebtedness of the Church to natural wisdom. Every putative thought of such wisdom as can be named is not extraneous to the Christian *mythos*, and without a role in the dramatic narrative, from Genesis to Apocalypse, in which that *mythos* is expressed. Also, all natural wisdom is legitimately liable to deconstruction. Only the Christian *mythos*, the Christian narrative, the Christian (ecclesial) community, can secure the human good – the beautiful pattern of living – which always eludes the secular ruler's grasp. Milbank's social programme is ... theocratic in that ... it seeks to restore Christendom. Unfortunately Milbank goes too far: in attempting to persuade to the faith of the Great Church it damages it, and not with some light scar but a grave wound.[44]

What is striking (and shocking) about this trenchant verdict is that Nichols identifies in Milbank's work the two features that I have argued in Chapter 8 are key to modern fundamentalism. Even if it is typically more militant and invariably more simplistic than Milbank, modern fundamentalism, in its different and various forms, does have a strong sense of counterculture and theological absolutism. Indeed this absolutism is upheld as a counter to modernity. Perhaps the charge of sectarianism that is so often levelled at Milbank and Hauerwas does after all contain a grain of truth.

In his response to these two critics, Milbank agrees that 'between my 'formal' or ideal descriptions of the Church (of an 'ideal' happening, and 'ideal' yet real, if vestigial transmission) and rather minimal attempts at 'judicious narrative', there may exist a certain tension'.[45]

---

[44]   Aidan Nichols, 'Non Tali Auxilio: John Milbank's Suasion to Orthodoxy', *New Blackfriars*, 73:861, 326–332, June 1992. See also Gregory Baum, *Essays in Critical Theology*, Kansas City: Sheed and Ward, 1994, p. 70, and Ian S. Markham, *Plurality and Christian Ethics*, Cambridge: Cambridge University Press, 1994, p. 146.

[45]   John Milbank, 'Enclaves, or Where is the Church?', *New Blackfriars*, 73:861, 341–352, June 1992.

This admission, although soon forgotten by Milbank,[46] raises again the issue of whether the focus in virtue ethics is primarily upon churches and churchgoers as they are or as they should be. For much of the time in both Milbank's *Theology and Social Theory* and in Hauerwas and Willimon's *Resident Aliens* it seems to be upon the latter. Nevertheless there are occasional indications in *Resident Aliens* that a virtue ethic does require a depiction of churchgoers as they are. Christian discipling of the young, for example, does seem to need the presence of actual, rather than idealized, 'saints':

> Christian ethics is, in the Aristotelian sense, an aristocratic ethic. It is not
> something that comes naturally. It can be learned. We are claiming, then, that a
> primary way of learning to be disciples is by being in contact with others who
> are disciples. So an essential role of the church is to put us in contact with those
> ethical aristocrats who are good at living the Christian faith. One role of any
> colony is to keep the young very close to the leaders – people who live aright the
> traditions of home. There is no substitute for living around other Christians.[47]

In line with virtue ethics, *Resident Aliens* recognizes that 'all ethics, even non-Christian ethics, makes sense only when embodied in sets of social practices that constitute a community ... such communities support a sense of right and wrong'.[48] Manifestly these must be actual and not purely idealized communities. Doubtless utopian images do have an important correcting and visionary function in many communities,[49] but it is difficult to see how they can act as primary means of socialization. In *Resident Aliens* there is also a clear recognition that actual communities can be dysfunctional: 'in a world like ours, people will be attracted to communities that promise them an easy way out of loneliness, togetherness based on common tastes, racial or ethnic traits, or mutual self-interest ... there

---

[46]   See John Milbank, 'Theology and the Economy of the Sciences' in Mark Thiessen Nation and Samuel Wells (eds), *Faithfulness and Fortitude: In Conversation with the Theological Ethics of Stanley Hauerwas*, Edinburgh: T&T Clark, 39–57, 2000. Interestingly Hauerwas (*With the Grain*, p. 233n) dissents from the 'stronger position' that Milbank takes there.

[47]   Hauerwas, *Resident Aliens*, p. 102.

[48]   Hauerwas, *Resident Aliens*, p. 79.

[49]   Cf. Karl Mannheim's classic *Ideology and Utopia*, London: Routledge & Kegan Paul, 1936.

is then little check on community becoming as tyrannical as the individual ego'. In contrast, Christian community is 'about disciplining our wants and needs in congruence with a true story, which gives us the resources to lead truthful lives'.[50] Both in Christian and in non-Christian contexts here, a process of socialization seems to be envisaged which involves empirical communities.

Now, of course, there is a proper theological concern with the church as it ought to be. All thoughtful theologians, from the beginning of Christianity, have recognized as much. This is not my point. Rather it is that the specifically sociological insight of virtue ethics is that the moral life is shaped by particular communities despite their actual frailties and ambiguities. Whereas there has been a tendency for moral philosophy to focus upon ethical decision-making as if individuals could act solely on the basis of autonomous reasoning, virtue ethics is more distinctly sociological in character. If MacIntyre has drawn particular attention to virtues as they are carried and nurtured within overlapping communities, Charles Taylor focuses more upon the tradition and community based antecedents of apparently autonomous choices. However, both philosophers have, in effect, a strong sense of the sociology of knowledge. Moral notions are socially generated and – even when this is not realized by the participants themselves – rely upon specific communities for their support.

Given this understanding, a sociological examination of specific moral communities becomes important – unless these communities are so idealized that they bear little relationship to empirical communities. Whereas many moral philosophers are interested in little other than the rational criteria used within ethical decision-making, virtue ethicists such as MacIntyre have an additional interest in social structures. Within virtue ethics, properly understood, the mechanisms of socialization become at least as important as formal rational criteria. An adequate understanding of social context is thus indispensible for virtue ethics properly understood.

This point forms a natural bridge to Volume 2. My task there is to explore ways that theology is shaped by society.

---

50   Hauerwas, *Resident Aliens*, p. 78.

Works Cited

Acquaviva, S.S., *The Decline of the Sacred in Industrial Society*, New York: Harper & Row, 1979 [Italian original 1966].

Algar, Hamid, *The Roots of the Islamic Revolution*, London: Open Press, The Muslim Institute, 1983.

Argyle, Michael, *Religious Behaviour*, London: Routledge & Kegan Paul, 1958.

Baker, Chris and Jonathan Miles-Watson, 'Faith and Traditional Capitals: Defining the Public Scope of Spiritual and Religious Capital – a Literature Review', *Implicit Religion*, 13:1, 17–69, 2010.

Barbour, Ian G., *Issues in Science and Religion*, New York: Prentice Hall and London: SCM Press, 1966.

——*Religion in an Age of Science*, San Francisco: Harper and London: SCM Press, 1990.

——*Religion and Science: Historical and Contemporary Issues*, San Francisco: Harper and London: SCM Press, 1997.

Barnsley, John H., *The Social Reality of Ethics*, London: Routledge & Kegan Paul, 1972.

Baron, Stephen, John Field and Tom Schuller (eds), *Social Capital: Critical Perspectives*, Oxford: Oxford University Press, 2000.

Barr, James, *Fundamentalism*, London: SCM Press, 1981.

Barry, F.R., *Secular and Supernatural*, London: SCM Press, 1969.

Barton, John (ed.), *The Cambridge Companion to Biblical Interpretation*, Cambridge: Cambridge University Press, 1998.

Bartsch, H.V. (ed.), *Kerygma and Myth*, vol. 1, London: SPCK, 1953.

Baum, Gregory, *Religion and Alienation: A Theological Reading of Sociology*, New York: Paulist Press, 1975 [reprinted Ottawa: Novalis, 2006].

——*The Social Imperative: Essays on the Critical Issues that Confront the Christian Churches*, New York: Paulist Press, 1979.

——*Theology and Society*, New York: Paulist Press, 1986.

——*Essays in Critical Theology*, Kansas City, MO: Sheed and Ward, 1994.

Beckford, James, *Cult Controversies: The Societal Response to the New Religious Movements*, London: Tavistock, 1985.

——*Religion and Advanced Industrial Society*, London: Unwin Hyman, 1989.

——with Thomas Luckmann (eds), *The Changing Face of Religion*, London: Sage, 1989.

——with Sophie Gilliat, *Religion in Prison: Equal Rites in a Multi-Faith Society*, Cambridge: Cambridge University Press, 1998.

Bellah, Robert N., *Beyond Belief*, New York: Harper & Row, 1970.

Berger, Peter L., *The Precarious Vision*, New York: Doubleday, 1961.

——*The Social Reality of Religion*, London: Faber & Faber, 1969 [US title, *The Sacred Canopy of Religion*, Garden City, NY: Doubleday, 1967].

——*A Rumour of Angels*, Garden City, NY: Doubleday, 1969 and Harmondsworth, Middlesex: Penguin, 1970.

——*Facing up to Modernity: Excursions in Society, Politics and Religion*, New York: Basic Books and London: Penguin, 1977.

——*The Heretical Imperative: Contemporary Possibilities of Religious Affirmation*, New York: Anchor, 1979 and London: Collins, 1980.

——*A Far Glory: The Quest for Faith in an Age of Credulity*, New York: Anchor Books, 1992.

——(ed.), *The Desecularization of the World*, Grand Rapids, MI: Eerdmans, 1999.

Bhardwaj, S.M. and G. Rinschede (eds), *Pilgrimage in World Religions: Geographia Religionum, Interdisziplinare Schriftenreihe zur Religionsgeographie*, Band 4, Berlin: Dietrich Reimer Verlag, 1988.

Black, Max, *Models and Metaphors*, Ithaca, NY: Cornell University Press, 1962.

Boulard, Ferdinand, *An Introduction to Religious Sociology*, London: Darton, Longman & Todd, 1960.

Bouma, Gary D., 'Recent "Protestant Ethic" Research', *Journal for the Scientific Study of Religion*, 21:2, 141–155, 1973.

——with Beverly R. Dixon, *The Religious Factor in Australian Life*, World Vision and the Zadok Centre: MARC Australia, 1986.

Bowden, John, *Karl Barth*, London: SCM Press, 1971.

Bowker, John, *The Sense of God*, Oxford: Oxford University Press, 1973.

Brewer, John D., 'Sociology and its strange "others": introduction', *History of the Human Sciences*, 20:2, 1–5, 2007.

——'Sociology and theology reconsidered: religious sociology and the sociology of religion in Britain', *History of the Human Sciences*, 20:2, 7–28, 2007.

Brown, Callum, *The Death of Christian Britain*, London: Routledge, 2001.

——with Michael Snape (eds), *Secularisation in the Christian World*, Farnham: Ashgate, 2010.

Brown, Judith Anne, *John Marco Allegro: The Maverick of the Dead Sea Scrolls*, Grand Rapids, MI: Eerdmans, 2005.

Bruce, Steve, *The Rise and Fall of the New Christian Right: Protestant Politics in America 1978–88*, Oxford: Clarendon, 1988.

——*Religion in the Modern World: From Cathedrals to Cults*, Oxford: Oxford University Press, 1996.

——*Choice and Religion: A Critique of Rational Choice Theory*, Oxford: Oxford University Press, 1999.

——*God is Dead: Secularization in the West*, Oxford, UK and Malden, MS: Blackwell Publishers, 2002.

——*Politics and Religion*, Oxford: Polity Press, 2003.

——*Secularization: In Defence of an Unfashionable Theory*, Oxford; Oxford University Press, 2011.

Buren, Paul van, *The Secular Meaning of the Gospel*, London: SCM Press, 1963.

Cairns, David, 'Peter Berger', *Scottish Journal of Theology*, 27:2, 1974.

Caplan, L. (ed.), *Studies in Religious Fundamentalism*, Albany, NY: State University of New York Press, 1987.

Carroll, Robert P., 'Ancient Israelite Prophecy and Dissonance Theory', *Numen*, 24: 2, 135–151, 1977–78.

——*When Prophecy Failed: Reactions and Responses to Failure in the Old Testament Prophetic Tradition*, London: SCM Press, 1979.

Casanova, José, *Public Religions in the Modern World*, Chicago: University of Chicago Press, 1994.

Childress, James F. and David B. Harned (eds), *Secularization and the Protestant Prospect*, New York: Louisville, KY: Westminster Press, 1970.

Cohen, Percy S., *Modern Social Theory*, London: Heinemann, 1968.

Cox, Harvey, *The Secular City*, New York: Macmillan, 1965 and London: Pelican, 1968.

——'The Prophetic Purpose of Theology', in Dean Peerman (ed.), *Frontline Theology*, London: SCM Press, 1969.

——*The Feast of Fools*, Cambridge, MS: Harvard University Press, 1969.

——*Religion in the Secular City: Toward a Postmodern Theology*, New York: Simon & Schuster, 1984.

——*The Silencing of Leonardo Boff*, Yorktown Heights, NY: Meyer-Stone, 1988.

Davie, Grace, *Religion in Britain Since 1945: Believing Without Belonging*, Oxford: Blackwell, 1994.

——*Religion in Modern Europe: A Memory Mutates*, Oxford: Oxford University Press, 2000.

——*Europe: The Exceptional Case*, London: Darton, Longman & Todd, 2002.

——*The Sociology of Religion*, London: Sage, 2007.

Davies, Christie, *The Strange Death of Moral Britain*, London: Transaction Publishers, 2007.

Davies, Douglas, Charles Watkins and Michael Winter, *Church and Religion in Rural England*, Edinburgh: T&T Clark, 1991.

Dawkins, Richard, *The God Delusion*, London: Bantam Press, 2006 and Boston: Houghton Mifflin, 2008.

Dekmejian, R. Hrair, *Islam in Revolution: Fundamentalism in the Arab World*, Syracuse, NY: Syracuse University Press, 1985.

Demerath, Nicholas J. III, 'In a Sow's Ear: a Reply to Goode', *Journal for the Scientific Study of Religion*, 6:1, 87–88, 1967.

Dennett, Daniel, *Breaking the Spell: Religion as a Natural Phenomenon*, New York: Viking and London: Allen Lane, 2006.

Ferguson, John, 'The Secular City Revisited', *The Modern Churchman*, April 1973.

Fergusson, David A.S., *Community, Liberalism and Christian Ethics*, Cambridge: Cambridge University Press, 1998.

Festinger, Leon, Henry W. Riecken and Stanley Schachter, *When Prophecy Fails: A Social and Psychological Study of a Modern Group that Predicted the Destruction of the World*, New York: Harper Torchbooks, 1956.

——*A Theory of Cognitive Dissonance*, Evanston, IL: Row Peterson, 1957.

Fichter, J.H., *Social Relations in the Urban Parish*, Chicago IL: Chicago University Press, 1954.

Finke, Roger and Rodney Stark, *The Churchgoing of America, 1776–1990: Winners and Losers in Our Religious Economy*, New Brunswick, NJ: Rutgers University Press, 1992.

——'Supply-Side Explanations for Religious Change', with Laurence A. Iannaccone, *Annals of the American Academy of Political and Social Science*, 527, 27–39, 1993.

Fischer, Michael M.J., *Iran: From Religious Dispute to Revolution*, Cambridge, MA: Harvard University Press, 1980.

Flew, Antony and Alasdair MacIntyre (eds), *New Essays in Philosophical Theology*, London: SCM Press, 1955.

Forrester, Duncan B., *Christian Justice and Public Policy*, Cambridge: Cambridge University Press, 1997.

——*Forrester on Christian Ethics and Practical Theology: Collected Writings on Christianity, India, and the Social Order*, Farnham: Ashgate, 2010.

Francis, Leslie J. (ed.), *Sociology, Theology and the Curriculum*, London: Cassell, 1999.

——*Gone for Good? Church-Leaving and Returning in the 21st Century*, with Philip Richter, London: Epworth, 2007.

Gager, John G., *Kingdom and Community: the Social World of Early Christianity*, Englewood Cliffs, NJ: Prentice Hall, 1975.

Gay, John D., *The Geography of Religion in England*, London: Duckworth, 1971.

Gellner, E. (ed.), *Islamic Dilemmas: Reformers, Nationalists and Industrialization*, The Hague, NL: Mouton, 1985.

Gill, Robin, 'British Theology as a Sociological Variable', in Michael Hill (ed.), *A Sociological Yearbook of Religion in Britain*, London: SCM Press, 1–12, 1974.

——*The Social Context of Theology*, Oxford: Mowbrays, 1975.

——*Theology and Social Structure*, Oxford: Mowbrays, 1977.

——(ed.), *Theology and Sociology: A Reader*, London: Geoffrey Chapman, 1987, New York: Paulist Press, 1988 (revised edition London: Cassell, 1996).

——*Competing Convictions*, London: SCM Press, 1989.

——*The Myth of the Empty Church*, London: SPCK, 1993 [revised as *The 'Empty' Church Revisited*, Aldershot, Hants: Ashgate, 2003].

——*Moral Leadership in a Postmodern Age*, T&T Clark, Edinburgh, 1997.

——and C. Kirk Hadaway and Penny Long Marler, 'Is Religious Belief Declining in Britain?', *Journal for the Scientific Study of Religion*, 37:3, 507–516, 1998.

——*Churchgoing and Christian Ethics*, Cambridge: Cambridge University Press, 1999.

——*Health Care and Christian Ethics*, Cambridge: Cambridge University Press, 2006.

Glasner, P.E., *The Sociology of Secularisation*, London: Routledge & Kegan Paul, 1977.

Glock, Charles Y. and Rodney Stark, *Christian Beliefs and Anti-Semitism*, New York: Harper, 1966.

——*American Piety: The Nature of Religious Commitment*, Berkeley, CA: University of California Press, 1968.

Gorenberg, Gershon, *The End of Days: Fundamentalisms and the Struggle for the Temple Mount*, New York: Free Press, 2000.

Gorsuch, Richard L. and Daniel Aleshire, 'Christian Faith and Prejudice: Review of Research', *Journal for the Scientific Study of Religion*, 13:3, 281–307, 1974.

Gottwald, Norman K., *The Tribes of Yahweh: a Sociology of the Religion of Liberated Israel, 1250–1050 B.C.E.*, Maryknoll, NY: Orbis Books and London: SCM Press, 1979.

——*The Hebrew Bible: A Socio-Literary Introduction*, Minneapolis, MI: Fortress, 1985.

Greeley, Andrew M., *Unsecular Man: The Persistence of Religion*, New York: Schocken Books, 1972 [English title *The Persistence of Religion*, London: SCM Press, 1973].

——'The LAM Religiosity Scale', *Journal for the Scientific Study of Religion*, 12:1–3, 1973.

Gustafson, James, 'The Sectarian Temptation', *Proceedings of the Catholic Theological Society of America*, 40, 83–84, 1985.

Hadden, J.K. and C.E. Swann, *Prime-time Preachers: the Rising Power of Televangelism*, Reading, MA: Addison-Wesley, 1981.

Halloran, J.D., *The Effects of Mass Communications*, Leicester: Leicester University Press, 1964.

Halpern, David, *Social Capital*, Cambridge: Polity, 2005.

Hammond, Phillip E. (ed.), *The Sacred in a Secular Age*, Berkeley, CA: University of California Press, 1984.

Hamnett, Ian, 'Sociology of Religion and Sociology of Error', *Religion*, 3,1–12, 1973.

——'A Mistake about Error', *New Blackfriars*, 67:788, 69–78, 1986.

Hardyck, J.A. and M. Braden, 'Prophecy Fails Again: a Report of a Failure to Replicate', *Journal of Abnormal and Social Psychology*, 65:2, 136–141, 1962.

Harned, David B. *Theology and the Arts*, Louisville, KY: Westminster Press, 1966.

——(ed.), *The Ambiguity of Religion*, Louisville, KY: Westminster Press, 1968.

Harris, Sam, *The End of Faith: Religion, Terror and the Future of Reason*, New York: Norton, 2004.

Hauerwas, Stanley, *Vision and Virtue*, Notre Dame, IN: Fides Press, 1974.

——*Character and the Christian Life*, San Antonio, TX: Trinity University Press, 1975.

——*A Community of Character: Toward a Constructive Christian Social Ethic*, Notre Dame, IN: University of Notre Dame, 1981.

——*The Peaceable Kingdom: A Primer of Christian Ethics*, Notre Dame, IN: University of Notre Dame Press, 1983, and London: SCM Press, 1984.

——*Suffering Presence*, Notre Dame, IN: University of Notre Dame Press, 1986, and Edinburgh: T&T Clark, 1988.

——with William Willimon, *Resident Aliens: Life in the Christian Colony*, Nashville, TN: Abingdon Press, 1989.

——*Naming the Silences*, Grand Rapids, MI: Eerdmans, 1990.

——*Against the Nations*, Notre Dame, IN: University of Notre Press, 1992.

——*Dispatches from the Front*, Durham, NC: Duke University Press, 1995.

——with William Willimon, *Where Resident Aliens Live*, Nashville, TN: Abingdon Press, 1996.

——*With the Grain of the Universe: The Church's Witness and Natural Theology*, Grand Rapids, MI: Brazos Press, 2001, and London: SCM Press, 2002.

——with Samuel Wells (eds), *The Blackwell Companion to Christian Ethics*, Oxford and New York: Blackwell, 2nd ed., 2011 [2004].

Heelas, Paul, Linda Woodhead et al., *The Spiritual Revolution: Why Religion is Giving way to Spirituality,* Oxford: Blackwell, 2005.

Hewitt, Margaret, 'A Sociological Critique', in F.G. Duffield (ed.), *The Paul Report Considered*, Chester: Marcham Manor Press, 1964.

Hill, Michael, *A Sociology of Religion*, London: Heinemann, 1973.

Hitchens, Christopher, *God is Not Great: How Religion Poisons Everything*, London: Atlantic and New York: Warner, 2007.

Hodgson, Leonard, *For Faith and Freedom*, Oxford: Blackwell, vol. 1, 1956.

Hogbin, Ian, *Social Change*, London: C.A. Watts, 1957.

Hoge, Dean R. and Jackson W. Carroll, 'Religiosity and Prejudice North and South', *Journal for the Scientific Study of Religion*, 12:2, 181–197, 1973.

Holloway, Richard, *Let God Arise*, Oxford: Mowbrays, 1972.

Horrell, David, *Social-Scientific Approaches to New Testament Interpretation*, Edinburgh: T&T Clark, 1999.

——*After the First Urban Christians: The Social-Scientific Study of Pauline Christianity Twenty-Five Years Later*, London and New York: T&T Clark, 2009.

Hudson, Liam, *The Cult of the Fact*, London: Jonathan Cape, 1972.

Jackson, M.J., 'Introduction to the English Edition', in F. Boulard, *An Introduction to Religious Sociology*, London: Darton, Longman & Todd, 1960.

Johnson, S.D. and J.B. Tamney (eds), *The Political Role of Religion in the United States*, Boulder, CO: Westview Press, 1986.

Jones, James W., 'Sacred Terror: The Psychology of Contemporary Religious Terrorism' in Andrew R. Murphy (ed.), *The Blackwell Companion to Religion and Violence*, Malden, MA and Oxford: Wiley-Blackwell, 293–303, 2011.

Jones, G. Vaughan, *Christology and Myth in the New Testament*, London: Allen & Unwin, 1956.

Juergensmeyer, Mark, *Terror in the Mind of God: The Global Rise of Religious Violence*, Berkeley, CA: University of California Press, 2000.

——(ed.), *The Oxford Handbook of Global Religions*, Oxford: Oxford University Press, 2006.

Kiki, Albert Maori, *Kiki: Ten Thousand Years in a Lifetime*, Westport, CT: Praeger Press, 1968.

Leach, Edmund R., *Political Systems of Highland Burma*, Cambridge, MA: Harvard University Press, 1954.

Lenski, Gerhard E., *The Religious Factor*, Garden City, NY: Doubleday, 1961.

Lewis, Bernard, 'The Return of Islam', *Commentary*, 61, 39–49, 1976.

——*The Crisis of Islam: Holy War and Unholy Terror*, New York: Random House, 2004.

Lewis, H.D., *Philosophy of Religion*, London: English Universities Press, 1965.

Luckmann, Thomas, *The Invisible Religion*, London: Macmillan, 1967.

Lundby, Knut (ed.), *Mediatization, Concept, Changes, Consequences*, New York and Oxford: Peter Lang, 2009.

Lurie, Alison, *Imaginary Friends*, London: Heinemann, 1967.

Lustick, Ian S., *For the Land and the Lord: Jewish Fundamentalism in Israel*, New York: Council on Foreign Relations, 1988.

MacCulloch, Diarmaid, *A History of Christianity: The First Three Thousand Years*, London: Allen Lane, 2009.

MacIntyre, Alasdair, *A Short History of Ethics*, London: Routledge & Kegan Paul, 1967.

——*After Virtue: a Study in Moral Theory*, London: Duckworth, 2nd edition, 1985 [1981].

——'A Partial Response to my Critics', in John Horton and Susan Mendus (eds), *After MacIntyre: Critical Perspectives on the Work of Alasdair MacIntyre*, Oxford: Polity Press and Notre Dame, IN: University of Notre Dame Press, 283–304, 1994.

Malina, Bruce J., 'Normative Dissonance and Christian Origins', *Semeia*, 35, 35–59, 1986.

Mannheim, Karl, *Ideology and Utopia*, London: Routledge & Kegan, 1936.

Markham, Ian S., *Plurality and Christian Ethics*, Cambridge: Cambridge University Press, 1994.

Marsden, G., *Fundamentalism and American Culture: The Shaping of Twentieth-Century Evangelicalism 1870–1925*, Oxford: Oxford University Press, 1980.

Martin, David, *Pacifism: An Historical and Sociological Study*, London: Routledge & Kegan Paul, 1965.

——*A Sociology of English Religion*, London: SCM Press, 1967.

——*The Religious and the Secular*, London: Routledge & Kegan Paul, 1969.

——*Tracts Against the Times*, Cambridge: Lutterworth, 1973.

——'The Secularization Question', *Theology*, 76:630, 81–82, 1973.

——'Ethical Commentary and Political Decision', *Theology*, 76:638, 527–536, 1973.

——*A General Theology of Secularization*, Oxford: Blackwell, 1978.

——*The Breaking of the Image: A Sociology of Christian Theory and Practice*, Oxford: Blackwell, 1980.

——with John Orme Mills and W.S.F. Pickering (eds), *Sociology and Theology: Alliance and Conflict*, Brighton, Sussex: Harvester, 1980 [reprinted Leiden, NL: Brill, 2003].

——*Reflections on Sociology and Theology*, Oxford: Clarendon Press, 1996.

——*Does Christianity Cause War?*, Oxford: Clarendon Press, 1997.

——*On Secularization: Towards a Revised General Theory*, Aldershot: Ashgate, 2005.

——*The Future of Christianity: Reflections on Violence, Democracy, Religion and Secularization*, Farnham: Ashgate, 2011.

Martin, Roderick, 'Sociology and Theology', in D.E.H. Whiteley and R. Martin (eds), *Sociology, Theology and Conflict*, Oxford: Blackwell, 14–37,1969.

Mascall, E.L., *Theology and Images*, Oxford: Mowbrays, 1963.

——*The Secularisation of Christianity*, Lutterworth: Libra, 1967.

Milbank, John, *Theology and Social Theory: Beyond Secular Reason*, Oxford: Blackwell, 1990 [revised 2006].

——'The End of Dialogue', in Gavin D'Costa (ed.), *Christian Uniqueness Reconsidered*, Maryknoll, NY: Orbis, 174–191, 1990.

——'Enclaves, or Where is the Church?', *New Blackfriars*, 73:861, 341–352, June 1992.

——*The Word Made Strange: Theology, Language, Culture*, Oxford: Blackwell, 1997.

——'Theology and the Economy of the Sciences' in Mark Thiessen Nation and Samuel Wells (eds), *Faithfulness and Fortitude: In Conversation with the Theological Ethics of Stanley Hauerwas*, Edinburgh: T&T Clark, 39–57, 2000.

Mills, C. Wright, *The Sociological Imagination*, Oxford: Oxford University Press, 1959.

Mottahedeh, Roy, *The Mantle of the Prophet: Religion and Politics in Iran*, New York: Pantheon, 1985.

Murphy, Andrew R. (ed.), *The Blackwell Companion to Religion and Violence*, Malden, MA and Oxford: Wiley-Blackwell, 2011.

Nelson, Benjamin, 'Is the Sociology of Religion Possible? A Reply to Robert Bellah', *Journal for the Scientific Study of Religion*, 9:2, 89–96, 1970.

Newbigin, Lesslie, *Religion for Secular Man*, London: SCM Press, 1966.

Nichols, Aidan, 'Non Tali Auxilio: John Milbank's Suasion to Orthodoxy', *New Blackfriars*, 73:861, 326–332, June 1992.

Obelkevich, J., L. Roper and R. Samuel (eds), *Disciplines of Faith: Studies in Religion, Politics and Patriarchy*, London: Routledge & Kegan Paul, 1987.

O'Donovan, Oliver, *The Desire of Nations: Rediscovering the Roots of Political Theology*, Cambridge: Cambridge University Press, 1996.

Olson, Joel, 'The Politics of Protestant Violence: Abolitionists and Anti-Abortionists', in Andrew R. Murphy (ed.), *The Blackwell Companion to Religion and Violence*, Malden, MA and Oxford: Wiley-Blackwell, 485–497, 2011.

Ossowska, Maria, *Social Determinants of Moral Ideas*, London: Routledge & Kegan Paul, 1971.

Owen, H.P., *Revelation and Existence*, Cardiff: University of Wales Press, 1957.

Pahl, R.H., *Patterns of Urban Living*, London: Longman, 1970.

Paul, Leslie, *The Deployment and Payment of the Clergy*, London: Church of England Information Office, 1964.

——'The Role of the Clergy Today–An Organisational Approach: Problems of Deployment', in C.L. Mitton (ed.), *The Social Sciences and the Churches*, Edinburgh: T&T Clark, 163–171, 1972.

Pickering, W.S.F., *Durkheim on Religion*, London: Routledge & Kegan Paul, 1975.

——*Durkheim's Sociology of Religion: Themes and Theories*, London: Routledge & Kegan Paul, 1984.

Pope, Stephen, *Human Evolution and Christian Ethics*, Cambridge: Cambridge University Press, 2008.

Pollack, Detlef and Daniel V.A. Olson (eds), *The Role of Religion in Modern Societies*, New York and London: Routledge, 2008.

Putnam, Robert D., *Bowling Alone: The Collapse and Revival of American Community*, New York: Simon & Schuster, 2000.

——*American Grace: How Religion Divides and Unites Us*, with David E. Campbell, New York: Simon & Schuster, 2010.

Rahner, Karl, *Theological Investigations*, vol. 1, London: Darton, Longman & Todd, 1961.

Ramsey, A.M., *God, Christ and the World*, London: SCM Press, 1969.

Ramsey, Ian T., *Religious Language*, London: SCM Press, 1959.

Reader, Ian, 'The Transformation of Failure and the Spiritualization of Violence', in Andrew R. Murphy (ed.), *The Blackwell Companion to Religion and Violence*, Malden, MA and Oxford: Wiley-Blackwell, 304–319, 2011.

Reimer, Samuel H., 'A Look at Cultural Effects on Religiosity: A Comparison Between the United States and Canada', *Journal for the Scientific Study of Religion*, 34:4, 445–457, 1996.

Rex, John, *Key Problems of Sociological Theory*, London: Routledge & Kegan Paul, 1961.

Robbins, Thomas, Dick Anthony and Thomas E. Curtis, 'The Limits of Symbolic Realism', *Journal for the Scientific Study of Religion*, 12:3, 342–353, 1973.

Roberts, Richard H., 'Theology and the Social Sciences', in David F. Ford and Rachel Muers (eds), *The Modern Theologians*, 3rd edn, Oxford: Blackwell, 370–388, 2005.

Robertson, Roland, *The Sociological Interpretation of Religion*, Oxford: Blackwell, 1970.

——(ed.), *Sociology of Religion*, Harmondsworth, Middlesex: Penguin, 1969.

——'Anti-global Religion?', in Mark Juergensmeyer (ed.), *The Oxford Handbook of Global Religions*, Oxford: Oxford University Press, 611–623, 2006.

Robinson, J.A.T., *Honest to God*, London: SCM Press, 1963.

——*The Human Face of God*, London: SCM Press, 1973.

——with David Edwards (eds), *The Honest to God Debate*, London: SCM Press, 1963.

Roy, Olivier, *Globalised Islam: The Search for a New Ummah*, London: Hurst, 2004.

Rudge, Peter, *Ministry and Management*, London: Tavistock, 1969.

Ruston, Roger, 'Apocalyptic and the Peace Movement', *New Blackfriars*, 67:791, 204–215, 1986.

Sacks, Jonathan, *The Persistence of Faith*, London: Weidenfeld & Nicholson, 1992.

——*Faith in the Future*, London: Darton, Longman & Todd, 1995.

Sandeen, E., *The Roots of Fundamentalism: British and American Millenarianism 1800–1930*, Chicago, IL: University of Chicago Press, 1970.

Scharf, Betty, *The Sociological Study of Religion*, London: Hutchinson, 1970.

Schillebeeckx, E., *Ministry: A Case for Change*, London: SCM Press, 1981.

——*The Church with a Human Face*, London: SCM Press, 1985.

Schumann, Friedrich, 'Can the Event of Jesus Christ Be Demythologized?', in H.V. Bartsch (ed.), *Kerygma and Myth*, vol. 1, London: SPCK, 1953.

Shaw, Graham, *The Cost of Authority: Manipulation and Freedom in the New Testament*, London: SCM Press, 1983.

Sheppard, David, *Built as a City*, London: Hodder & Stoughton, 1974.

Sivan, E., *Radical Islam: Medieval Theology and Modern Politics*, New Haven, CT: Yale University Press, 1985.

Smart, Ninian, *The Phenomenon of Religion*, London: Macmillan, 1973.

Song, Robert, *Christianity and Liberal Society*, Oxford: Clarendon Press, 1997.

Stark, Rodney and William Sims Bainbridge, *The Future of Religion: Secularization, Revival and Cult Formation*, Berkeley, CA: University of California Press, 1985.

Stark, Werner, *The Sociology of Religion*, (3 volumes), London: Routledge & Kegan Paul, 1966–67.

Thompson, Kenneth A., *Bureaucracy and Church Reform*, Oxford: Oxford University Press, 1970.

Towler, Robert, *Homo Religiosus: Sociological Problems in the Study of Religion*, London: Constable, 1974.

——*The Need for Certainty: A Sociological Study of Conventional Religion*, London: Routledge & Kegan Paul, 1984.

Treacy, Eric, 'Approaching the Report', in F.G. Duffield (ed.), *The Paul Report Considered*, Chester: Marcham Manor Press, 1964.

Troeltsch, Ernst, *The Social Teaching of the Christian Churches*, (2 volumes), New York: Harper, 1960 [1912].

Turner, Bryan S., *Secularization* (4 volumes), London and New York: Sage, 2010.

Vaihinger, H., *The Philosophy of 'As If'*, London: Kegan Paul, 1924.

Voas, David and Alasdair Crockett, 'Religion in Britain: Neither Believing nor Belonging', *Sociology*, 39, 11–28, 2005.

Vrijhof, P.H. and J. Waardenburg, *Official and Popular Religion: Analysis of a Theme for Religious Studies*, The Hague, NL: Mouton, 1979.

Weber, Max, *The Protestant Ethic and the 'Spirit' of Capitalism*, New York, NY: Scribner, 1958 [1905].

——*The Sociology of Religion*, London: Methuen, 1965 [1920].

Whiteley, D.E.H. and R. Martin, *Sociology, Theology and Conflict*, Oxford: Blackwell, 1969.

Williams, Rowan, 'Saving Time: Thoughts on Practice, Patience and Vision', *New Blackfriars*, 73:861, 319–326, June 1992.

Wilson, Bryan, *Religion in Secular Society*, London: C.A. Watts, 1966 and Harmondsworth, Middlesex: Penguin, 1969.

——'A Typology of Sects', in Roland Robertson (ed.), *Sociology of Religion*, Harmondsworth, Middlesex: Penguin, 361–383, 1969.

——*Magic and the Millennium*, Oxford: Heinemann, 1973.

——*Contemporary Transformations of Religion*, Oxford: Oxford University Press, 1976.

——*Religion in Sociological Perspective*, Oxford: Oxford University Press, 1982.

——*The Social Dimension of Sectarianism*, Oxford: Clarendon Press, 1990.

Yinger, J. Milton, *Religion, Society and the Individual*, New York: Macmillan, 1957.

Index